Family Court HELL

Mark Harris

Pen Press Publishers Ltd

First published in Great Britain by
Pen Press Publishers Ltd
25 Eastern Place
Brighton
BN2 1GJ

ISBN 978-1-906206-12-3

Printed and bound in UK by Cpod, Trowbridge, Wiltshire

A catalogue record of this book is available from
the British Library

Cover design by Jacqueline Abromeit

CONTENTS

INTRODUCTION

I hope this book may give some support to the many thousands of separated fathers who have entered or are entering the farcical secret family courts of the UK and much of the western world. Everywhere, family courts proclaim their actions and decisions are always made 'in the best interests of the child'. However, in reality, the wishes of the mother and the bank accounts of the court players are the usual benefactors.

This book details my personal battle with the United Kingdom's family courts after my marriage broke down. The case went on for almost ten years, spanned 133 hearings before 33 different judges, including two presidents of the UK Family Division. In this book, I have detailed only some of the most farcical moments; otherwise this book could have run to many thousands of pages. My case and subsequent actions led directly to international protests by fathers uniting under the Fathers 4 Justice banner.

No one can do anything to stop a former wife or partner becoming obstructive over access to the children, but likewise, no one expects the legal system to assist her on such a mission. But it does, and with monotonous regularity. If the obstructive parents' support mechanisms were removed, and orders for contact enforced, most cases would resolve quite quickly.

In my case, the higher up the court hierarchy the matter ascended, the more farcical it became; we had court proceeding tapes of a circuit judge's absurd comments mysteriously erased while in the safe keeping of the court service. A year later, our very first High Court judge was caught wine drinking with the Official Solicitor's representatives (who were supposedly independent parties to the proceedings) between adjournments. Earlier in that same case, the judge heard the mother's boyfriend make five separate threats to kill me from the witness box, but sent him home to live with my children while sending me off to prison for waving to them.

At another hearing, my ex-wife passed our first Lady High Court judge a letter supposedly from our youngest daughter (then aged eight) telling the judge she 'never wanted to see Daddy', which the judge readily accepted. When a Home Office handwriting expert later examined the letter and other samples of handwriting and reported "the mother was the probable author of the letter," the appeal court readily accepted the process had been corrupted – but refused to intervene. Unbelievably, Lord Justice Matthew Thorpe then had the gall to call this "…a very simple contact dispute…" even though it was our 105th hearing.

This 'very simple contact dispute' was believed to have cost the UK taxpayer almost £1 million.

Less than a year later at another hearing, a very eminent and well-known expert witness was brought in to assist the case. But when he admitted, on oath, to having been 'very economical' with the truth in his court reports, his fatally flawed recommendations were still accepted by that judge – with disastrous consequences to us all.

That particular High Court judge, our 29th, on the back of this expert witness's deceit, soon experienced a fathers' protest outside one of his homes. To defuse the anger, he went public with the child psychiatrist's admissions to try and justify not calling a mistrial, only to then quickly arrange for his words on this deceit to 'disappear' from the published law reports.

Only in 'secret courts', hidden away from the press and public could *any* of this have happened. Yet all of this, and much, much more, *did happen* to me and my children. Public accountability of the judiciary is the only 'quality control' of any court. Government and parliament have no say in how the courts operate, and they do not intervene in proceedings or outcomes. Parliament simply put the laws in place, and the courts are trusted to implement them. Therefore, it follows that the family courts, with no public accountability, have *no real* quality control.

I never accepted the farce and injustices that were handed down by these various judges or ever considered walking away from my daughters, so I battled on. Then, in 2000, I decided to take my battle public.

Upon going public, tens, hundreds, then thousands of other abused fathers came forward with similar experiences and the protest group Fathers 4 Justice was conceived. Other countries around the world that base their legal system on the British model soon witnessed fathers coming together in public protest against their individual nation's secret family courts. However, the UK authorities' reaction to this growing dissent was not to listen to the discord or try to put matters right, but instead raid the homes and bug the phones of members, infiltrate meetings, subvert public perception and destroy lawful protests in ways more in keeping with a cold war communist state than 21st century Britain.

I was jailed twice for contempt of court during the family proceedings; I served a total 129 days at two Category B prisons for simply trying to maintain a relationship with my daughters against their mother's wishes. The mother's breaches of all court orders were consistently ignored. Her new boyfriend's multiple assaults on my children were simply brushed aside and covered up while my daughters' well-documented wishes to be with me were trampled over for years.

The case plunged rapidly from farce to outright human rights abuse, with more injustices piled on top of previous ones to try and make me go away. But I refused to go away.

There is a happy ending, but only when my children became old enough to take the law into their own hands. Then the courts immediately allowed me to return to being the full time father of my daughters once again. The press in 2003 dubbed the case 'Britain's worst ever'.

A mother can move *any* new man into the home of your children. 'New man' (and any subsequent new men she may move in) need undergo no background checks, make no court applications; he just moves in, no questions asked. New man is presumed fine to be with your kids from day one. At that point, the process natural Dad has to enter and endure just to try and see the children he loves and once lived with becomes a crime against humanity.

As the divorced father Sir Bob Geldof said on national television in 2002 when asked of his personal experiences of fighting to see his daughters through the family courts, *"I cannot believe what they do to parents in the name of the law."*

Personally, I believe future historians, probably well after even my own children's lifetimes, will look back at what currently masquerades as 'in the interests of the child' by the family courts and will place what's routinely happening today alongside other historic, authority-led western world crimes against its people such as slavery and the holocaust.

OBITUARY
SHEILA HARRIS
1937-2005

During my epic struggle with the family court's to see my three daughters, my mother, Sheila Harris (far left), was huge support, not only to me, but to the many fathers who campaigned against the family courts.

Sheila Harris attended a number of Fathers 4 Justice protests in the London area and helped collect signatures outside the Royal Court's of Justice, London, for the petition that was handed into 10 Downing Street in October 2000.

Thanks solely to the bravery of my daughters who took on the Family Court Judges and won, Sheila got to see her granddaughters again in 2003, and my daughters were reunited with their much loved grandmother.

Tragically, just over one year later, my mother was diagnosed with cancer, and died from the illness a few months later on 1 March 2005.

CHAPTER 1

My Marriage, Our Break-up, and How the Court Farce Began

Back in 1983, when I was 24, I was working as a self-employed driving instructor in Plymouth when I met my future wife. She was a pupil six years younger than me that I was teaching to drive. There was a mutual attraction. We dated, we lived together, we planned our first child, Lisa, and, 18 months after we moved in together, we got married just before Lisa's birth.

It was a simple, small wedding as my wife was six months pregnant and money was a little tight. We were young, but back then getting married and having a family seemed like the most natural thing to do in the world. She had actually proposed to me on leap year's day in 1984 and seemed to want nothing more than to have children and settle down. To me, it all seemed wonderful, even though with hindsight I can see it was a serious mistake.

For my age, I was financially secure. I had moved to Plymouth, where my father's side of my family originally came from, after growing up in Romford, Essex. I'd traded up a small flat near London to a three-bed semi in Plymouth. My new girlfriend and future wife chose to give up her work as a clerical assistant in a local garage from soon after we started dating.

Lisa was born in 1986. Nothing prepares you for the arrival of your first child, even though I had been so excited during the pregnancy.

When that child is plonked down in your arms, just a minute or so old, well, it just blows your mind. I've never experienced anything like it before or since. Suddenly the whole world looked so different, scary and threatening to this tiny baby. I can remember how nervous I was driving her home for the first time.

We moved from my modest semi near the city centre to Yealmpton, a more up-market part of South Devon eight miles outside Plymouth nearly a year later. I had worked hard and made good gains in the booming 80s property market which enabled us as a family to buy a very nice four-bedroom detached house with an average-sized mortgage for that time. Our middle daughter was born in 1989, and our third daughter arrived in 1991.

By 1993, the marriage was not particularly happy. I have no wish to put into print any complaints I had about my ex-wife here. Given everything that's happened since, it's tempting to, but that is not the purpose of this book. (The main purpose of this book is to try and bring about some change in how the British family courts [mis]function and operate.) But essentially my ex was a woman still in thrall to her parents. She was always desperate for their approval and, as far as I could see, never got it. Her own father never sent her a birthday card throughout our marriage, which may seem a small thing, but it wasn't to her and used to upset her very much. Her own parents were having marriage difficulties and got divorced themselves in about 1988. I honestly believe her mother had an agenda about our marriage – she didn't want her daughter to be happily settled when she herself was not. She interfered on an almost daily basis and soon found she could get at her daughter through me.

In the end, we banned my mother-in-law from coming to the house as she caused us such problems. It was my idea, born out of desperation, but supported by my wife at the time. But, after three peaceful years of me not seeing the mother-in-law, I suggested we relented and let her come around again. But she was soon back to her old ways and within eight months my wife and I were apart. I would even go so far as to say that if her parents had been even just fairly normal, we would never have split up at all.

My ex had her own demons; soon after she had our third baby she developed a terrible eating disorder, even though to my mind she wasn't at all overweight at a trim size 10/12. She used to take laxatives by the bucket-load, binged on chocolate and became obsessed with aerobics and going to the gym. It was a very unhappy time for her, I am sure, but she was extremely difficult to support and help, no matter how hard I tried.

For the record, I am quite happy to state that the marriage breakdown was probably due to faults on both sides. Although I was never unfaithful, and I don't believe she was either, we did become very unhappy together. This was despite the fact that we had three lovely children, a nice house, new car and even a boat. Outwardly we looked like a happy family, but the truth was very different.

Then, on Saturday November 6th 1993, my life came to an abrupt halt. I left home to watch my local football team, Plymouth Argyle, play Brentford. I was a season ticket holder then and I am again now. Little did I know that while I was watching a pretty mediocre game of football my wife was putting into action her plan that was to tear apart my family. Her actions that day destroyed my home, my finances, my life – and propelled me into the ten-year farce that passes for family law in this country.

I drove home from the match. I turned in my street and as I neared my house I noticed my father's car outside my house. As I turned into my driveway, I noticed my father, who lived in Plymouth, standing in front of my garage. Just by the look on his face, I could see there was something seriously wrong.

My immediate thought was something had happened to my wife or daughters. It was every parent's nightmare – maybe a car accident, injury in the home, or worse. Grim-faced, my father told me to come indoors. By now I was screaming at him to tell me what was wrong. All I had expected to find waiting for my return to home was my daughters and their mother, and perhaps, if I was lucky, something nice for tea.

As I opened the front door, the beautiful home I had left just over three hours earlier was unrecognisable. Entering the large hallway, there were pictures missing from the wall, curtains gone, plant pots knocked over and their contents spilled across the carpet. Wires hung from the ceiling where a light fitting had been.

Staggered, I entered the lounge with my father to sit with him on a sofa that I immediately discovered was simply no longer there. The comfortably furnished room was now almost empty and barren. There were just marks in the carpet to hint at where the furniture had been when I last went into that very room, three hours before, to kiss my children goodbye as I left for the match. Burglars would not have caused this degree of destruction – shelves had been ripped off the wall with such force that half the plasterboard had gone with them. I was now not just confused, but disorientated.

My father started to tell me that he received a phone call from my wife half an hour before. She told him that she had left me and taken the children with a few household items and was setting up a home without me. She asked him to also tell me not to look for her or the children. I was in total shock. Everything I had called family and home at 2 pm had vanished by 5 pm. The house was almost completely empty and what little furnishings left were damaged. Worse still, where were my children?

It took several minutes for all of this to sink in. I stood in this empty room in physical shock. Everything I had worked for was gone. I felt as though I had been physically attacked. After some careful thought I started to work out the only place my wife and children could have headed off to was her mother's vacant (and unfurnished) second home that the last tenant had vacated some weeks before. It had struck me as strange that my mother-in-law had not made any attempts to find a new tenant on this occasion for several weeks, where previously she had moved new tenants in as soon as old tenants vacated. Suddenly this began to make sense to me.

I started to suspect my mother-in-law – and probably my father-in-law too – who both now lived with new partners, had to be involved somewhere in all of this. I could not possibly see anywhere else my wife could have gone, or how she could have done all of this without organised help in just over three hours.

My mood was surprisingly calm and rational; I think in truth I was in severe shock at the turn of events. Talking my suspicions over with my father, he offered to go to my mother-in-law's second home and take a look, saying it would be more helpful if I just stayed where I was for now. He drove to that address (about five miles away back in Plymouth) where, sure enough, he found my wife, her mother and father, both their new partners and other relatives on my wife's side, settling her into that house. There was no sign of my children, who I later discovered were being looked after by a cousin of my wife's.

Not for the first time, my wife let her mother do her talking, while her father was fixing the very light fittings into her new home that I had bought and fitted to our house just weeks before. My wife, through her mother, made it clear she was not coming back; she now had all she wanted, demanded the family home be sold off as soon as possible and declared I could see the children 'sometime'.

To cut a very long story short, over the following weeks, I got to see the children only when it suited my now-estranged wife and her mother. I was bombarded from the start with letters from her solicitor; divorce petitions, statements and demands for this, that, and every other. I seemed powerless even to take part in what was happening. I was having a divorce I did not want and had no say in anything that was happening. I could only ask myself just what had I done to deserve being stripped of everything that was my entire life for the last seven years and before? I sought legal advice. And I hardly saw my children. On the first occasion I saw my children after her leaving, the girls seemed to think it was, at first, some big adventure and appeared confused as to just when would we all be going home. Like me, they had no warning of this life-changing day coming, they were simply taken to a relative's from their home, without explanation or reason and returned to another home three hours later – minus Dad. As the days and weeks passed, the penny dropped with each of them and the realisation of the life change took hold – they no longer lived in their home with their father.

I had to wait for legal aid so that I could begin to afford to answer the barrage of demands from my wife's solicitors. She, it seemed, had arranged for her legal aid and briefed her solicitor well in advance of her departure. Then, a month after she left, my now-estranged wife telephoned me, quite unexpectedly, and said she wanted to meet me, but without the children. I picked her up from around the corner from her house and drove about a mile away to talk in my car as she did not want her parents to know we were meeting up. She told me she thought that her leaving was "a terrible mistake," that things between us could be worked out and she wanted to "try again."

I was confused. By now, after so much hurt, part of me wanted to get out of the marriage. On the other hand, part of me wanted my family, my home and my life back as it was. But my wife's actions and her way of leaving, the way it was done (the 'few household items' she took, as detailed in the divorce petition, in fact needed two trips in a seven-ton self-drive lorry loaded by three men) had destroyed what little regard or trust I had left for her in our unhappy marriage. I did ask myself just how could I possibly have anything to do with her now?

And her parents, my in-laws, had taken part and helped to plan this deception and destruction of my life behind my back. How could I ever bring myself to even speak to these people again, let alone welcome them into my home, visit them, or even to wish them a happy Christmas?

I had made the effort with them in the past but they were quite clear from the day of our wedding in 1986 they didn't like me but were never able or willing to give any reason. Be that as it may, during our marriage it seemed to me they enjoyed causing friction between me and my wife.

Now, when they had assisted and encouraged my wife to leave in such a damaging and cruel way, with such underhanded viciousness, I asked myself how could I seriously even have any contact with these people, and her wider family, ever again. Simply, I reasoned I could never again.

And aside from my wife's relatives, I asked myself just how could I ever go out of the house to work or go to another football match without wondering if my home, belongings, children were all being moved out again? Could I really ever see myself replacing all of the fittings, shelves, wall units, everything she and her family had removed that I had already once fitted with loving care to the home? How could I possibly go around making good all of the damage to the decoration they had collectively caused to our home without fearing it could happen again at any time?

It did even cross my mind just how could I confidently even eat anything my wife cooked for me after this if she decided she simply wanted rid of me again? To me, this was not just about my wife, there was a conspiracy from her entire immediate family trying and wanting to break us up. I was up against a small army wanting us apart.

I slept on her 'proposition'. The next day I decided I could not possibly ever have her back. After all, I reasoned, after a month apart the children were appearing to slowly be coming to terms with their new home, new schools, new friends. They missed me, of course, and I missed them, but hostilities from my estranged wife had been easing, allowing me to see them one evening in the week and most weekends.

For me, there was now no way back, and ironically, I now actually wanted the divorce she had instigated. The next day, I rang her and told her there was no going back. She was furious and it was from that moment that things turned really ugly surrounding our children.

On the practical side, I agreed to sell the family home off, as she had previously demanded. I was happy enough to split the proceeds – despite her having not made any financial contribution to it at all – and for the kids to live with her, as long as I could see them often. I wanted to keep things friendly but go our own ways.

But when I broke this news to her, hostility instantly returned with a vengeance. I went to her new home to pick the girls up as arranged on the Saturday. I was met with both her mother and father giving me abuse and telling me "you won't be seeing the children." By now my legal aid was in place. Oh well, I thought, I'll go off to court and sort this out. Little did I know what was in store…

CHAPTER 2

The Court Process Begins

My first solicitor, a rather pessimistic character, wanted to try and reach agreement without a court hearing, which sounded fair enough. This was all a new world to me. I had no clue about courts or the legal system. Who really wants to go to court anyway? But my estranged wife's solicitors were just not responding to letters and phone calls asking for discussions over the children. So, after some days with no progress, I instructed my solicitor to take her to court to get the ball rolling. An application was immediately filed and we were booked in for a directions hearing in Plymouth County Court just before the Christmas 1993.

My estranged wife had never been to any form of court in her life. Knowing her, I sensed that when we got to the court door she might well take the easy option, agree something and we could all go home.

Well, I was right on this occasion. Once at the court, we swiftly agreed, through our solicitors, that I would have my daughters every weekend from 10 am Saturday to 4 pm Sunday and every Wednesday teatime after school for two hours. We agreed they would reside with her. The two school-aged girls had already settled into their new school and the pre-school girl was happy in her new playschool. To me, it seemed there was positive light somewhere at the end of this very dark tunnel. The court rubber-stamped the agreement, my solicitor billed the Legal Aid Board for more than £2,000 and everyone went home as happy as can be expected in the circumstances.

Now my ex-wife had immediately gone on income support at the point of leaving the home, I stopped work the day after and did the same. The CSA got in touch with me about three weeks after she went, but by now as I was on benefits too, so they got nothing.

This was all just before Christmas 1993. I had now taken a smaller, rented, furnished house in Plympton, the same district where she had moved with my kids. The family home, now in the hands of an estate agent, was being sold. Even in the stripped-out state it was, it sold quickly and for a good price, such was the desirability of the neighbourhood it was in.

My new rented home was small but fully furnished and had two bedrooms. It was a base from which to pick up the pieces of my life. I knew now it was time to start to try and build a future for myself as a divorcing father. My mind turned to the matter of purchasing another home near to the children. I even started to think about a tentative venture into the dating game once again and even went out for drinks with a couple of women, although it came to nothing. Just who wants to listen to a man miserably talking about his divorce all evening?

I also returned to work for the driving school I had just abandoned the day my wife left. The proprietor was most understanding about my ten-week absence and kindly took me back. I felt I was just about becoming fit to rejoin the human race.

Needless to say, Christmas 1993 was pretty grim for me. I saw the kids for nearly half of that Xmas – the afternoon, about three hours, by agreement in the court – it was a horrible day, all alone apart from the girls' visit; I recall my Xmas dinner was a tinned Fray Bentos meal, horrible!

Shortly after Christmas, the children told me, "Mum has a boyfriend." It was a very strange feeling at first, I must admit. I was still married, admittedly unhappily and divorcing, but still married to this woman who now had a new man in her life. I told myself though this could perhaps be a good thing and it was time to move on, and that my only concern should be for my children and how they took to her new man.

By March 1994, the new man had moved into my children's home. I didn't mind; things seemed to be working out for all of us. I too had started seeing someone for a short while just after that Christmas, but it had been blatantly clear to me it was far too soon to think of anyone as long-term. My new relationship soon ended, not with a bang but a whimper. I can't say I blame her for dumping me either, I wasn't exactly good company.

As for my estranged wife's new relationship, well he, Wayne Taylor, was a store man at the dockyard in Plymouth, the same age as my wife at that time, 28. He was a rather tall, skinny chap, who apparently caught the bus to her home from the dockyard most days as he couldn't drive and I can't say that from what I heard I thought very much of him. At first though, I didn't worry about his role in my daughters' lives. But that was soon to change…

By late spring 1994, my wife applied to the court to reduce my contact with my daughters to just once a fortnight from the 'every weekend and Wednesday teatime' order agreed just four months before. She wanted this reduced to just alternate weekends only, because, she claimed, the kids came back 'overtired'. Soon after her new boyfriend moved in, the children began to say that they wanted to live with me as Mum's new boyfriend "isn't very nice." From what they said, he shouted at them lots, he always asked them about me and, all in all, they just didn't want to live in a house with him. They also hated his smoking, something their mother and I never did. They were clear in one thing; they loved their mother and they were happy to live with their mother. But not if he was there.

It was a really sick feeling to have to take them, protesting, home to him after every time I saw them. I even began to have fantasies about snatching the kids and going off on the run. But, if I did this, I reasoned after I had used up all the limits on my credit cards, what then? I had no cash to go with. And what if one of the children got ill? No, it would be madness to do such a thing. But little did I know what insanity the courts were about to inflict on us over the next decade.…

So, as we were going back to court anyway, not by my choice, and the girls were unhappy with their new living arrangements at home, I cross-applied for residence of the children. They were all continually saying with growing force that they want to live with me and their reasons had not changed. They were now aged three, five and seven. The family home had been sold and I was in the process of buying my next house, the one I still live in to this day. I reasoned that I could easily have the children live with me. In my work as a driving instructor, I could easily go part-time or I was even quite prepared to live wholly on benefits, as my wife was doing from the day she left, and be a full time carer.

The hearing took place at Plymouth County Court in December 1994. It was a day and a half hearing. My ex-wife had a solicitor and barrister, funded by legal aid. I represented myself. The judge, Recorder White, decided the children "cannot make decisions to change residence," but opted instead to maintain 'status quo' with their residence, and adjusted my time down with the girls to coincide more with the mother's wishes. In court, my wife claimed her boyfriend "hardly sees the children" but got on with him well when they did. This the judge readily accepted, so my residence application was then deemed to be 'without grounds'. I argued in court with much force that the court welfare officer had been seriously mislead by the children's mother about her boyfriend's role in my children's lives, and failed to investigate the merits of my residence application seriously, or even at all. In his summing up prior to making the order, Recorder White did observe that Mr Taylor, the mother's boyfriend, should have 'at least been seen' by the court welfare officer, but did nothing to rectify this unbelievable defect in the process regarding this man's living arrangements with my children.

Well, we kept with the weekly teatime contacts, but weekends became alternate from Friday at 5 pm to 6 pm Sunday night, with half of all school holidays each through the final days of 1994 and beyond. This was meant to be the definitive order.

Almost immediately, my ex-wife broke the arrangements, in the first week of January 1995. I went to the mother's home to collect the girls for the midweek contact, and the house was deserted, no one was home. The next day, as the court office opened, I was there filing for enforcement proceedings, got the papers stamped up with the court seal, and drove to her solicitor's office and served her solicitor direct. The enforcement hearing was listed for early February 1995.

The next midweek contact resumed, and things continued as ordered. We both were in court three weeks after, again before Recorder White.

At first, Recorder White seemed angry. He started by asking of my ex-wife's solicitor just as to why her client broken his order 'barely after the ink had dried'. Her solicitor came up with feeble excuse that after the half Xmas holiday contact her client had 'got the days mixed up'. But what nonsense – Tuesday, as always, was still followed by the Wednesday, the day specified for midweek contact. After more frowning, and the most feeble attempt of a threat by Recorder White to move the kids to me if she broke more orders, he then accepted the claim of 'confusion' on the mother's part and closed the hearing down. We went home, but that most feeble of threats to move the girls to me held well for over 18 months before the mother broke any further court orders for contact.

So contact continued – and so did the children's complaints about the mother's new man. These complaints had now gone on for months, and the children's complaints about Taylor 'not being very nice' now included complaints of being hurt by him on occasions months prior to the hearing before Recorder White – and these complaints mushroomed after it.

One particular occasion of these assaults by Wayne Taylor on my children the court welfare officer and Recorder White chose to ignore dated back four months prior to the residence hearing . This was back in August 1994. It was on a Wednesday teatime in early August after I picked the girls up that I heard about this particular occasion of my youngest two daughters being hit by this man for making noise, one of the most serious complaints about the mother's new man up to that point. Worse though subsequently followed. Now on this occasion the girls were clearly distressed about what took place the day before. Upon returning the girls home, I passed a message back through the children to the mother's boyfriend, Wayne Taylor, after this latest assault, that if he kept hurting my children he would have me to answer to, hoping that would deter him from physically hurting my children anymore. It actually did, in a way, for a short while at least, but not as I imagined or intended.

On the next weekend contact that August, I arrived to collect my daughters at 9 am, the Saturday. Upon arrival, my ex-wife came down the drive with my daughters. This was unusual as for months, the children were simply let out of the door as I arrived. She brought a message for me – that being I return the girls to her at lunchtime. I told her it was a full weekend contact, and I would be returning them on Sunday evening, as detailed in the court order.

As I ended that sentence, Wayne, dressed in combat trousers and a muscle vest, runs down the drive from the rear of the house directly towards me, clearly shaping up to attack, in front of my children, in what was obviously a planned ambush of me – with the mother somewhat complicit in this ambush it appeared.

Sensing imminent attack, I pushed Lisa out of the way, who had now come and stood beside me, and punched Taylor squarely in the face as soon as he approached. He staggered back, completely stunned. Now seeing red, I punched him over and over again, partly to ensure he could not attack me, and partly through anger that he'd been hurting my children and now had the cheek to interfere with my collecting of the children. We both ended up on the floor, exchanging blows, although none of his connected. I recall both my glasses I wore then and my watch coming off, and at that moment I wanted his blood. The fracas lasted several seconds before I felt myself being lifted off of Taylor from behind, by someone lifting me from under my arms. Meanwhile, Taylor was now laid on the floor, not moving much.

I turned to see who had lifted me up from behind, at first thinking Taylor had an accomplice, and he too would attack me. But no, it was a neighbour of my ex-wife who was washing his car in the road, who, having seen what was going on, decided to intervene and break things up. I'm glad he did, as I really don't know to this day where it or I would have stopped.

"Not in front of the children, not in front of the children," reasoned the neighbour with me, now positioned between me and Taylor as he slowly got off the ground and hid behind my ex-wife. The neighbour was a large, possibly Greek or Middle Eastern man in his 40s – he only wanted this all to stop and his intervention was completely as 'peacemaker'.

Now the fight had stopped, my children were distressed, and my ex-wife was consoling Taylor, who was looking somewhat the worse for wear. To this day I still clearly recall Taylor's look of shock on his face when he clearly set out to attack me, but ended up the worse for it. If he had simply stayed indoors, nothing would have happened. By now, Lisa had picked up my glasses and watch; I told the girls to get into my car, while their mother took a rather bloodied boyfriend back into her house. I then took my daughters to the local police station where I reported his approach and intended attack on me. My thinking was to do this properly, through the right channels. But that proved to be a brick wall that we immediately ran into.

At Plympton police station, which was about a quarter of a mile away, I reported the attempted attack on me by Taylor, and his assaults on my children in the days and weeks before. The police officer, at first had some sympathy for my plight, having just arrived to collect my children and being attacked by Mum's new man in the process. He refused to take any statement off my children, though, but suggested I "take it up with Social Services" on the Monday if this man had been hurting my children.

We were in the police station for about 45 minutes; I gave a statement about what had happened, and I insisted in that statement my children's allegations of assault by Taylor were included, much to the police officer's reluctance.

But just before we left, another policeman at the station passed a message to the officer I was seeing that Mr Taylor had just phoned in and cross-alleged assault by me upon him, and the police would have to take a statement from him too regarding what he was claiming.

The police officer went on to tell me his 'gut instinct' was that we would both get cautions. It seemed to him that although Taylor had appeared to have come off worse, he should not have come out in such a threatening manner in the first place, or even come out at all when the father was just picking up his children. The policeman said that they had already established through checks that neither of us had any criminal history for violence of any kind either. Hearing the police officer's words and gauging his attitude suggested to me that we would both end up being told off, and Taylor would in all probability never come out again when I picked the kids up. Also, I thought, Taylor would in all probability stop hurting my children, and that would be the end of it all.

But, like most things that happened in this part of my life, nothing went as expected. The police officer I reported the attack to went to interview Wayne Taylor later that day to get his side of the story. Upon meeting him, it transpired that they were both work colleagues when the police officer previously worked in Devonport Dockyard himself prior to joining the force.

To say this reunification of former workmates coloured the police officer's attitude was an understatement to say the least. Gone went the 'caution' all round thinking, as was the sympathy towards Dad picking up his kids and being interfered with by Mum's new boyfriend. And a mystery witness, who just so happened to be opening her curtains opposite when I arrived and 'seeing' all the incident unfold, appeared too.

Well, later that Saturday the police officer phones me, and tells me to report to Plympton police station at 7.30 am on the Sunday morning to be interviewed 'on tape'. I told him I had my daughters with me for the weekend and I asked if we could make the interview later that day. The police officer simply told me that if I did not attend Plympton police station at 7.30 am sharp, he would come and arrest me, kids there or not. So, I made a point of enjoying the rest of the Saturday with my children, put them to bed that evening while arranging for my father to baby-sit them on the Sunday morning while I went and gave the taped interview.

To cut a long story short, Wayne Taylor, my ex-wife and the invisible at the time behind-the-curtains-witness opposite had all made statements later on the Saturday afternoon. The statements, all taken by Taylor's former work mate/now police officer, concurred with each other in that Taylor had walked peacefully down the driveway to 'chat' to me – and I attacked him. To this day I never could work out just how the neighbour on the opposite side of the street, behind closed windows and opening her curtains 25 yards away could tell just what Wayne Taylor had in mind when coming down the driveway to me, but there you go. Of course, the matter of Taylor's assaults on my children was suppressed completely out of the magistrates' hearing weeks later, the mother was deemed an honest witness who backed Taylor's 'only wanted a chat' claim, despite it coming out that she was dishonestly claiming single parent benefits while living with Taylor – a working partner – that had not been declared to the benefits agency, and I was convicted after trial by a single stipendiary magistrate of common assault, given a suspended four-month prison sentence and ordered to pay Taylor £150 compensation at £2 a week.

The stipendiary magistrate observed that while there was "some doubt" over Mr Taylor's motives and manner in approaching me, he deemed I had gone "beyond the levels of self defence" and found me guilty. So, there we have it, I now left the Magistrates' Court with a criminal record for violence.

Surprisingly, before Recorder White in the contact/residence hearing several weeks later, the mother's barrister chose not to bring up any mention of this conviction for assault by me on her boyfriend, in front of the children, which I really expected to be used against me with venom. Lets face it, I now had a criminal record for violence, and in front of the kids. Of course, if she had chosen to use this, Taylor's true position of residence with her in the children's home would have altered the entire investigation by the court welfare officer in my residence application, who would have then had to look into the children's relationship with him. As, too, the benefits agency may have investigated her 'lone parent' income support claim. Although I brought up Taylor's residence with my children not only to the court welfare officer when she interviewed me, but with Recorder White during the hearing, both chose to completely ignore it. As I said earlier, at the final hearing all Recorder White observed was, "Mr Taylor should have at least been seen by the court welfare officer," but nothing was done to rectify this defect in the process.

To be fair, Wayne Taylor did not assault my children for quite a few weeks after the residence/contact hearing before Recorder White. However, in early March 1995, Taylor, in a fit of temper, pinched Lisa, who was then aged just eight. When I heard about this on the next contact I was outraged. I wanted to go and pinch him, or worse, but guessing the mother and her lover would concoct another story against me, producing yet more invisible witnesses to back her claims, I took the police officer's advice and called Social Services. Funny, although I was charged by the police for assault on Taylor months before, assaults on my children by him did not seem to warrant the attention or time of the police, they'd rather pass it off to a council-employed social worker. Anyway, I entered the recommended process. I also immediately reapplied for residence of each of my children to the Plymouth County Court. The girls each told me they wanted to live with me because Wayne was so nasty to them.

Anyway, a Devon social worker, Ms D (the social workers cannot be named, by order of the court) was contacted, and she interviewed Lisa about the pinching a day or so later. Lisa revealed the pinching of her by Wayne Taylor and his previous assaults on her and her sisters. The social worker shortly later interviewed the mother, who at first admitted that Taylor had indeed pinched Lisa but "only to show her what it was like" because she had just pinched one of her sisters. The mother at first further admits he has smacked them "once or twice before," but added "never hard." The social worker promptly interviews Taylor, who flatly denied ever pinching Lisa, or ever hitting any of the children. The mother then withdrew her previous statement, and then denied Taylor had ever touched any of the children. Immediately, the social worker convenes a child protection meeting to consider the risk to the children at the Plymouth NSPCC offices in Plymouth, as it was clear the mother was unwilling or unable to protect the children. At last, I thought, someone is listening.

So in May 1995, a child protection case conference was convened. Myself, my ex-wife, Wayne Taylor, the children's school's head teacher, a health visitor, an NSPCC representative, the social worker (Ms D) and a police child protection officer are invited to the meeting to consider registration of my children on the 'At Risk' register. All attend the meeting around this very large table. The social worker reads her report out to the meeting, which now detailed each of my daughter's claims against Taylor, and the mother's conflicting accounts regarding the pinching incident. The NSPCC chairman asks Taylor direct about the assaults, which are all met by him with flat denials. The mother is asked about why she gave conflicting accounts of the pinching incident, and other assaults, to which she simply answered, "no comment." I was then asked my views on registration, and I said that while the children lived in a house with him, risk was obvious, especially as the mother seemed unable or unwilling to protect the children adequately. Taylor then piped up and said the only person present with a conviction for assault present was me – for assaulting him! This brought an immediate response from the chair of the meeting, who told him that they were only interested in who was assaulting the children. I then told the conference that I was reapplying for residence of all three children, with contact to the mother – but only when Wayne Taylor was not present.

This statement of mine somewhat disturbed the social worker, Ms D, who then changed course somewhat. She then said she now recommended the children be registered on the At Risk register for *emotional abuse* instead of *physical risk*, because the parents were fighting over custody. My reply that we were only fighting over custody because of the physical risk in the mother's home did not move her one bit, and to maintain the meeting's united front, each child was then registered for being at emotional risk by the people empowered to vote.

When I protested about the change of risk category, I was told that the category of registration was irrelevant, as the children would receive the same degree of protection whatever registration status applied. But it was clear to me that once the residence of the children with the mother was in any form of jeopardy, the professionals, led by Ms D, seemed to weaken their resolve to adequately recognise the risks posed.

Within weeks, the children reported yet another assault by Wayne Taylor to me. They claimed Taylor had again hurt the youngest one (now four) when she got out of bed and came downstairs. Another call to the social worker prompted a further interview, this time of all three children, but no action taken, despite Ms D telling me afterwards that she believed what the children had said about this particular incident too.

Still trying to do things 'the right way', I then applied to the court for an injunction banning Mr Taylor from not only assaulting any of my children, but keeping him away from their home when they were there, and I supported my application with copies of the Social Services' reports and the case conference report. His Honour, Judge James Wigmore, issued an immediate injunction upon Taylor not to assault the children, but unbelievably left him in their home, despite the court records showing him as having a home elsewhere. The injunction was immediately served upon Taylor by a court official, and everyone was ordered back to the court two weeks later.

At this next hearing, Mr Taylor, again denying any wrongdoing, agreed to give the court an undertaking not to ever touch my children after the injunction expired.

But, as now was the norm, within days the youngest was assaulted by him once again in their home. This time he smacked her at the dinner table in front of her sisters for refusing to eat something. Once again I informed the social worker, who once again interviewed the children individually, heard their complaints first hand and saw the mother and Taylor who both flatly denied any smacking or assault took place. Ms D tells me that she is unable to do anything yet again, but will note what has been said.

Not happy with this, I sought enforcement from the court of Mr Taylor's undertaking to the court not to assault my children. Within days we were before His Honour Judge Wigmore. Despite claiming all innocence of wrongdoing to my children, Taylor turned up in court with a barrister funded by himself to defend him.

But, like so much that takes place in the family courts, utter farce rather than the interests of any child unfolded. Judge Wigmore refused to read the Social Services' reports of what the children had ever said. Instead, Judge Wigmore started the proceedings with the question to me: "Did you fill in these application forms, Mr Harris?" which he obviously knew I did. I replied, "Yes, of course." Judge Wigmore then said, "Well, you haven't filled the forms out correctly, have you?" I asked him to explain as to what was wrong with them, to which the judge replied, "Well, it's not for me to give you legal advice."

Judge Wigmore then went on to say he was going to dismiss my application to protect my children without any further consideration, and ordered me to pay Mr Taylor's barrister's costs and time off work. To say my exchange with Wigmore at this point was heated is an understatement. I told him that there was documentation from Social Services, confirming these children were being regularly assaulted by Mr Taylor going back at least a year. I told him these assaults were escalating in force and frequency, often over the most trivial of issues. I made the point that the mother clearly could not be relied upon to protect the children, in no small part because she supported Taylor against the children – referring him to her conflicting accounts of the pinching incident – but also her denials that he even lived there. My point that whether the forms were correctly filled in or not was irrelevant as to what was happening and Taylor's broken court undertaking not to touch these children. I asked Judge Wigmore if the forms really did need redrafting, he should simply adjourn the hearing for a day or two, so I could amend the forms, then the real issue – protecting the children from further assaults by Mr Taylor – could be addressed by the court.

Unfortunately, Judge Wigmore of the Plymouth family court was having none of it, he simply did not want to listen – or protect my children. He dismissed my application without any further consideration and ordered that I pay all Mr Taylor's full costs for coming to court that day. I told Wigmore that I wouldn't be paying him anything. I then asked him to point me in the direction of how I appeal his appalling decision. Again, Judge Wigmore refused to tell me the appeals process, and closed the hearing down, leaving Mr Taylor with a huge smile on his face – and free to go back to my children's home and continue assaulting them.

So, after leaving the courtroom totally shell-shocked, I sought out the avenues of appeal. This farce dished out by Judge James Wigmore I reasoned could not possibly be right. Wigmore's absurd handling of the matter that day proved quite wrong on appeal too.

There was, at that time, much publicity of a case in South Wales where a mother's new boyfriend, after numerous assaults on her five-year-old daughter, killed the child and was convicted of manslaughter. Much press coverage was made of the fact the authorities in South Wales, the police, the social workers and the family courts had heard numerous complaints from the child about being hurt by her mother's boyfriend, but did nothing. The father's residence application to move his child to him was also shunned by the South Wales family court. The boyfriend got ten years' prison, but as the press at the time reflected, that child's death could so easily have been prevented if only the authorities had listened and acted. So I left the courtroom to seek out the appeals system.

CHAPTER 3

Britain's Top Two Judges Get Involved

Acting in person, I made numerous enquiries at the reception area of the Plymouth court and a clerk explained the appeals process. I then applied to appeal to the Court of Appeal in London. It took over three months to get the appeal heard. In December 1995, the matter went up to the appeal court. Myself, alone, I took my case to London. Taylor, who was supported by my ex-wife, her parents and his parents were summoned up too. So, at 10.30 am we all went into Court 66 before Lord Justice Thorpe and Lady Justice Butler-Sloss. It is a daunting place to go; there was a big libel trial on there that day, many TV cameras and a number of familiar TV reporters were outside the building interviewing various people.

In the appeal court, which is held in an open courtroom, Lady Justice Butler-Sloss started to go through my application to appeal with me. I had provided the Social Services' reports detailing what my daughters were saying, the same reports I provided to Judge Wigmore. It was clear they had studied the decision of Judge Wigmore in detail. The lady appeal judge asked Wayne Taylor what he had to say for himself about these reported assaults on the children, but all she was met by was his outright denials. It was clear she did not believe him and asked him to sit down.

Lady Justice Butler-Sloss then turned to me. I stood up. She asked was my main concern to protect my children, or to see the boyfriend in prison. Of course, the protection of my children was my only concern, and I told her so. Butler-Sloss then told me that the best channel to do this was to apply for residence. I told her I had done this at the Plymouth court nearly a year ago, but the application seemed to be going nowhere.

Butler-Sloss said that if I were to agree to let the appeal court simply substitute the award of costs against me by Judge Wigmore for a no costs order, meaning I had not got to pay the boyfriend for his time or representation in the court, they would promise to put pressure upon the Plymouth court to expedite my residence application.

This seemed a reasonable response at the time. But that was to be my first serious mistake in trusting a judge at any court to honour their word, or even do their duty.

In their judgement, which is given in public and is on public record and runs to eight pages, Lord Justice Thorpe gave the first reading. After disagreeing with Judge Wigmore's dismissal of my application back in Plymouth to commit the boyfriend to prison for assaulting my children on a technicality, Thorpe said, "…there was some independent evidence to suggest that, technicality or not, Mr Taylor was in breach…" [of the order not to assault my children.]

Thorpe went on to say, "If there was an assault on August 1st, that was something of crucial significance in the determination of the outstanding residence application."

And further on he added, "It seems to me vital that the outstanding issues between Mr and Mrs Harris as to residence, and incidentally as to the protection of the children while Mrs Harris is in relationship with Mr Taylor, be promoted to a much higher place in the priority order of waiting cases."

And further again Thorpe observed in regard to the way Judge Wigmore dealt with my application in this way: "It seems to me that it would be hard to define what greater particularity could have written into the application as a litigant in person on the appropriate County Court form…I have some misgivings as to whether the learned judge was on sure ground to dismiss the application summarily."

Sounds fair enough. My gut feeling on the day was Wigmore

got it all wrong, he should have dealt with the application. Thorpe simply confirmed Wigmore was wrong.

Lady Justice Butler-Sloss then said, "It would have been far better if Judge Wigmore had been able to reason with Mr Harris, recommend to Mr Harris that he really did not want to put Mr Taylor inside; what he wanted was to be sure that his children were protected from what Mr Harris believes was the unjustified smacking of his children, and there is an undertaking [which replaced the injunction when it expired, but carries the same weight] not to smack or touch these children."

Well, protect the children, move them if Mr Taylor remains in residence with the mother if they cannot be protected from him. That was all I sought and what I was all about and at last a court seemed to agree.

So in January 1996, I sent the above court judgement from the appeal court to the NSPCC, asking if the children's risk registration – emotional abuse – was appropriate in the light of what the appeal court had said. Many weeks later, a child protection officer at the Plymouth NSPCC wrote back and said she had read the Social Services records since At Risk registration in May 1995 and the appeal court judgement, and was recommending that Social Services in Plymouth should convene another case conference to consider registration of each child for physical abuse as well as emotional abuse.

The new social worker, Ms A, rejected the NSPCC recommendation, stating further registration was "unnecessary". Meanwhile, the promise of Lady Justice Butler-Sloss to put pressure upon the Plymouth court to get on and deal with my residence application back in December 1995 started to look like a lie intended just to make me go away quietly. Four months on, it was now April 1996 and still no listing.

Then in early May 1996, while still awaiting for the Plymouth court to actually list my residence application, the middle child reported yet another slapping by Taylor upon her, for messing around at the dinner table. I contacted Social Services once again, another social worker, a Ms A, told me they would note it, but nothing more.

Her sole concern seemed to be to ensure the mother kept residence, not protecting the children. The promise of Lady Justice Butler-Sloss to put pressure upon the Plymouth court to actually getting on with my application, now nearly six months before, proved by now to be an untruth from the court just to make me go away. Nothing happened at all.

My feeling then was me and my daughters were being shafted by not only the appalling anti-male feminists of Social Services, but by each judge in each court, with the subsequence that sooner or later one of my children would be seriously hurt, or worse. The abuse of my children had now gone on for well over a year, and it was increasing in frequency, as well as force. I decide to take this out of the secret courts and into public. Doing things 'the right way' was pointless, there was a clear gender issue going on here, wherever I turned. In desperation, I then decided to stage a roof top protest at the Plymouth Social Services' office. I was going public. So I alerted the local TV, press and Radio on the morning of the day of 8th May 1996 of my intentions. Plymouth is a fairly sleepy backwater, protests are rare events, so the attention of the press was easily attracted. I also bought two large cans of white automotive spray paint from my local car accessory shop.

So, with TV cameras rolling, press photographers and radio in attendance, I climbed onto the roof of the Plymouth Social Services' office in the Efford district of Plymouth, where the social worker I wanted removed from the case, Ms A, was based. It was handy in the sense that out of all their offices in the city, the Efford branch where she was based had a roof easily accessible by way of a small ladder. I parked, I took my ladder off my car roof rack and simply went up with spray cans in hand. I climbed and sprayed various statements on their pitched roof including 'My kids are in danger, ask the NSPCC – they've read your files'. Another sprayed statement of mine was 'Sack *** *****' (Ms A, another social worker, who cannot be named, by order of the court) and 'The court of appeal read your files too last year and deemed my kids are at risk, so why don't you?' and 'Are you really waiting for a body to be thrown out – listen to my kids'. I sprayed much more, but after all this time I really cannot recall accurately what else I sprayed, but all statements were of the same theme. It was a large roof, which gave wide scope for many statements. I used up the two large cans of automotive spray paint.

After an hour, the relevant press attention had departed and with promises of Social Services' senior management to investigate the case, I came down from the roof and was arrested by waiting police and taken to Plymouth's Charles Cross police station. I was later charged with criminal damage, to which I pleaded guilty, received a conditional discharge and ordered to pay £50 towards the £300 worth of damage caused. I now had a first criminal conviction for criminal damage.

Rooftop protest father in court

A PLYMOUTH man, described as a loving and concerned father, staged a rooftop protest against Devon Social Services over concerns for his three young daughters, a city court heard.

The 37-year-old man, who cannot be named for legal reasons, painted demands like: "My kids demand the right to be heard" on a wall of the DSS office in Douglass Road, Efford, on May 7, which cost £300 to clean off, city magistrates were told.

The father was protesting at delays by social services in investigating his claims that his daughters were being sexually abused by his ex-wife's boyfriend.

And the rooftop actions of the "desperate" father,

'My kids deserve the right to be heard'

who pleaded guilty to criminal damage, achieved what he set out to do, defence solicitor Anthony Daniel told magistrates.

The defendant was first spotted on the roof by Social Services District Manager Elizabeth Hitchings, the court was told.

And before he was coaxed down by police, he threw down to her a written list of demands in connection with the safety of his children.

Mr Daniel said: "Later he was interviewed by police who were also concerned about the information he gave about physical molestation of his children by his ex-wife's some-time live-in boyfriend

Feminist

"He had tried for months for some investigation by social services, he enlisted the NSPCC and even went to the Court of Appeal in December last year– which was concerned that matters were not proceeding – and he even came to blows with the boyfriend.

"He is a concerned and loving father and felt his desires were being put on the back-burner by social service workers who, he

felt, were being feminist and not even-handed when they told him the children were better off with their mother."

Mr Daniels said that in desperation the father staged the rooftop protest to get someone who was independent of himself, his ex-wife or social services, to talk to his children and find out what was happening.

"He achieved what he set out to do. Social services have complied with a new case worker and he feels that things are going in the right direction and his children's welfare will be safeguarded."

Magistrates gave the father 12 months' conditional discharge, and ordered him to pay £50 compensation to Devon Social Services towards the cost of getting the wall cleaned.

In what was believed to be the first father ever upon a roof in protest over his children in the UK, Mark Harris climbed upon the roof of the Plymouth Social Services department that consistently ignored his children's complaints of abuse by their mothers boyfriend. - June 1996, reproduced by kind permission of The Herald Plymouth.

Believing, like most UK citizens, that 'the system' will protect my children, all I simply sought was protection through the courts and through the social workers, time and again for my children. Back as far as late 1994, after my altercation with the mother's boyfriend, I tried to do things 'the right way'. I obtained an injunction forbidding him from assaulting my daughters through the civil courts. When he breached that order, I sought his committal to prison for contempt, this being 'the right way' to go. But it was clear that in the realms of the secret family courts of the UK, the agenda, especially where young children are involved, is to do nothing to undermine the mother. And the anti-male brigade from the local Social Services' office seemed hell bent on promoting the same twisted cause.

Anyway, my rooftop protest did have two effects. One was that the Plymouth court immediately listed my residence application, now some 18 months after I had applied, within weeks, for early June 1996. I sensed they feared the court rooftop was next. But, unfortunately, my protest enraged the anti-dad/male brigade at Devon Social Services. They immediately convened another case conference within days in the May, but with the NSPCC case worker who recommended physical abuse registration excluded. Instead, the social workers chaired the entire meeting, wrote a five-page report that was read out, of which four were pages were entirely devoted to my rooftop protest and pending conviction for criminal damage. They unanimously voted that I was emotionally abusing the children by taking my complaints public, and continued the registration of each child for emotional abuse, now caused by my court applications and rooftop demo. I pushed with great venom the point that they were ignoring not only their own reports that my children were complaining of assaults in their home, now going back nearly two years, but the NSPCC recommendations of physical risk in the mother's home. I passed out copies of the judgement of the appeal court six months prior too. Unbelievably, the Social Services' chairperson (Ms C) simply said the meeting was now closed, and if I'd got anything to say, to tell the family court next month! They were simply not for listening. The whole process now degenerated into farce and sham, the process was corrupted to engineer a desired outcome. The mother and Mr Taylor left the conference with the parting comment they were now stopping contact between myself and the children until the court case. In other words, she was intending to break the court order, and she did.

Anyway, a couple of weeks later in June 1996, the residence hearing was listed before a Judge Audrey Sander in the Plymouth County Court. Social Services, without any request from the court, filed a report recommending the mother kept residence, and they would keep the children on the At Risk register because I'd taken to protests in public, thereby, was their view, I was undermining the mother's home, which they deemed emotional abuse! Nothing then, at all, was included in their report about the catalogue of assaults the children told them directly about what they were enduring in their home with their mother and her boyfriend. They simply pretended Wayne Taylor did not exist.

Anyway, we all went to the court. Now I had, for this hearing, obtained legal aid, so I had a solicitor and barrister. Again, naively, I thought 'right' would eventually prevail, surely. I had all the reports of these assaults, which were passed, to my legal advisor, going back now almost two years. I had the printed judgement of the appeal court six months before which was clear: if the mother was still with Mr Taylor ANY assault by him on my children would be 'crucial' as to deciding if the children remain with her. Taylor was still in residence, this time he actually came to court for the first time with the mother, so there could be no dispute over his existence or role in her life. The children had now also told the second court welfare officer, just appointed, they would like to live with Dad and see Mum lots. Just how much more of a case did I need, I thought.

However, this just proved to be just one more false dawn. My barrister, down from London and full of bluster and self-importance, told me outside the court door that I had a hopeless case to move the children, as the court welfare officer made no recommendation to move the children to me, and the social workers were actually recommending residence stayed with the mother. We had a heated exchange in the conference room. I went through the court of appeal judgement with him, as well as the NSPCC recommendations and the social worker reports of the assaults on my children, as told to them by the kids. But he was unmoved. He told me that with no recommendation, the court would never move my children to me, and unless I accepted the recommendations of the court welfare officer regarding my time seeing my children, I would probably never see my children ever again. In other words, go away quietly, I see the kids. Rock any boats, never see them again.

This was the gun held to my head, by my own representative who's meant to be fighting my case. The mother had refused all contact for the past couple of weeks, and my own adviser was telling me that unless I backed down, I'd never see my children again. What do you do? At first, I told him to stick his advice where the sun does not shine, I'd go into court and fight my own case, and appeal any decision that did not move the children to me. Four letter words were used by me to him, with frequency. At this point I expected my barrister to just dump me and exit the court, but strangely he did not. Instead, he went out and conferred with the court welfare officer.

Some minutes later, he came back into the conference room, we were now well past the time we should have been in the court before the judge. It seemed to me as if he was acting on some sort of direction, possibly sent out by the judge I wondered, to get some agreement between myself and the mother. My barrister announced that as the protection of my children was my reason for being in court, he asked how about if I agreed that the mother kept residence, I got lots of contact back, and a family assistance order is made, where the children will be seen by the court welfare officer regularly for the next six months. If there were further assaults, he reasoned, they could tell him and we would all come back to court in six months' time – at another review – via the court welfare officer to see how it'd all worked out.

Under extreme duress, I eventually accepted this. I did reason if the assaults upon my children by the mother's boyfriend stopped and I saw the kids lots – well, mission accomplished, I suppose. So we all then went in about an hour late before Judge Sander, who rubber-stamped up the agreement, and we all went home. By now,

I had little faith that any of this would protect my children, but I thought we would give it a go.

So, residence of the girls stayed with the mother, Mr Taylor remained in residence, and I regained regular contact within days. However, Judge Sander also made the family assistance order to last until the next court review listed for December 1996 so the children would be seen by the court welfare officer so they could raise any 'matters' they wished with him. And speak to him they did.

Just five weeks later, the court welfare officer made arrangements to see the children under the terms of the family assistance order. My youngest child started crying when he sees them. He enquires as to what was wrong with her. The youngest started to tell him (she was now five) that the night before, Wayne came into the bedroom she shares with her middle sister at her mother's, put his hands around her face, and squeezed it until she cried, because she was making a noise. The middle sister confirmed the account of this, and the youngest pointed out a bruise to her face that he inflicted.

The court welfare officer reported this assault the next day to the two social workers now assigned to the case, Ms D and Ms P. Once again, the children tell them what happened, too, but Taylor, backed by the mother, simply denied anything at all happened. So, armed with the report of both the social workers and the court welfare officer, I immediately reapply for residence of each child on the basis of this latest attack by Taylor on my children that the court welfare officer saw as serious. Nothing was going to knock me off course now, so I dumped my Barrister, menace the Plymouth court for a listing, and we get before Judge Sander again a few weeks later, in early September 1996.

Then in court, I told Judge Sander that last year the mother's boyfriend's assaults on my children were, in the eyes of the Court of Appeal, crucial in determining the issue of residence. I also pointed out the NSPCC view, and that these children for over two years had reported numerous assaults by Taylor to myself, two social workers and now a court welfare officer, so just what more did she need? I then backed this up with the written judgement from the Court of Appeal (public) records to prove to her their view was if a *single* assault took place, it was unequivocal; if he was still with the mother, the children should live with me. Unbelievably, Judge Audrey Sander's blunt reply was, "I'm not interested in what they [at The Court of Appeal] say up there!" Unbelievable, but true. I was gobsmacked.

Judge Sander then simply adjourned that hearing until December 1996, and left once again everything as it was, with Mr Taylor still regularly breaking his court undertaking not to touch my children – and still living with them.

Then, weeks later, the children made a point of speaking to the court welfare officer again in October 1996 when he visited them . This time they elaborated about what was going on in their home. Unfortunately, he passed the buck back to the social workers. The girls reported a catalogue of assaults by Taylor to him, and told him, "We all want to live with Dad." They were now aged five, seven and nine. I already had yet another adjourned residence application before the court after yet more assaults on my children during the summer of 1996. Now the children had told the right person, while in their mother's home, where they wanted to live – and why.

Then the social workers, Ms D, a Ms P and a Ms C (not the Ms C chairing the case conference back in May, but the line manager of Ms P, whom by chance I later discovered she lived in relationship with!) heard about this the next day and called an emergency case conference for the day after. Usually, case conferences are arranged many weeks in advance, but this one was put in place within a record 24 hours. And neither did the mother or Wayne Taylor attend. At the conference, again minus the NSPCC representative, nothing was mentioned or reported about the now two-and-a-half years of assaults by Taylor upon the children. Not only was nothing reported to the conference about the children's statements to the court welfare officer just a couple of days before, but instead the social workers conspired to falsely report that the children were refusing to speak to anyone anymore, *including* the court welfare officer about anything. So they then wanted to reduce my contact to two hours a fortnight for six months while they undertook a comprehensive assessment of the children. At this emergency conference, I was not aware of what the children had just told the court welfare officer, although it later emerged that he had told Ms P and Ms D the day before the conference just what the children had said. Clearly, they were now perverting the course of the outcome to obtain a desired result by misleading the conference. Anyway, the conference, more kangaroo court, was abruptly ended and the next day we were all in court, minus the court welfare officer, before Judge Sander, sitting in Truro, Cornwall.

This was November 1996. It was a short hearing in Truro court. The mother had, overnight, surprisingly made an application to the court which coincided with what the social workers wanted at the case conference – namely to reduce my contact to two hours a fortnight, supervised, while social workers did a comprehensive assessment, to last six months, to see what the kids really wanted. I was served with a copy of her application in the court reception area. Social Services had a supporting statement pre-prepared at the court to support her application, too. They, too, served me with the papers in the same manner. The social workers are clearly now not only working against the children's well-being and corrupting the process, but they are clearly advising the mother on legal manoeuvres, such as making the court application. Not only that, the social workers Ms C, Ms P and Ms D even have the gall to sit with the mother and her solicitor in the court during the proceedings.

Again, I reiterated to Judge Sander that without any evidence of what the children were telling the court welfare officer, nothing should be done until we heard what he had to say. Nothing about the now two-and-a-half years of assaults by Taylor upon them was in the Social Services report, so I asked that the court welfare officer be brought to court before anything was done. But Judge Sander refused everything I wanted until the next month's full hearing. I asked why my last residence application took 18 months to list, but the mother's application to reduce my contact to almost nothing gets listed in 24 hours. Judge Sander refused to answer that point, too. But looking back, I believe Judge Sander, like it turned out the three social workers who lied firstly in their report to the case conference and now the court, which reiterated the false phrase "the children are not speaking to anyone, including the court welfare officer..." knew full well what the children had really told him. I believe Judge Sander deliberately scuppered my residence application, which was still live because she simply did not want to deal with the huge mess this was all becoming. Also very strange, the court welfare officer was 'unavailable' to attend the Truro court that day...

So for the next month, my children and I had to undergo the humiliation of 'supervised contact' of two hours a fortnight by the cohabiting Ms P and Ms C. (Their living arrangements and relationship was not known to me at this time, although by now I had suspicions...)

The next hearing was where my contact with my daughters was effectively ended for years by Judge Sander. This was now December 1996, a whole year after the Court of Appeal decision. This is the judge who 'did not care' what they said up in the Court of Appeal a year ago. She also seemed ambivalent as to what the children said, too, even when it was dragged from the court welfare officer that the children complained about Taylor assaulting them and they wanted to live with their dad. Judge Sander's excuse to disregard what the kids said to him then was "...the comprehensive assessment is underway, let that run its course, and review again then in six months...' In other words, the children stay with the mother, no matter what they said or what they wanted.

During the December 1996 hearing held at Exeter court, during my stint of being cross examined in the witness box, I turned to Judge Sander and asked was I understanding this correctly, that my contact with my children was to be restricted because the mother's boyfriend was assaulting my children. Unbelievably, Judge Sander said, "Yes, that is the case". She said it clear, she agreed in unequivocal terms, MY CONTACT WITH MY CHILDREN WAS BEING RESTRICTED BECAUSE WAYNE TAYLOR WAS ASSAULTING MY CHILDREN! She then went on to make an order putting me on supervised contact for six months, and leaving the mother's boyfriend still living with my children!

Now, all cases before circuit judges' cases are taped by the court loggers. Even my then latest solicitor said I had grounds to appeal, not only for being put on supervised contact, but on the residence issue too. But, after all the time limits expired to launch any appeal they said they would not apply for it anyway. Something sinister was going on below the surface, but I just could not work out what.

Well, I thought, quite naively, I will apply for an appeal without my solicitor, who by now was proving pretty limp. Appeals can be done out of time, and I will show Butler-Sloss and Thorpe at the Royal Courts of Justice just what Judge Sander had to say. I applied through the court service, which is the only channel, for a transcript of my evidence in the witness box and Judge Sander's comments, from start to finish. The hearing was held at Exeter County Court on 17th December 1996. This was to be the basis of my appeal.

The court transcribers, Smith Bernal of London, days after I placed the order, telephoned me. They said they had listened to the tapes, started the transcription of what was said, but then discovered the tape went blank near the end. *They told me they had to return the tape to the court because it appeared to have been tampered with*. I wrote to the Exeter court asking for an explanation and requested to hear the tape for myself, which is allowed.

Days later, I received an appointment to hear this tape with a court logger at Plymouth County Court, where the tapes for our case were stored. Hearing my evidence and the cross examination of myself before Judge Sander was a slightly strange experience. However, I got to my question to the judge "Is this correct that my contact with my children is being reduced to supervised contact, two hours a fortnight, because the mother's boyfriend is assaulting my children?". Then, unbelievably, the tape went blank as I started to speak! Only the beginning of my question "Is this…" can be heard. The tape then just went blank to the end. The court logger present and in charge of playing this tape back to me looked confused. He rewound the tape and played it again. Same again, start of my question, then the tape went blank. He couldn't explain what had happened, but he stated, "Something's very wrong, this just doesn't happen."

Once again, leaving a court shell-shocked by what had taken place, I set about the complaints procedures. I was furious. I sent letters to the County Court, the Court Service Headquarters and the Lord Chancellor's Department as the tape had obviously been sabotaged. Clearly, if one of my children were to have been seriously assaulted, or worse, by the mother's boyfriend after Judge Sander's comments, just how would that reflect upon her? No one responded with any answer to this for over one year. And of course, my appeal could not be started.

For nearly 18 months of endless letters, no response was given. Only then, when I threatened to get upon the Plymouth court roof in protest, were responses given.

The first response, from Plymouth court said:

"In reply to your letter dated 10 June 1998, I can confirm that tape number 701 from the hearing at Exeter on 17th December 1996 is blank from counter number 3061 to the end of the tape, but I am unable to give an explanation as to why.

Yours sincerely,

N Locock (Mrs)
Listing section."

Then, just four days after Plymouth court's response to the threat of a rooftop protest, I received a letter from the Court Service Customer Service Unit, London, saying:

"Further to your letter dated 15 June 1998 and your call today I am sorry for the delay in sending you a full reply but our enquiries into the issues you raise are taking longer than expected. However, I can assure you that a member of this unit will write back to you again as soon as possible.

Yours sincerely,

Casper Kennedy
Customer Service Unit."

Nine days after this response, the Court Service wrote again, dated 24ᵗʰ June 1998.

Now this letter went into a very long-winded explanation from them of how these court tapes are just *not* tampered with. They went on to say in that letter the clerk on duty operating the tape machine that day on 17ᵗʰ December 1996 had, unfortunately "left the court service" so they simply could not explain what had happened, but they did apologise for the inconvenience caused!

With this feeble 'apology', but no reason, now nearly 19 months after I first complained, the letter concluded with the now time honoured get-out phrase that takes place with secret family courts when you ask for investigation into any judicial or court behaviour:

"I should also add, due to the independence of the Judiciary, neither the Lord Chancellor, nor any Government official, can comment on how a Judge conducts a hearing, the evidence that he takes into account or the weight he gives to such evidence.

Yours sincerely,

Faqir Nawaz
Customer Services Unit."

These tapes are, we're told, kept safe and secure. A court logger sits with the machine at all times during hearings. He ensures as one tape expires, another is *already running*. The machines that record have two tapes so continual recording is maintained. The logger writes down who says what and when, noting the tape counter and time. He is the first into court with the tapes, and last to leave. He never leaves the machine during recording. The tapes are held in a secure room. Yet this particular part of taped evidence, kept for at least three years by law, becomes erased just at this most crucial time, with the judge saying the most ridiculous, and nobody can explain why. No other part of the two days of taped evidence is affected by erasure or fault, just my question to Judge Sander her absurd reply. I probably cannot say here, for fear of this book being stopped by the court, that I think this tape was deliberately erased to cover the judge's back in case something serious one day happened to one of my children in the mother's home. But it does leave an enormous suspicion to me that this is the case when no one can explain just why this particular portion of secure recording goes missing...

This was the point which confirmed to me that the family courts were indeed corrupt to the core, and whether you got what you wanted or not depended on not if you were right or wrong, not what was in any child's best interest, but dependent only on if you were either the mother or the father.

However, little did I know that the farce regarding Judge Sander and the erased tape on 17th December 1996, together with the order putting me on supervised contact because the mother's boyfriend continually assaulted my children, was just the start of the very steepest ascendancy to the nonsense that was take over my life for the next seven years.

On my second fortnightly two-hour supervised contact at my home (this was to go on until the social workers had completed their comprehensive assessment – about May 1997) after the last Sander hearing, the two social workers brought my children over for my two hour contact session. This was January 1997. About five minutes into the visit, my youngest daughter, then aged six, took her sock off and showed the social worker a cut to her foot. No prompting, no encouragement. She then told the social workers, *in my presence*, that her mother's boyfriend had pushed her into her bedroom door and caused this cut the night before. Her middle sister, who shared a bedroom with her, confirmed the story as it was told as she was in the room when this happened. I asked the social workers what they intended to do – or were they waiting for a child's body to be carried out of that house before they accepted what was going on?

I was assured by the cohabiting Ms P and Ms D, "We will be

taking action." I now had to watch my three daughters shortly afterwards be transported home by these two social workers, back to the home where they were receiving continual and escalating physical abuse, and I was powerless to do anything about it.

Now it was to be another two weeks before I was due to see my children again. A couple of days passed, and no update from Social Services, so I phoned to see what 'action' was being taken. I was told by Ms P that the mother had been visited regarding the cut foot to the youngest child. Ms P said the mother had bought new shoes that very week for the youngest (now six) and the new shoes had caused the cut to her foot. When the mother's boyfriend was approached about the claim, he simply denied ever pushing the child into the bedroom door and repeated, as usual, that he would never do such a thing. In other words, mother and her boyfriend were calling my children liars – and the social workers were siding with them against the children.

I saw red. I demanded to see the manager of Social Services' office. I got an appointment the very next day. When I arrived I was told by Ms P that Social Services were no longer prepared to supervise my contact and they were not having anything more to do with me. They then asked me to leave their offices and refused to talk to me anymore.

This was January 1997, and the social workers were now deliberately breaking the very court order they sought just four weeks ago – and my young daughters were still being physically abused in their home by a man who never even had to ask a court if he could see them, let alone live with them.

Cut off from my girls, I applied to court immediately for resumption of my previous order for staying contact. The reason the social workers put up to supervise my contact for the next six months (the comprehensive assessment they wanted to do) was now invalid as they had refused to take part in the very court order they sought.

Now, I was totally frustrated by all of this. Being put on supervised contact because *someone else* assaulted my children, then my supervised contact order being broken by the dishonest local authority through no fault of my own – and all because the mother's boyfriend assaulted my children yet again. So, I reapplied to the court to restore the contact I previously had, and whilst I waited for that hearing, I took to waving to my daughters, who lived about a quarter of a mile away from me, as their mother drove them to school most mornings. I just wanted them to know I still cared and I had not given up on them.

Twelve weeks later we went back to court before His Honour Judge Wigmore, a West Country circuit judge, sitting at Truro court in April 1997. In the West Country, family cases, although based in one court, can be moved anywhere around the area to accommodate the judge's workload. I applied to Judge Wigmore for immediate reinstatement of my regular staying contact and interim residence of my children, to be determined at the earliest hearing available. I also asked the court to move the case up to the High Court as I was unhappy with the County Court's inaction to resolve matters and protect my children. Representing myself, I told Judge Wigmore I thought he and his fellow circuit judges were appalling and I wanted a "better standard of judge." presuming a High Court judge would be better.

The mother, through her legally aided barrister, Mr Robert Alford of Exeter, asked the court to keep the case in the County Court, end all my contact and place an injunction on me to stop me waving to the children.

Judge Wigmore, acknowledging each child had now for years stated the mother's boyfriend was hurting them and making them unhappy, immediately transferred the case up to the High Court Family Division, and invited the Official Solicitor to act as guardian ad litem for the children. In other words, the girls would now have their own representation in the court, independent of my ex-wife, myself – and these appalling social workers, who once again were in the court. It sounded good, like a breakthrough I thought, but that proved a very false dawn indeed.

But at this hearing, Devon Social Services asked to also be party to the proceedings, as they were there to support the mother's applications to stop me ever seeing my children – and applied for a care order for each of the children. Judge Wigmore questioned them on this point of them seeking to put the children in care. Quite shockingly, the Devon Social Services' solicitor, Miss Vanessa Richardson, told Wigmore that the local authority did not actually want to put the children in care at all, but by them filing a care application – a false application – they could be attached to the proceedings as party. Unbelievable corruption now actually articulated into words by the Social Services solicitor. Judge Wigmore, luckily, gave Miss Richardson short shrift in that attempt to make such an illegal move. He deemed their attempt to join the proceedings as unlawful, and simply could not be allowed. He refused their application to file these bogus care applications (more good news, so I thought). He directed that if the local authority were not seeking to put any of the children in care, but merely make such an application to support the mother, and interfere in private law matters, then their application "cannot succeed in law." He was clear, they *could not* be a party to these private law proceedings. Yet more good news, so I thought...

However, after seeing off the Social Services, Judge Wigmore soon reverted to type. He then went on to award the mother her injunction forbidding me from going on the 'school route' when she drove the girls to school as the mother claimed this made her feel harassed when most mornings I stood and waved to the children. He also took away the now broken two-hour a fortnight contact order and replaced it with a 'no contact' order. In defence, I told the judge that he was taking away my contact order for no reason at all; my limited supervised contact order was being flouted by the local authority, and he should enforce it. He agreed the local authority had no status to break a court order, but then removed the order anyway. I told him my motivation for waving to the children since the breaking of the contact order was trying to assure my girls, who always waved back happily, that I had not just deserted them. I pointed out the waving would only stop when my contact was restored.

Judge Wigmore was having none of it though. Whatever the mother wanted, he laboured to deliver. It was also clear to me that whatever the children wanted was only going to be respected by him if it coincided with what their mother wanted. He then went on to order that I had no contact, and placed the injunction on me not to go on the 'school route' until it was all sorted out.

Now, in the space of just four months, I had gone from twice a week staying in contact with my much loved daughters who told the court welfare officer they wanted to come and live with me, to nothing, and the only thing that had consistently happened was the mother's boyfriend kept assaulting my children. I was incensed, and who wouldn't be? I told Wigmore I intended to ensure my daughters would know Dad still loves them no matter what corruption he wanted to dispense, and I made it very clear what I thought of the nonsense that he was inflicting upon me and the girls.

I further told him that I'd been the only one obeying court orders all this time, and I was the only one – along with my children, of course – that was being shafted. I said I'd be waving them off to school tomorrow morning, and every morning, until this farce was stopped. I recall telling him he could please himself – and what, with anything, he cared to do about that. Wigmore's response was to tell me to wait until a High Court judge came and sorted it all out; he then promptly closed the proceedings down, and once again I had to go home empty handed.

CHAPTER 4

The High Court –
and a Higher Level of Farce

The next month, May 1997, the Official Solicitor accepted the invite to represent the children. At last, I thought, the children's views and complaints will reach the court and be investigated properly. I phoned a friend of mine who was a member of Families Need Fathers and told him my 'good news'. The father, who does not want to be named in this book, but spent years battling the courts to see his son and assisting other fathers, instantly sounded most despondent. He told me the presence of the Official Solicitor in a contact and residence case was "the very worst thing that could happen, he simply acts as the mother's back-up advocate." The Families Need Fathers member next day posted me a copy of a Mail on Sunday article, which can be seen opposite from another case that's quite self-explanatory.

In the May, Mr Justice Wilson of the Family Division arrived at Plymouth court for a directions hearing. He strode into court, full of self-importance and things at first looked hopeful. Unbelievably, in court, Devon Social Services were sat there with a barrister representing them. They had just gatecrashed the proceedings. They had *assumed* party status, despite being refused it four weeks before because they had no legal basis for it. And they had made no further application.

Law chief trounced by boy of 13

By ALISON BRACE

Son in family tussle wins fight to have his guardian removed

A 13-YEAR-OLD boy has made legal history . . . by having the Government's top lawyer removed as his guardian.

He claimed that Official Solicitor Peter Harris failed to follow his wish to let him live with his father after his parents split up — forcing him instead to live with his mother.

And last week's landmark ruling highlights once again the controversial Children Act, which was designed to protect youngsters' interests but in this case ignored the boy's wishes. Under the act, Mr Harris was appointed to represent the American boy — who cannot be named for legal reasons — after a lengthy custody battle between his parents which cost the British taxpayer more than £300,000.

But now High Court judge Mr Justice Johnson has overturned the appointment, ruling th t the boy does not need a legal guardian because he has sufficient maturity to instruct his own private lawyers.

Although the boy must remain a ward of the British courts until he is 18, he will be allowed to return to his native country next year with his father.

The boy set a legal precedent last year when he became the first child ever to apply for Mr Harri 's removal from his case — but a Court of Appeal ruled at the time that he was not mature enough to understand the consequences of his legal actions. He tried to sue Mr Harris — but was told that the Official Solicitor was immune from such actions.

Mature

So the boy told his story to The Mail on Sunday and appeared on TV to explain the plight of youngsters misrepresented by the law meant to help them. And last week the courts acknowledged the boy's actions and said he was articulate and mature for his age.

His father said last night: 'By talking to the newspapers and appearing on TV he clearly demonstrated that he is very articulate and understands the issues extremely well.

'But this whole case throws into question the Children Act. It was supposed to give children a substantial say in their future, yet the children are still not being heard. Judges are failing to follow Parliament's wishes.'

The Mail on Sunday revealed last December how, after plenty of protests, the boy took the law into his own hands and ran away to his father's North London home to be with him for Christmas.

The boy — who only holds an American passport — plans to continue his secondary education in the US from next summer and attend the same university as his father and other relatives.

From The Mail on Sunday in December last year

The Mail on Sunday, December 1994. The Official Solicitors office claims to represent the children in Court cases, but above & as in my children's case, if the children DO want to see their father, the Official Solicitor often refuses to follow the instruction. - Reproduced by kind permission by The Mail on Sunday.

I immediately raised with Judge Wilson this wrongful and unlawful act by them; they had just been refused the right to be here, but here they are again. Judge Wilson heard me out but then let them remain in court as a party. Judge Wilson, however, did set up phone contact between my girls and I, but this was to be monitored and taped by the social workers, on the condition I promised to stop going on the 'school route' and waving to them, while we awaited the full hearing.

I agreed not to go on the 'school route' while we waited for the full hearing that was promised for a few weeks' time. I disputed the mother was harassed by this at all, and told him as we all lived within a quarter of a mile of each other, we would inevitability cross paths and I was bound to see the kids. Wilson simply told me to keep off the 'school route', which I reluctantly agree to.

However, months before all of this, after the Judge Sander debacle, I found I simply could not work after the loss of my children from my life. I was totally preoccupied, so I became, by choice, unemployed. I left the driving school again. One of the conditions of receiving unemployment benefit at that time was you had to be 'actively seeking' work. This 'actively seeking' work condition entailed visiting the nearby Jobcentre at least two or three times a week.

After waving to the children most mornings for the last three months going one way en route to the Jobcentre, I now started walking the most direct way to the Jobcentre, ensuring the staff there saw me 'actively seeking' work, i.e. looking through the latest vacancies. So, after Judge Wilson set up the phone contact, I started going this most direct way to the Jobcentre from my house, thus avoiding the 'school route' that I had deliberately placed myself upon most mornings each week, in hope of seeing my daughters when their mother drove them to school.

After a week or so of missing my children being driven to their school, the mother then started to drive the children to school the way I'm now walking to the Jobcentre. I could not believe my luck. I was keeping off the 'school route' she had told Judge Wilson she wanted me kept off, going directly east from her house – and here she was now driving my children to school on a far more indirect route – which was on my 'Jobcentre route' – where she knew I would be. I again waved to the children as they passed and they waved back. Little did I know, though, her solicitor had arranged for a private detective – all fully paid for on legal aid – to film me most mornings while she drove by with the girls and I waved.

On many occasions, the mother and her new man would drive by most mornings with, and occasionally without, the children and shout abuse and gesture at me. Trying to prove that my now ex-wife was not harassed at all, I took a camera with me on one occasion.

The next day, mother and new boyfriend hurled abuse at me, once again, with boyfriend gesturing out of her car window. Quick as a flash, I pulled out the camera I brought with me this time and I snapped them in the process.

As can be seen in the photo, this 'harassed' mother is actually WAVING and laughing at me while her boyfriend has opened her car window and gestures to me. Gotcha! Well, so I thought.

She – they – were on my 'Jobcentre route' while I was keeping off the 'school route'. My thinking was I must now have nipped this harassment nonsense in the bud, see you in court. Now, because of the publicity injunction in her favour, the children's mother's identity in the following photo had to be hidden. But, please be assured, she was broadly smiling at the time!

The children, unsighted but in the rear of the mothers car, pass me on the way to school, 14 July 1997. Judge Wilson found I was harassing the mother on this occasion and jailed me for four months. In defence, I produced this photo of the mother and Wayne Taylor smiling and waving back, which I thought proved there was no harassment at all. Wilson said of this 'people who are harassed do not always look harassed'. Unfortunately, he never responded to my question back; "But do they smile and wave back?"

Pre-court, the Official Solicitor's representative, Mr Szulc, asked to see me, prior to the hearing. So I arranged with him to go to his London office as I could combine a visit to my mother in Horn-church while making the trip. Thinking these people were there to represent the children and their interests, I turned up at his Central London office full of optimism. However, that illusion soon came crashing down to earth. Mr Szulc's very first question to me after my 200-mile drive was, "Why are you not paying maintenance for your daughters?"

Now, I'd arrived laden with all of the Social Services/court welfare reports detailing the mother's boyfriend's assaults, court judgements accepting these assaults were taking place and the children's stated wishes to live with me. So I asked myself just why this man's first question to me was querying why I was not paying, out of my unemployment benefit of £60 a week, for someone (fully employed) to live with my kids and assault them?

My answer to Mr Szulc, which I have to admit did include the

'F' word, was, "Just what the f*** is that to do with what you are here for?" He didn't answer that, I don't believe he really could. It was none of his business. Realising his question would remain unanswered, Szulc then moved swiftly on to ask my reasons for applying for residence of my daughters, and any reasons why I should even see them ever again if I didn't get their residence.

I left his office two hours later somewhat confused. Here was a massive, expensive, professional, legal organisation, funded by the taxpayer, brought into our lives to represent the children – my children – in the High Court, but all this man handling the case seems to be interested in is the mother's application to remove me from my daughters. Still, I'm thinking to myself, we have a High Court judge down from the Royal Courts of Justice in London involved now, not some local judge from the backwaters of Devon, *surely* things have got to get better?

Now, just before we went to court in July, the Official Solicitor, after seeing the children and mother, files his report to the court. It runs to over 150 pages. Nowhere does the report deal with the mother's boyfriend's assaults on my children at all, which is THE reason why I've applied to the court for residence. Neither has he investigated the claims of assault the children he represents made to three past social workers and a court welfare officer either. He also ignored the findings of fact from the past Court of Appeal hearing in 1995 that the mother's boyfriend IS assaulting my children. All he focused on was, does the father harass the mother by waving to the children and making court applications for residence? My friend from Families Need Fathers gloomy predictions about the workings of the Official Solicitor's Office came flooding back.

One small paragraph in his 150+ page court report dealt with the children's wishes and feelings. In that solitary paragraph the Official Solicitor described himself as "on the horns of a dilemma, as he represents three children who all speak with one voice, they want regular contact with their father, but if the court finds the mother's claims of harassment are found true, the Official Solicitor recommends no contact." The Official Solicitor then devotes over

100 pages of his and his appointed child psychiatrist's report, in a variety of ways, to my waving at the children and seeing them on the way to their school.

I was in stunned shock when I read this. Here was an organisation that was coming to court in Plymouth from London, for a one-week hearing, with an entourage of a barrister, a top consultant child psychiatrist and a solicitor, staying in a top local hotel, all expenses paid by the taxpayer, to represent my children. But they were not representing my children at all, they were just planning to simply back up the mother, who had a very competent legal team of her own anyway, together with the illegally – but allowed into the case after being refused lawful entry – Social Services people. They were NOT representing the children or even investigating the years of abuse in the home. Again, everything degenerated into a sham.

Now, the court system is set up to work in an adversarial way: mother and father fight their respective cases, whether their individual merits are just or not. The children's representative, if engaged, is (supposed to be) there to fight the children's corner. The judge is (supposedly) sat there, in the middle, weighing up both (or all) sides, and finding the correct and just position, taking into account the Children Act checklist. But in this and so many other secret family court cases, this just does not happen. If people are allowed to illegally join a case with an agenda to back up one party (in this and most cases, the mother), and the representative of the children can go against his instructions from his clients, as in this and other cases, to back the mothers cause too, *and the judge allows this to happen*, then undiluted farce and injustice is the inevitable result, and that's just what we got.

The judge alone is (supposedly) there to decide, after hearing *all views and opinions*, what's right and what's wrong. He's employed to decide matters in family cases 'in the child's best interests'. At the very top of the Children Act checklist, the judge has an overriding duty to consider, when deciding outcomes, "the ascertainable wishes and feelings of the child."

The hearing went on for nine days instead of the intended five because Mr Szulc caused a huge administration error through sheer incompetence. He failed to deliver documentation on time to his own child psychiatrist, who needed time to read matters. There was a potential investigation needed that involved a time when the mother took one of my daughters to the doctors that warranted closer consideration. We started the hearing in July 1997 and the hearing concluded in November that year because of this.

On the July day this administration error arrived in the case, Judge Wilson put up what appeared a credible appearance of rebuking Mr Szulc for causing the four-month adjournment by his failure to administer the children's medical documents to his own child psychiatrist. Wilson adjourned the hearing until November, as he was not back in Plymouth until then, a matter that would have taken 48 hours to resolve now had to wait four months. At the end of the first day back in court in November 1997, the documents having been read by the child psychiatrist during the four-month break (which, incidentally made no difference to the outcome, or anything whatsoever, and his investigation proved negative), I accidentally went home with the Official Solicitor's barrister's (Miss Catherine Wood) case notes & Mr Szulc's personal notepad amongst my documents. I was representing myself, we were all sat next to each other. When I got home I realised I had something not mine. But reading them both proved riveting.

After Judge Wilson had lambasted Mr Szulc in the court for his administration cock-up back in July, Mr Szulc's notepad detailed how they had all caught the same train back from Plymouth to London as the judge. Mr Szulc's notes described how on the train, Judge Wilson approached them, bringing Mr Szulc and the Official Solicitor's entourage a bottle of wine and told them "no hard feelings." The Official Solicitor's representative, Mr Szulc, clearly saw this as very improper, and detailed a note to himself on the train to report the matter to the Official Solicitor himself, upon arrival back in London, presumably because it compromised the independence of the judge so compendiously.

The next day at the court, I handed both sets of notes to Miss Wood, asking if she would hand Mr Szulc his notes for me. Miss Wood and 'the team' were visibly panic stricken, they knew I undoubtedly read everything. They cornered me in the entrance hall of the Plymouth court and demanded to know if I had photocopied any the notes. I said no…

In court, Miss Wood started to tell the judge what had happened and what I must have read. Wilson looked totally blown away. I was wondering to myself if yet more court tapes were about to get erased. There was a deafening silence in the whole court. Judge Wilson was now scarlet red. I stood up, representing myself, tail slightly up. The rat I smelt was now reeking. I told Judge Wilson what I'd always suspected; they were all in league with each other anyway and now it was clear from the contents of the case notes that I had read. I asked him to leave the case as his position as judge was untenable and he should be replaced – unless of course he was willing to resolve this farce and sort out the children matters today. Wilson said nothing, but adjourned for about five minutes, leaving the courtroom a shaken and embarrassed man. Upon his return, he composed himself somewhat and prepared his explanation.

I can still recall his first words after he re-entered the court: "Never, in 30 years at the bar has anything like this been allowed to happen." Wine bar or bar counsel, I asked myself. He was clearly furious with Miss Wood and Mr Szulc for not only writing the wine episode down, but far more aggrieved for her leaving these two sets of notes anywhere I could find them. However, he then went on, clearly for my benefit, to explain that when he was a barrister he represented the Official Solicitor in cases like this, knew the individuals in court from there and bought them all wine, more in a 'reunion like' way than the apologetic way as written. But, either way, there we had it, the charade of family courts pretending to be independent, neutral, unbiased places is just a front – they are all mates just playing a game.

I stood up and bluntly re-iterated my view that he should either cut through this nonsense and sort the case out with no further ado, or simply go home and let us have an independent judge, if one existed. I pointed out that when I asked for the case to be transferred to the High Court, I expected something better than what we had in the County Court, but this now was clearly not the case. Unfortunately,

Judge Wilson was unmoved. Judge Wilson announced he was staying and his reaction was to place a lifetime injunction on me preventing disclosure of Miss Wood's files to anyone outside the secret courts. In other words, Mr Justice Wilson sought to cover his contemptuous behaviour with a gagging order. Luckily, Wilson omitted to include Mr Szulc's notepad in that order, or I would not be able to write about any of the wine drinking here. So, the brief contents of Mr Szulc's notepad re the wine-drinking episode can be written about here, not because of the openness of the judge, but because of his error.

Without doubt, Miss Wood's file contained far more about her out of court activities with the wine drinking judge, but it cannot be written about here, or anywhere. The broader detail of this fiasco still, unfortunately, remains covered in secrecy, forever, by order of the court.

Now, on the last day of the hearing in November 1997 before Wilson, the mother's boyfriend, Wayne Taylor, gave evidence to the court in support of the mother's application to end my contact with my kids.

During Taylor's stint in the witness box (I had no solicitor and was acting in person) I started to question him about all the catalogue of assaults the kids were reporting to the social workers and the court welfare officer over the last three years. The Official Solicitor's people had ignored his behaviour towards my children so far, as did the judge and the Social Services' legal team – despite Taylor's assaults on my children being the only reason why all these people had become involved in our lives in the first place. So I took it on.

At first, Wayne Taylor simply denied all wrongdoing. As I started to go though the Social Services' documentation with him about the children's claims, one by one, he snapped. Quite unbelievably, Wayne Taylor then threatened, from the witness box, to come around my house and kill me. The court fell into total silence. Jaws visibly dropped, including Judge Wilson's. Sensing I had something here, I expanded on what he had just threatened to do. Wayne Taylor then made four more separate threats to kill me, from the witness box, while under oath during my questioning of him.

Although I personally saw these threats as all mouth and little else, Judge Wilson conceded afterwards he saw these threats as serious. When Taylor left the witness box, he returned to sit with my ex-wife in the court. But Judge Wilson was not having this at all. He immediately ordered Wayne Taylor to leave the court in light of his "*murderous threats*" (Wilson's words). The look on Taylor's face at this point was of disbelief; he *really was* so unintelligent to think he could make repeat threats to kill someone in a court, and no one would take issue with it. So, despite him being ordered from the courtroom by Judge Wilson, this judge still allowed Wayne Taylor to return to my children's home that night, despite my application in the court to keep him away from my kids.

Anyway, that day the proceedings finished, and Judge Wilson said he would give his "compendious judgement" the next day at 1 pm. Being a rational person, I thought Wayne Taylor, with his threats to kill me in the court, had helped my case no end, not only for me to at least see my children again, but have them removed from anywhere he was likely to be. I reasoned to myself that this judge must now have to end the utter farce the case had degenerated into and sort all this out, and that it was likely to either go in part or in whole in my favour. My point for being in court this time and so much in the past too, was the danger Wayne Taylor posed to the children – and he had just put himself on a plate for me. Even the mother's barrister, Robert Alford, seemed to be back-pedalling in his closing speech because of Taylor's threats to kill. The threats to kill by Taylor certainly seemed to me to make the 'crime' I was also in court for, of waving to my children, pale into the insignificance it really was.

Well, 1 pm judgement day had arrived. Taylor was not at the court, but everyone else was. We all sit and await Wilson's grand entrance, and we don't have to wait very long.

Judge Wilson soon after enters and sits. He starts off by detailing all the applications before him that he was to deal with, and it was quite some roll call: "The father's application for residence, the father's application for contact, the father's application to remove Wayne Taylor from the children's home, the mother's application to end contact between father and the children, the mother's application to commit the father to prison for waving to the children, the mother's application to restrict the father's right to apply to the court for anything (a Section 91 (14) order), Devon County Council's application for a care order to end the father's contact if the mother does not pursue the same application, the paternal grandmother's application for contact and the paternal grandfather's application for contact with the children."

Wilson's first words were to warn us all that his judgement would be long, and it was – it went to 65 pages. The first minutes were encouraging indeed. He immediately dismissed Devon County Council's whole position in the proceedings as being of one "without logic", and dismissed everything they sought in the proceedings, even though Judge Wigmore had dismissed the very same application seven months prior. So, Devon County Council, it was estimated at a later date, had wasted around £20,000 of taxpayers' money in gatecrashing the proceedings which they simply had no logical – or legal – role to take part in. So far, so good, I was thinking, but that view of mine did not last very long at all.

Wilson then went on to give the rest of his judgement, which he promised would resolve the case for the future.

Needless to say after the promising start, total and utter farce soon prevailed. Judge Wilson 'found' for the mother on everything. He 'found' I was indeed harassing her by my waving to the children between May and July of that year, despite accepting she had changed her 'school route' from the original route that I agreed to keep away from. He 'found', from the photo of her waving *to me from her car* with her boyfriend, that she was being harassed even on that particular occasion in July and stated, "People who are harassed don't always look harassed." A fair comment on the surface maybe, but would a judge, sitting in an open court, with press and public hearing the proceedings, be able to say that when not only has the 'victim' changed her route to one she knowingly will find her so-called harasser present on, but waves back at him and smiles too?

The rest of Wilson's judgement soon became an attack on me, as a man, not a father, while the mother was held up as a model citizen. The farce started to unfold through the next hour or so of his attack upon me. Firstly, Wilson acknowledged that, "the deep wishes of the three intelligent children aged six, eight and almost ten… are to have regular, face to face staying contact with their father…" He went on to describe their deep wishes to see me as a "yearning". Powerful terms indeed. OK, fine, I thought, the ascertainable wishes of the children are, according to the Children Act checklist, the first consideration in these cases, he's got to give us something, surely? Just how can he not harm these kids by not at least restoring what we had, and I waited in anticipation as to what he was to make of Wayne Taylor's assaults on my children, and his threats to kill me in the court the day before.

Because of the 'harassment' of the mother by me, Judge Wilson used this to justify why he was now going against "the deep wishes of three articulate, intelligent children now aged six, eight and nearly ten to see the father they love" and ordered no contact between them and me. He then jailed me for four months for the contempt of court of breaching the order of going on 'the school route' and waving, despite the mother having changed the school route! In Judge Wilson's view, *any route* the mother took to the school was, for the purposes of his court 'the school route'. She clearly had no responsibility to stick to one route, no responsibility to keep a reasonable distance if she did not want to see me, or even avoid any route that she knew I used.

To take this nonsense a small step further, should the mother have chosen to have detoured past my house on the way to the school, that would have become 'the school route' and I would have been in breach had I waved to the children even from my lounge window. This heinous farce simply could not happen in an open court.

But not content with this complete garbage, Judge Nicholas Wilson then promptly revealed to us that day the true ills of the British secret family courts for what they are. He unbelievably justified cutting off these three "intelligent children" from me, their father, because the effect of them seeing me would be "catastrophic" upon the mother, and therefore that would "indirectly" affect the children. Catastrophic upon the mother if the children see me? So Wilson had now successfully corrupted the entire process of law by placing the wishes and feelings of the *mother* over the children's by deciding it best to have a happy mother, for the sake of the children. I wondered if had I heard this correctly at the time, but the printed version of what he said that was issued to us all that day confirmed so, *he really did say this.*

My immediate thoughts on this were simple: if the mother was to be so 'catastrophically effected' by her children seeing their father, a man *she once married*, how could that mother be considered stable enough to have the children live with her anyway?

But there you have it, the Children Act 1989 was successfully bypassed to please the mother, despite the Act's – and parliament's – intent is to put the child's welfare first. So, Judge Nicholas Wilson had substituted the law of the land to benefit the mother (at the time aged 30), as he saw fit, and devastate the children instead – in their best interests, of course.

Wilson then promptly moved on to Wayne Taylor, his threats to kill me, and his assaults upon the children. Wilson accepted a number of these assaults had taken place, describing them as "a minor but inappropriate degree of force in helping the mother to keep order…" Now, Taylor and the mother in court had both denied he had ever touched the children. By saying this, though, Wilson had automatically deemed not only Taylor a liar, but the mother a liar for lying *against the children* to support him. But none of that mattered to this judge one iota. Breathtakingly, Wilson concluded in the same paragraph by saying Devon Social Services must maintain "a keen vigilance" to ensure the children's safety.

Wilson then dealt with what he called, yet again, the "murderous threats" by Wayne Taylor towards me in the court. He instructed Devon Social Services to pass Taylor's threats onto the police as he viewed what had happened as 'criminal offences'. He seemed to anticipate possible criminal charges could be brought, and authorised immediate police access to the court records of what was threatened, which I presumed to include the court tapes.

Shell-shocked, I then sat through the concluding part of Wilson's judgement, which dealt with my waving to the children. Judge Wilson then rose, left the courtroom for about a minute, then reappeared in what could only be described as a frilly shirt and a judge's wig.

Upon his return, he declared the court was now 'an open court' to announce the sentencing before proceeding to announce he found that I had breached the order not to harass the mother by waving to my children on 30 occasions between April and July 1997, which was almost four months before. Wilson acknowledged the mother had *changed her route* to school in the May to a new route she knew I was now using, but still ruled that I was harassing her by simply being there, or indeed anywhere or any route she went to the school on. He then proceeded to sentence me to four months in prison for *each breach*, a total of *ten years* in prison, for waving to the children. Ten years of sentence, for waving to your own children. More Monty Python than any legal system, Wilson now even had the comedy outfit on too. To me, he was now dispensing the comedy lines. However, Wilson then went on to say, in a tone (well, almost) of 'compassion' he would make all the 30 sentences concurrent, therefore one four-month sentence covered them all. He then proclaimed the court was immediately 'closed court' once again.

Wilson then concluded by telling me I could reapply for contact with my children "maybe next year," and set up this absurd exclusion zone I was not to enter around the children's home.

Before being swiftly whisked away to Exeter prison by the three security staff Wilson had summonsed to the courtroom, I asked him for permission to appeal each of his absurd orders. In family proceedings, if you want to appeal a judge, you have to ask his or her permission to do so against each single order he makes. If (as is usual) the judge refuses, you have to ask for the permission to appeal to a single judge at the Court of Appeal, and if that judge gives you permission, then you have a right to appeal to two, or sometimes three, judges there. If he, or they, say no then there is no further recourse. Wilson, clearly enjoying his moment of absolute power, predictably barked "refused" as I asked for permission to appeal on each order. My request for bail, pending appeal of his committal order, met with the same barked response. I was then handed a copy of the eight-page committal order by the court clerk, handcuffed, and within seconds, I was off to Exeter prison in a secure van that day, November 7th 1997, four years and one day from when my family were removed from my life by my ex-wife. Now I'm removed from my liberty as well – while my children, cut off from me, are made to live with a mother prepared to lie to cover her boyfriend's hurting of them.

The journey to Exeter prison from Plymouth court is about 40 miles. I had three security staff escort me there in a secure van. The van inside was divided into six small, approximately 2 ft x 2 ft, locked enclosures, and I was locked in one of these. I was the only inmate on board, the van and three-man escort was just for me. On the journey, I could see out of the blackened side window where we were going, and as I knew Exeter town centre fairly well, I realised exactly when we arrived at the prison gate.

So, the van pulled up at the gate, and a prison officer came out to speak to the driver. Then the gate opened, and the van drove through to a second gate, where the first was closed behind the van. I was now in prison grounds. More prison staff came out, and what appeared to be the senior officer at the gatehouse was handed a copy of my committal order, which he read. I clearly heard laughter between my escorts and the prison officer. One of my escorts says, very clearly, "He must have really p****d the judge off!" to which I clearly heard the prison officer reply, "Or he must have caught him seeing his Misses!" The inner gate then opened, the van drove through into the prison reception area, where it stops, and I was then released from the enclosure in the van that I was transported in.

Now, prison staff do an unpleasant job, in unpleasant conditions, and often dealing with very unpleasant people. They don't really talk much like gentlemen at all, they are, in reality – while at work at least – every bit as crude and foul mouthed as the inmates in any prison. Now I'm then sat in the prison reception area, awaiting the process of being booked in. The senior reception officer walked over to me with a copy of my committal order in his hand. He said, "Just what the f***'s this s**t all about, mate?" I replied, "Good question – only went to court for access to my kids." He replied back, "Did you have a brief in court?" I said, "No, I acted in person." He laughed out loud, then advised me to see the legal aid officer on the wing the next day and get a solicitor pretty quick. I just nodded.

The committal order soon got passed all around the staff and caused much amusement amongst the prison staff. There soon surfaced a visible degree of disbelief of what I was in for, and I sensed a little sympathy too.

Anyway, the booking-in process took place, I was issued with some bedding, a plastic mug and toothbrush (but no toothpaste!) and I was lead to the remand wing and placed in a cell occupied by another inmate. I was ushered in, and the solid steel door with no handles on the inside of it was slammed shut. The inmate, a man about my age, looked me up and down, nodded without saying anything, and continued to read his book. He's laid upon the top bunk, so I put my prison bedding on the lower bunk, and made the bed.

After a while we started to chat. It turned out he's in for persistent shoplifting, and he's out in a couple of days. He asked what I was in for, and I told him he should just read the committal order as he just wouldn't believe me. He did, and a smile appeared across his face. Turned out his name was Jeff, and over the next couple of days we mainly chatted about football, the only thing we both shared any interest in. I also took the advice of the prison officer in reception and started the ball rolling to get some legal representation to sort out my plight.

Now, my first weekend in Exeter prison was somewhat disturbed by much commotion outside the walls. There were police helicopters hovering nearby most of the night, police cars with sirens blaring racing by, and what certainly appeared to be much activity outside the prison. I thought that perhaps there may have been an escape as most of the attention appeared to focus just outside the prison walls.

However, the next day on local radio the story that dominated the news was that a child of 14 had been found murdered nearby, killed while walking her dog in the early evening. Her throat had been cut. It became quite obvious that the police activity that night around the prison had stemmed from this dreadful discovery, and not an escape at all. This in a strange way compounded the absurdity of my own personal plight in that while the authorities had been imprisoning me for waving to my children, a sub-human lunatic had murdered an innocent child almost within sight of the prison I'd been sent too.

Despite the massive police search and subsequent investigation that followed, over nine years later no one has ever been arrested for the murder of that poor young girl, Kate Bushell.

Over the next days, I got frequent changes of cellmate, comprising of a variety of petty thieves, drug addicts and eventually, a celebrity inmate, Albert Walker, a Canadian fugitive who was on remand awaiting trial in what was later described in the nationals as the 'Rolex watch murder'.

During my time sharing with Albert, who preferred to be called Andrew, he was adamant – and quite convincing – that he was the victim of a miscarriage of justice, and was eagerly awaiting his pending trial for murder where he would clear his name.

His case came to trial, several months after my release. However, when it did, I followed the case with interest due to my cell-sharing time with him on the run up to Christmas 1997. All the national papers followed his trial, as did the regional and national TV.

Albert Walker was found guilty of the murder of a college lecturer he had befriended while on the run from the Canadian police. Walker had befriended the lecturer in Essex, and went on the lecturer's yacht for a sail in the English Channel. It transpired that while at sea, Walker murdered the lecturer, and dumped his body overboard, then assumed his victim's identity to replace his own. Walker then moved into his victim's home, and lived as the man he murdered.

However, many weeks later the victim's body washed ashore along the Devon coastline in a very decomposed state. The only identity on the body was a Rolex watch the deceased still wore. The police were able to trace from this the purchaser of the watch from the registration of the Rolex, and when they called at the dead owner's home to inform any relatives of their find, Albert Walker answered the door – as the deceased!

To cut a very long story short (a story ITV made into a film that was shown on TV in 2000) Walker was arrested for murder, sentenced to life, with an extradition warrant issued to the Canadian police for numerous crimes he was on the run from in Canada, should he ever be released from a UK prison. It did make me smile after Walker was sentenced that I, Britain's first dad jailed for waving to his own kids, shared a cell with what turned out to be Interpol's third most wanted person.

Anyway, during my days in Exeter Prison, I got legal representation and applied to purge my contempt of court on legal aid. My first purge application heard by the then president of the Family Division, Sir Stephen Brown, failed because I had talked to the press by phone from prison and the secret family courts really don't like any exposure of what they get up to. On my second purge application, Sir Stephen Brown, sitting at the Royal Courts of Justice in London, set early release date, 22nd December 1997. Although the mother, again fully funded on legal aid, side by side with Devon Social Services and the children's representative from the Official Solicitor, opposed my release (this despite them not ever asking the children – who they were still meant to be representing – for their views) the early release date was set.

I was released from Exeter prison that Tuesday, the 22nd. I served a total of 45 days in that Category B prison for waving to my children. The Daily Mail tried to do the story a month before, but when the court heard about their intentions, they placed an immediate gagging order on them too. The Daily Mail had to 'pulp' 10,000 printed copies of their paper that was set for nationwide distribution – and the court successfully 'buried' what it did to me and my children.

All subsequent appeals failed and I did not see my children other than in passing for several months. I now also had police officers at my door investigating my ex-wife's claims to them that I was following her and harassing her. This was nonsense, and it transpired the police did not really believe her anyway.

Between my release from Exeter prison and our next children hearing, the only occurrence between my ex-wife and I was when my former mother-in-law got herself warned by the police about loitering *outside my house*, which is in a cul-de-sac. Then, a few weeks after that, with me still keeping well out of the way, my former father-in-law was arrested and accepted a caution for following *me* around and making threats to kill me in a police station.

So, this mother, found by Judge Wilson to be harassed by me, was actually proving to be the harasser, but I wondered whether the secret courts would want to hear this. I intended to test this quite soon.

Then, a few more weeks passed, and a summons arrived in my post. Wayne Taylor was trying to sue me for £20 (yes, £20) through the Plymouth County Court, a hearing my ex-wife chose to attend to assist and support him. He was claiming I caused him these 'losses' by him having to come to court in the past. The claim was thrown out. This, after Judge Wilson found the mother had been brought to court too often by me...

But luckily, the police were not accepting my ex-wife's now ongoing claims against me at all – unlike the family court. They started to actually investigate all what she was saying. Later in the summer of 1998, four local officers, unbeknown to anyone, placed my ex-wife under a series of covert observations during the course of a two-day surveillance operation. A pattern over time, since the Wilson hearing, had developed where she went to the local police station and made complaints about me following her at regular intervals. It became a daily claim, it transpired. I was later told about these observations by a friendly local police officer who suggested I take steps to find out the full results of their observations.

Weeks later, after letters to the local chief inspector, I received the four police statements and operations records detailing their covert observations on my ex-wife. They concluded that she had made repeated false allegations to them about me for harassment, including times she was under their covert observations, and they were able to confirm I simply *was not there*. I was told she had received a warning about wasting police time.

Armed with this, I sensed that I must now be able to blow the whole of Judge Wilson's lunacy orders to stop me and the children seeing each other clean out of the water. His whole decision to end my children's relationship with me was based solely on his absurd findings that the mother was harassed by me waving to the kids, something I knew was completely bogus and never accepted at all. Now, armed with the police evidence that the mother WAS making multiple false allegations, something no genuinely harassed person would ever do, I went back to the court. She was simply milking the corrupt UK family court process to keep my children from me; all this was all funded by the British taxpayer too.

It took months, but I managed to get the case back to court for reconsideration in November 1998, a whole year after Judge Wilson had denied my children and I a relationship we all wanted because he wrongly 'found' I harassed their mother. The Official Solicitor and local authority, all backing the mother the year before to cut off contact and because she was 'harassed' by me, now backed her counter application to 'delay' restoration of contact as "there has been too much litigation…and the mother needs a rest from it." Unbelievably, these legal people actually managed to keep a straight face in court when submitting this absurd angle to prevent the restoration of justice. Mr Justice Holman, the then chief western circuit judge, clearly embarrassed by the wine-supping Wilson verdict of finding the mother harassed, now proving so false (something I forcibly reminded him of throughout the hearing while acting in person) granted me leave to apply to see my children. The children's representation, still aware of the children's instructions that they wanted to see me, opposed this throughout and sought leave to appeal. Luckily, they were refused.

So in April 1999, the full hearing eventually took place. As always, a father's application takes months to get listed, and listing for this hearing followed the usual course. We were now to get a Judge Kirkwood. The children's representative changed consultant child psychiatrist to Dr Hamish Cameron, an eminent expert witness well known on the family court circuit and famed for giving speeches supporting the concept and virtues of shared parenting. Just a pity, when he claimed his hugely exorbitant fees for coming into court in this contact and residence dispute, he seemed to forget those concepts and virtues.

The Official Solicitor and his new privately fee paid expert wrote a further report that once again exceeded 150 pages. Dr Cameron and his fee payers recommended contact to return, but "not for at least six months more." Dr Cameron and the Official Solicitor reported to the court that I had sent various letters of complaint about Judge Wilson, the Official Solicitor and the local authority to the Lord

Chancellor's Department and others. They recommended, again against all wishes of the children they were supposedly in court to represent, I (and the children) should be made to wait at least a further six months before seeing each other. They quite incredulously recommended that during this further six months I should not write any complaining or confrontational letters about anyone involved in the case, before my children and I should see each other.

So the children's representatives from the Official Solicitors' office still sought to work against the children they represented. They continued to work against the children's instructions and wishes, on the ludicrous excuse this time being because their dad wrote letters of complaint regarding what nonsense is taking place. So, in the offices of the Official Solicitor, a mother's boyfriend could live with the children, make them unhappy and abuse them, no problem, but Dad writes letters of complaint, so Dad must be kept from the kids. It's the insanity of secret court – and this is exactly what they did.

Not surprisingly, not one word was written about harassment that so dominated the last report (well, how could they now?) But now the new excuse not to go against the mother was because I had wrote letters of complaint about the past poor conduct of people in the court through the proper channels! The interests of any child was simply not on their radar anywhere.

Now, as had blighted this case for years, more wrongdoing and farce immediately arrived in Judge Kirkwood's court on that April 1999 day too. The local authority, whom even Judge Wilson at the end of his 1997 hearing said there was "no logic" to them being a party, were still there and had behaved illegally yet again. Now, a solicitor I once briefly employed to fight my case in 1996, Ms Fiona O'Leary, had since gone to work for Devon County Council as a solicitor – and had taken over the role from Vanessa Richardson as solicitor for Devon in this very case. Her name appeared on Social Services' letters to me and on court documentation for the case just days before.

Yes, my former solicitor who had worked *for me* to try and fight my case to see my children, had now changed sides and was working *against me*. Not only are fraudulent care applications made by these people to further their personal agendas, now they ignored the rules on conflict of interests too.

This is completely illegal. There are clear rules about conflict of interest in any legal proceedings. No legal representative can 'change sides', taking confidential information and knowledge with them to fight the person they once represented.

Just before the hearing was about to commence, outside the court door, I approached the Devon Social Services' barrister, Miss Melissa Barlow and dropped the bombshell that I'd spotted this malpractice and would be raising this in court with a view to getting them removed. A very red faced Miss Barlow raced off, presumably to speak with the social workers.

Now once again, as this hearing commenced, we had another barrister, Miss Barlow this time, on her feet, explaining to a stunned courtroom that something "very wrong" had happened. I somewhat got the feeling of déjà vu! She admitted to Judge Kirkwood that this serious breach of legal rules had compromised their position, and sought his direction.

Judge Kirkwood asked me what I thought, so I told him. I said, tail well up, that Devon Social Services should never have been in the proceedings in the first place, they had corrupted the entire process throughout, they were failing my children in their basic duties to listen to them and this was just the latest wrongdoing that these people had brought to us. I wanted them thrown out of court – and now. I also told the judge about my concerns that the two female social workers writing these bias and misleading reports – and bias not only against myself, but my children too – Ms P and Ms C, were actually living together in a relationship. I questioned their objectivity.

Judge Kirkwood, although ignoring the concerns I had about the social workers living together in a gay relationship and their obvious viewpoint against me and in favour of the mother, told Devon that they had made their own position untenable by engaging one of my former solicitors to act in this case. He gave them a long lecture about rules and proceedings, and sent them packing. They were now no longer party to the proceedings.

Now, the hearing lasted two days. Dr Cameron and the Official Solicitor still wanted at least six more months of no contact so I could go this period of time to prove that I could refrain from writing letters of complaint before I should see my children. Again, if this was held in an open court, could such undiluted nonsense ever be uttered as reason not to let a father see his children, especially when they want to see him as well? Of course not, it would bring the entire court process into disrepute if this sort of thing ever got out.

I pushed and pushed upon Judge Kirkwood the police statements, the waving photo of the mother and the children's still stated wishes of wanting to see me. I reminded Judge Kirkwood that despite Judge Wilson cutting me off from the kids to please their mother, the mother's parents had each since got themselves arrested and warned regarding their actions towards me by the police. Then, of course, the mother herself, who told Judge Wilson she was so "fed up" with coming to court back then, chose to come to court when her boyfriend tried to wrongfully sue me for £20. I made myself clear I was not going to go away and he should start to put right the utter wrongdoings and farce that had now plagued the case for years. The mother was still firmly opposed to my seeing of our children, as always, and that was never going to change.

Luckily, more through sheer embarrassment than any sense of justice, Judge Kirkwood started contact again, but just once a month, where all past recommendations (including Dr Cameron's, though after a further six months' delay of course) were for alternate weekends plus once weekly teatime. Kirkwood, instead of simply putting things right, tried to appease the mother with a feeble 'half way measure' that was destined to run into trouble. And it soon did.

May, June, July 1999, I had three monthly supervised contacts of six hours' duration at my home. Strange this, Dad does not see his children for a while, be it weeks, months or years and the family courts see need to 'reintroduce' him to his kids. Yet, when servicemen return to their families after months or even years away fighting for their country, no one sees fit to 'reintroduce' Dad then, he just comes home. Or even if Dad comes home from a long prison sentence, whatever the crime, no one thinks of reintroducing him to his kids, again he just comes home. But the divorced father has to be 'reintroduced' by way of supervised contacts, an invention of the absurd that ply their trade in the secret courts.

Of course, no one ever sees fit to 'introduce' the mum's new boyfriend or boyfriends to the by way of supervised contact. He just turns up, perhaps even moves in, and the kids just have to get on with it – even in cases where their dad might have the indignation of being on supervised contact to those same children, visits which are so very much like a prison visit.

By now, I had not seen my children for two years. Unfortunately, only my two youngest arrived. Lisa, then 12, felt 'shy' about coming, but sent her love via her sisters. The younger two said their mother was making it awkward for Lisa, so I went straight back to court seeking the mother be compelled to send Lisa, exactly as stated in the court order. All that was needed was encouragement from the mother to Lisa, who at just 12, could easily have been sent by her mother should she chose (or even be made) to use her authority as her mother.

Unfortunately, Judge Kirkwood refused to compel the mother to do anything. Her instead made a bizarre order that 'hoped and expected Lisa would come to contact'. What rot. That's not a court order, it's a request. I sought an order, but by now it was apparent family courts simply don't order a mother to do anything. And it was apparent the mother was going to sabotage what little contact I was getting, and the judiciary would do nothing to stop her.

For the August, September and October 1999 visits, we had moved on to six hours a month unsupervised contact, at my home – but with Lisa still not coming. We had another hearing listed to review it all at the end of that October. On each of the three unsupervised contacts, Social Services' care staff (not social workers) brought the two children who actually arrived, and collected them from me to return them to the mother. They wrote reports on the children's views on each visit.

I cannot reproduce those reports here in full as they are privileged to the secret courts, but, like the past four court welfare reports, they could not have been wrote in any better or more positive terms: "The two girls happily came out for the visit to Dad's…", "We picked the girls up from their Dad's house at 6 pm…each were looking forward to their next visit…", "The girls asked if they could stay another half hour…", etc, etc. These were just brief extracts from the general text of those reports.

So, I was before Judge Kirkwood again, October 1999 on this 'review'. Dr Cameron and the Official Solicitor, both of whom refused to ever come and see a visit, produced yet another report, spread over 100 pages, stating that the two youngest children "did not really like seeing their dad…and Lisa was not going to see him again". This latest report of theirs was not only so far from reality, but totally conflicted with the growing number of reports that had accumulated over the years from people who had actually bothered to come and see me with my kids. I did start to wonder if these appalling people really had these 'hostile to the father' reports already pre-prepared at their offices in bulk, and all they did was fill in the names of the latest case…

So, Judge Kirkwood was again confronted with a mother hostile to contact and supported by the so-called children's representative – who had worked from day one against the children's well documented wishes to see me. This time he had the care workers' reports detailing two children who liked seeing Dad so much and had told them they wanted to see me lots more.

Unfortunately, Kirkwood, like so many other family court judges before him, took the easy way out. He ignored the very latest six positive contact reports, together with the now four historic court welfare reports, all recommending fortnightly staying contact and weekly teatime visits plus half of school holidays – and instead continued the once a month 'prison visit' type regime, of care workers fetching and carrying the children to my house, while I spent the day with them. And of course, he still refused to take action with the mother on Lisa's non-arrival.

I was outraged. Now Dr Cameron had wrote a most damming report on contact – even though he chose to never come and see even one session. To further the mother's cause, he then decided to falsely degenerate me. He reported that both a previously involved probation officer and a previously involved child psychotherapist involved in the case from years back had told him I had a 'personality disorder' that impinged on my relationship with everyone, including my children. He claimed in his report, dated 30th September 1999, that these previously involved professionals both said this to him on the phone. This was Dr Hamish Cameron's sole justification not to increase contact, and it worked.

Now I knew this was false. I asked Judge Kirkwood at the hearing to order these two past professionals into court to see just what they had said to Dr Cameron in that phone call just days before. It would have been easy, both were based nearby in Plymouth, they could have been ordered to the court that day. I had checked on their availability that morning with phone calls to their respective offices and both were available. But Judge Kirkwood was having none of it. He simply went with six more months of this once-a-month 'prison' visit regime, moved the imaginary exclusion zone set up by Judge Wilson around the children's old home to an area around the children's new home in another part of Plymouth, unbelieveably made a critical comment about my re-decorating of my daughters bedrooms at my house as he judged this undermined the mothers' home and left the case.

Weeks later, after much letter writing and phone calls, both the probation officer and child psychotherapist put in writing that they had *never* told Dr Cameron that they thought I had a personality disorder at all. The child psychotherapist, of Plymouth NHS Trust, went further. He copied to me his letter to Dr Cameron where he asked Dr Cameron to withdraw this report from the court because of this false representation of himself that I had made him aware of.

Now, I sent this 'proof' that Judge Kirkwood had been misled by Dr Cameron's report to the appeal court and to Judge Kirkwood himself at the Royal Courts. Despite being so seriously mislead by Dr Cameron, Judge Kirkwood never responded despite the entire outcome that day being so fatally flawed. The appeal court was not any better either, they just wrote back saying that I was now "out of time" to appeal and best I raise this with the next judge to look at the case in March 2000, a Mrs Justice Bracewell.

I immediately wrote to the late Mrs Justice Bracewell, explaining what had happened, forwarding copies of Dr Cameron's report containing these serious defects, and the letters from the probation officer and child psychotherapist identifying the serious defects that mislead Judge Kirkwood, together with copy of the request from the child psychotherapist for the report of Dr Cameron's to be withdrawn from the court record. *I also explained Dr Cameron had ignored this request to withdraw his report.*

Mrs Justice Bracewell, through her clerk, replied with the following letter on 15th December 2000 in regard to this serious matter:

"Dear Mr Harris,

Mrs Justice Bracewell has seen your letter dated December 12th 1999 and asks me to inform you that as the hearing on March 31st 2000 is a review of contact *since* the last hearing, it is not appropriate to have a directions hearing in advance, nor to consider historic material which has been the subject matter of previous hearings and decisions.

Yours Sincerely,

Eric Davis,
Clerk to the Hon. Mrs Justice Bracewell"

So, despite having well surpassed our 100th appearance in the family courts in the last seven years, this 'top of the range' lady High Court judge, made a Dame for services to the country, was planning to start our next hearing off from the position of yet another gross mistrial – caused this time by the false evidence of the expert witness.

So we had the further six-monthly visits from just my two youngest daughters, all still loving to come and see me and each still telling the care workers who fetched and carried them each month that they wanted to come over and see me lots more. Still no Lisa coming, and the two youngest girls also told the care workers that Mum and Wayne made Lisa feel guilty about ever coming. The care workers, to their credit, reported all of this to the court.

So, now we were before Judge Bracewell, 31ˢᵗ March 2000. We now had 12 care worker reports from the last year detailing the youngest two enjoying coming to see me, and wanting to see me much more. There was not one adverse report on any contact since this had all started nearly seven years before in 1993. All of the past court welfare reports also detailed the children wanting to see me lots – with the last one in 1997 even stating the girls' wishes were to actually come and live with me.

But just what do the appalling Official Solicitor and Dr Cameron do, still having never come to see the children at any contact ever? They file another joint report exceeding 100 pages, which, as always, coincided exactly with the mother's wishes and against the children they are supposedly there to represent. They now recommend my visits are cut down to just six per year, with a review the next year. They jointly reported, despite never seeing any occasions of me with my children, or even interviewing the children away from their mother, that the girls "don't like seeing Dad."

In court, I started to try and cross examine Dr Cameron about his false representations of the child psychotherapist in his last report before Judge Kirkwood. I was in person, I couldn't get legal aid for representation and I couldn't afford the requisite barrister that has to represent you before a High Court judge. (Solicitors cannot represent anyone before a High Court judge, you have to have a barrister with a solicitor sat behind him or her.) Dr Cameron simply refused to answer any of my questions. I asked Judge Bracewell to intervene as Dr Cameron was simply not answering questions I raise regarding his last false court report. Judge Bracewell simply IGNORED MY REQUEST and instead asked me rather impatiently if I had finished my cross examination yet! It is clear Judge Bracewell was simply going to place more farce upon me and the children. Injustice heaped upon injustice – with Dr Cameron successfully perverting the course of justice.

But before we finished in court that day, the mother then went into the witness box to give her evidence as to why contact should be halved, or better still, ended. The mother, from the witness box produces a letter she claimed is from the youngest daughter, then aged eight, addressed to 'the judge'.

Now the secret family court rules forbid me putting word for word into print the content of that letter, but I can state that the letter detailed my youngest daughter apparently saying she did not like Dad, she did not like seeing Dad and she did not want to come to see me anymore. The letter was at first handed to Judge Bracewell, then passed all around the court, getting to me last. Immediately, I spotted the letter was written by the mother – I recognised her handwriting! Spotting this letter from the child as a forgery, I immediately asked for this letter to be sent to a handwriting expert, together with samples of the mother's own handwriting, and I offered to fund this. I pointed out to the judge that if she were to let even more false documentation and claims into the court, we would all be back again very quick with nothing resolved. I immediately took her through the way both Judges Wilson and Kirkwood were mislead and said that now if she was not careful, she would follow them on this path too. I was actually pleading for her to take action.

Unfortunately, in the true tradition of the Family Division, Judge Joy-Anne Bracewell refused this request for expert examination of the letter, just like she also chose to ignore all of the very good contact reports before her too. Judge Bracewell, of course, immediately believed the mother's claim that the child wrote the letter. Bracewell then went on to halving my time with my children to just six times a year, six hours each school holiday, unsupervised, at my house.

As I sat hearing Judge Bracewell dispense this utter nonsense and farce in her secret court judgement which ran to nearly 30 pages, which had Dr Cameron and the mother smiling at each other throughout, I decided enough was enough and this was the day I decided that public protest was the only option. Trying to do things 'the right way' for almost seven years had not worked and was clearly never going to work. I had been to court well over 100 times, so why should the next hearing or hearings change anything, I reasoned. It was clear to me that I couldn't be the only dad up against this corruption. All of these judges were doing exactly the same thing. Truth, justice, evidence and fact simply did not matter, only the mother's wishes and well-being bothered anyone. If the mother agreed to something, anything, that was what you would get. If she opposed something, or everything, likewise, that's what Dad would eventually end up with. That day was where the public protest was to start, and I decided I would be the one to start it.

The Children Act, although far from perfect, is good enough to be made to work. Likewise, the Contempt of Court Act, available to enforce *any* court order, is also more than sufficient for making court orders work. The problem was now clear; the people dishing out these absurd findings and allowing the course of justice to be interfered with all of the time – the judges – *were the problem*. It was plain outright gender discrimination against fathers. I therefore decided before I left the court in Plymouth that day while hearing this nonsense that the protest group to be formed would be called DADS – Dads Against Discrimination. I had no plan of action in mind, but 'something' was to be done, done soon, and done publicly.

So when I went home, angry and determined, I lodged the customary appeal at the Royal Courts. I planned to fight my case at the same time as bringing other court-abused fathers into lawful protest. I had plenty of spare time anyway, I was now only seeing my children one day every school holiday (six times a year) for six hours. Although I had returned to work at another driving school about a year prior, I would ensure protest would be accommodated around my work. I planned to fight now on two fronts: in the courts, for what it was worth, and on the streets, while trying to be the best marginalised father to my much loved daughters possible.

Despite Judge Bracewell refusing the involvement of a handwriting expert to examine the youngest daughter's letter to the judge, I took the step upon myself of employing the highest qualified handwriting expert I could find immediately after the case concluded, a Mr David Jones of Alvechurch, Birmingham. He agreed to do this work. I asked him to look at the letter claimed to be from my youngest daughter, a sample of my daughter's handwriting I had in my possession and my ex-wife's handwriting which appeared in the court documentation regarding the financial settlement of the family home. Mr Jones, BSc, FSS, Dp, is a consultant document examiner and forensic handwriting expert who was employed by the Home Office Forensic Science Service between 1964 and 1987.

Mr Jones, after examining what my ex-wife claimed was my youngest daughter's letter to Judge Bracewell, a copy of my daughter's handwriting that was at my house and previously handwritten documentation of my ex-wife's, wrote a three-page report which, after detailing his scientific forensic examination of the documents, concluded that:

1) The child did *not* write the letter to the judge.

2) My ex-wife was the probable author of the correspondance, that being the 'childs' letter to the judge.

I had told Judge Bracewell at the time that I thought the mother had forged this letter and this report more than suggested I was right. Bracewell's inaction and unwillingness to listen once again meant that justice was unreachable for me and my kids.

With Dr Cameron having corrupted the process before Judge Kirkwood with his defective report about my fictional 'personality disorder' in the previous hearing, we now had the mother compounding this interference of the process, by producing a totally false document that was passed off to a judge and accepted as true. This at least warranted further investigation, if not a complete retrial – or a successful appeal.

The day after I received the handwriting expert's report, the first planned fathers' rights protest was to take place outside the Plymouth court under the DADS banner. The protest received much regional TV and press coverage as it was believed to be the very first fathers' rights protest outside a family court anywhere in the country, possibly the world (pictured opposite). Our first protest was attended by a handful of protesters (about 20), but little did any of us there know how this very small, rather disorganised protest, deep in Devon, would grow into a worldwide campaign – and cause the authorities to rise up and smash it.

After our successful first protest, I traced Judge Bracewell to her country home in Somerton, Somerset, via the 192.com directory enquiries service and research of the Who's Who directory. Judge Bracewell co-owns a country hotel in the town with her husband. I drove there at the end of April, with a copy of this report and a covering letter to the judge. Although a very up-market, smart and quite exclusive country hotel, it was obviously a fairly small and well run family establishment. The lawns outside were immaculate, manicured and kept like bowling greens. The driveway, after crossing the cattle grid at the entrance, was gravelled and my car tyres made that 'manor house' crunching sound as I entered the small car park.

Mark Harris, foreground, leads the first group of campaigners on protest outside Plymouth County Court, April 2000. This is believed to be the United kingdom's first fathers' rights protest ever. This group was named 'DADS-Dads Against Discrimination'.

Upon arrival I found the main entrance, entered and approached a man I found stood at the hotel reception. I asked the gentleman at the reception desk if by any chance he was Mr Copeland. I had previously found out through the Who's Who listing that Judge Bracewell works in her maiden name but Copeland is her married name – and the name she resided in at the hotel with her husband. The man at the reception rather proudly confirmed he was indeed Mr Copeland. Without further comment, I instantly passed him the envelope addressed to Mrs Justice Bracewell, family court judge, and I bluntly asked him if he would be kind enough to pass the envelope to his 'Misses', the High Court judge, as she'd messed my case up big-time and I wanted her back in Plymouth to sort it out. The absolute look of shock on this man's face was a picture and I can still vividly recall, years later. Looking back, if Mr Copeland had had a weak heart, the shock of his judge-wife being rumbled in this way at home may have caused him serious harm. He just could not speak, he just nodded slowly and walked away like a stunned snail, with my envelope in hand.

In reality, I did not expect this woman judge to do much or anything at all. Her attitude to me and her indifference to my children's plight in the court told me she really did not care at all. But turning up at her home with the evidence was part of my plan now to get more in these people's faces. In court she simply ran through the motions, happily endorsing what the mother wanted as usual, supported by Dr Cameron, then went home.

However, my 'master plan' was that with my appeal coming up at the Royal Courts of Justice in a few weeks' time, surely it would be time for the court to intervene. I was going there armed with not only the police reports confirming Judge Wilson was mislead about the mother's claims of harassment over two years ago, but I was able to follow that up with Dr Cameron's proven unreliable reporting causing the huge mistrial before Judge Kirkwood 18 months after and, of course, the handwriting expert report confirming another mistrial before Judge Bracewell so very recently. I asked myself how could they possibly let this farce go on further, *they must surely have to bring us some sanity.*

So, June 2000, and up to the Court of Appeal before Lord Justice Thorpe once again. I was seeking permission to appeal the order of Judge Bracewell. Most of my appeals seemed to go to Lord

Justice Matthew Thorpe or Dame Elizabeth Butler-Sloss. I asked Thorpe to appeal not only Bracewell's order, but every nonsense order past and present, but, as usual, all were refused. Lord Justice Thorpe started his terse three-page judgement, including this now unbelievable phrase, which can be quoted verbatim as appeal court cases are held in open court, with the children's identities kept to just initials:

"Although it is, in essence, a very simple contact dispute…"

Thorpe, true to form, refused to get involved or do anything to help in sort out this "very simple contact dispute" but instead chose to let this "very simple contact dispute" rage on for another three years. He disposed of the mistrial caused by Judge Bracewell wrongfully accepting the 'letter' from my youngest daughter thus:

"…the father has sought to introduce evidence from a handwriting expert…he heard the judge say that she did not grant his application permission [to instruct this expert]…his subsequent instruction of an expert seems at least, wilful, if not defiant…and it's very unlikely that this court would grant permission for the admission of such evidence."

So, there you have it from the country's most senior family court appeal judge of the day. It does not matter if faked documents change the entire course or outcome of a family court case, it does not matter if someone, anyone, deliberately perverts the course of justice, if the father or the kids lose out because of it, tough luck. He must simply just go away quietly and accept it, and if he does not, he's defiant. If errors, mistakes, or deliberate acts in family courts causes miscarriages of justice, Matthew Thorpe confirmed their attitude – so what?

Inevitably, the bi-monthly contact visits, with just the two youngest transported to my house by the care workers, still without the eldest girl, was open to sabotage by the mother and her boyfriend. And, of course, sabotaged it was. April, then the June visits, each during school holiday or half term break went fine. The care workers openly reported the joy of each child coming to and leaving Dad's home on each occasion. They also reported the two youngest asking them to help get more visits to Dad's, as they didn't want to go so long without seeing him. The girls also detailed pressure placed upon them and the eldest girl, Lisa, then 13, from their home to say they didn't want to come. All of this was accurately documented by the care workers, which all went to the next court hearing.

In August, the inevitable happened. The youngest child succumbed to the pressure not to come. Only the middle daughter arrived, escorted by two care workers. When they left us, my daughter told me that it was getting "too difficult" to keep coming; the less they came, the more difficult "mum and him" (Wayne Taylor) were making it for them at home. Still naively, I told her to tell the care workers on the way home (this was still fully unsupervised contact, but the care workers still had to fetch and carry them over, by order of the court) and they should help. She asked if I could "tell the court next time" that they wanted help to making seeing me easier. It was quite distressing to hear my child ask for this simple right to be able to freely see me with her sisters, but finding I was so powerless to help her, as a father should.

I blamed Dr Cameron for causing all these problems for me and my daughters. I had seen off the harassment nonsense that caused Judge Wilson to stop contact nearly three years before, but Cameron's introduction of false material to the court caused these monthly, now bi-monthly visits to continue, rather than progress into the regular visits and stays that the care workers previously recommended. Dr Cameron, with his untruths to Judge Kirkwood, deflected that judge from sorting the case out by telling what can only be described as lies. He not only lied, he refused to withdraw that defective 1999 report of his that went before Judge Kirkwood from the court as he was asked to by the Plymouth NHS Trust child psychotherapist. I now viewed Dr Cameron as the enemy.

Months after Dr Cameron refused to withdraw this report, about September 2000, and the inevitable gradual breakdown of contact because of it's infrequency, levels *he* recommended to Judge

Bracewell, I sought the attention of the criminal courts to what he had done. The family courts simply brushed over what was happening and let him continue wreaking havoc in our lives.

I, as so many times in the past, had tried to do things 'the right way' and reported Dr Cameron to my local police months earlier for perverting the course of justice, but they were just not interested. A father restricted from or not seeing his children gets no sympathy from anyone. You sense the assumption is, there must be a reason. So, heartbroken and frustrated beyond endurance, I decided to get what Dr Cameron was up to into a criminal court. I drove 200 miles to Dr Cameron's exclusive home in Richmond, tied a note with my name and address around a brick with my reasons for my actions and threw it through his car window which was parked in his driveway. I then drove the mile or so to Richmond police station with copies of his court report and the letters confirming his misrepresentations to Judge Kirkwood to give myself up for the offence of criminal damage.

At Richmond police station, I told the officer manning the front desk what I had just done, and why. I was informed that they had received a 999 call just moments before I had arrived, from the address where I had lobbed the brick. I was promptly arrested and escorted to the cells.

During my subsequent interview for the criminal damage, I told the officers that I wanted to explain my actions in a proper court (The Magistrates') with all the press and public as witness. I was by now into public protest anyway and I intended bringing into the open just what was going on in my secret court case.

I was later bailed from Richmond police station to return six weeks later on October 2nd 2000, conveniently the day after I had arranged with others a protest against the family courts in the capital, that being a march from Trafalgar Square to conclude with the handing in of a petition to No 10 Downing Street demanding equal parenting after divorce or separation and the end to closed family courts. I led a march of over 150 parents from Trafalgar Square to No 10, carrying, amongst other messages, a banner detailing the farce in my case and naming the two most senior judges currently involved, accompanied by my late mother, Sheila Harris.

The day after what is believed to be the first Equal Parenting march seen in the UK or worldwide, I answered my bail at Richmond police station. I was informed by the officer in charge of the case, WPC McCormack, that Dr Cameron did not wish to press charges regarding the criminal damage – and I was free to go. I was somewhat gob-smacked. Now, it's open to speculation, but I guessed Dr Cameron, despite calling 999 when his window was smashed, thought of the ramifications for him when I explained just why I did it. I cannot think of any other reason why he should drop all charges...

Mark Harris, far left, leads the United Kingdom's first march on 10 Downing Street on October 1st 2000 to hand in a petition demanding equal parenting & the opening up of the Family Court's to public scrutiny. Thanks Dave Ellison of Warrington for the photo.

A couple of days later, my middle daughter arrived for the mid October half term visit, alone and clearly worried about what was waiting for her at home with the mother and Wayne Taylor because she insisted on coming to see me. She told me there's just "no point" telling anyone about what goes on at her home as nobody takes any notice. Here I am, her father, unable to protect her from this emotional abuse that the mother and boyfriend are inflicting upon her, yet, I'm the one with restricted access to her, why?

I sensed this poor child of just 11 was not going to be able to stand up, alone, to the pressures at home trying to put her off of seeing me for much longer. She said the less they came over, the worse it was made. She said when her and her sisters used to see me lots, everyone just got used to it. I told her before she left that day I would try and sort this lot out for her and her sisters, that I loved them all, and I hoped the mother and boyfriend would not upset her too much for coming over. I remember thanking her for being so very brave. She again told me to "tell the courts we just want to see you lots."

The next day, I went straight to the court office in Plymouth and re-applied to the court to restore contact, fully, as all the recommendations since 1993, now nearly eight years ago, had recommended – that being alternate weekends staying, half all school holidays, plus weekly teatime visits. Infrequency became the trouble, and, as my daughter had told me the day before: "we see you lots, everyone just got used to it." Everything else did not and had not worked, and this current order, like so many of the half measures tried, failed us all too. I also applied for enforcement of Lisa's attendance to be brought upon the mother.

Strangely, the mother, quite outside of the court order and presumably hearing of my applications to restore full contact with enforcement 'offered', through the care worker service, another day-long contact, less than four weeks later. I wondered if it was because she just didn't fancy facing the court after she had broken yet more court orders, had just seen sense at last, or realised just what harm she was inflicting upon the children, so of course I readily agreed

However, the Saturday for this extra contact came round, and I prepared a snack for my daughters ready for their mid day arrival, not really knowing if one, two or all three would actually turn up. Then the care worker people carrier pulled up outside my home, but with only the two care workers inside.

I went straight out to meet them, at the bottom of my driveway. The male worker, for the first time with a tape recorder in his hand and directed at me, told me that each of the girls had come to the door when they arrived to collect them at Mum's and each had said they did not want to come over to see me anymore. My previous view that the mother may well have seen sense, or even relented by offering this extra visit proved completely unrealistic; she simply wanted a report from the care workers 'pre-court' where the children would be saying, even though it was in her presence and at her front door, they did not want to see me again. Thus, she got exactly that.

That was just before Christmas 2000 and we also got yet another High Court judge, Mr Justice James Munby, assigned to our case. I researched him as best I could, I found he's only been appointed a judge just a couple of months prior. He's allocated to come to the Plymouth court for a five-day 'trial' at the end of January 2001.

Strangely, Judge Munby's first action was to appoint the Attorney General as party to the proceedings – because I had previously put the brick through Dr Cameron's window and led the DADS protest group outside courts. Munby said he was concerned this could interfere with the administration of justice. Unfortunately, the Attorney General chose to ignore the evidence that the expert witness himself had interfered with in the administration of justice. He also ignored it when Dr Cameron did it again.

Now, this bizarre course of action by Judge Munby at the outset of his involvement seemed to inspire my ex-wife to return to type almost immediately. A day or so after the Attorney General was appointed, I got two very young policemen knock at my door early one evening.

When I open the door, they asked to come in regarding an allegation they had received from my ex-wife. With little real concern, I let them in.

We got to my lounge area when one of them started to explain that they had received a phone call earlier that day from my ex-wife who complained to them that I had phoned her up and threatened to damage her car if she did not let me see the children. I explained to them that not only was this yet another untrue allegation by her, but there was quite some history of her making false allegations against me on the weeks prior to these contact hearings in the family courts to the police. But these two new recruits to the Devon and Cornwall Constabulary were just not for listening. They informed me that as I had a past conviction for criminal damage (the roof-top protest at the Social Services' area nearly four years prior) I was being arrested on suspicion of threats to cause criminal damage. I stood there in utter disbelief. I was then placed in handcuffs and put in the back of their waiting riot van that they had parked outside my house.

After the five mile or so journey from my home, we arrived at Plymouth's Charles Cross Police Station. It's now about 9 pm. There was the usual queue of drunks and petty criminals ahead of me in the custody office being gradually processed by the duty sergeant behind a desk. Eventually, it's my turn to be processed.

As we got to the sergeant, the two young constables explained to him that earlier in the day they had received a phone call from my ex-wife and they repeated to him what they had said to me; that she had alleged that I had phoned her and threatened to damage her car if she did not let me see my children.

The sergeant turned to me, reminded me I was still under caution, and asked if there was anything I wanted to say.

Angry that a simple false phone call from my ex could get me arrested and brought to a police station together with the frustration of my child access problems, I clearly recall saying to him, "Yeah, I've got something to say, alright, this is just a load more bo**ocks from my ex-wife that she will want to use in the next court hearing over seeing my kids, and arresting me like this just gives her credibility."

The sergeant appeared to write down my comments, and asked if I wanted the duty solicitor. I replied, "That's right, I do!"

I was then led off to the cells where I was detained overnight.

Although next morning I was given a pretty good breakfast, and a not so good lunch followed later, I was not seen again until nearly 3 pm later that day, when I was informed by a civilian member of the custody staff that my duty solicitor had arrived and would see me shortly.

About 20 minutes later I was taken from the cell to meet my solicitor, Miss Sophie Hodge, who introduced herself to me and explained that the police had informed her of the allegations made against me – and that they had searched my house during the night.

Before I could even comment upon this, Sophie went on to say that there was just something not right about all of this, the fact I had been arrested on the strength of just a phone call, that I had been held for nearly 18 hours without interview and my house had been searched. I then immediately told her about the covert police observations the same police force had undertook on my ex-wife in 1997 which concluded she made multiple false allegations of harassment against me and that this was just another false allegation of hers.

Sophie Hodge was unaware of the history and seemed genuinely stunned by this news, so I elaborated with the detail. Miss Hodge, despite her youthful appearance, was now convinced an abuse of the process was taking place and told me so. Sophie had been informed that during the police search of my home, they'd recovered two address books with DADS members' contact details and some press clippings of recent protests. She asked me where I had kept these books and I told her in a desk drawer in my dining room.

Sophie told me that the police had obtained a search warrant to 'spin' my house under the pretence of looking for materials that could have been used to damage my ex-wife's car, such as paint stripper, brake fluid, etc, the crime I had been arrested for. I told her that in my garage there was paint stripper, brake fluid and plenty of tools that could easily be used to commit damage to a car if I had had a will to do so. Miss Hodge went on to explain that it appeared to her from what they'd said that the police search had only been through documentation in my house related to the DADS protests and nothing more and there appeared no search of my garage, the first obvious place such items would be kept. She then said it appeared to her the arrest, detention of me and search of my home in the way it was done looked unlawful, in particular with regard to the history of my ex and her proven false allegations.

Miss Hodge then prepared a short statement for me to read out during the pending interview which detailed the covert observations of the police in 1997, which she predicted would end in my immediate release. She advised me to speak about nothing more, just reply to all further questions with 'No comment'.

The taped interview soon commenced, but not with the two young officers who arrested me the previous evening, but two detectives from the CID. After my rights were read to me, Miss Hodge, who was present throughout, stated that I wished to read out a prepared statement, and one of the officers asked me to proceed.

So I read out the prepared statement, detailing from memory all the facts about the Police covert observations on my ex wife, dates, times, places and named the four officers involved. I concluded the statement with the police conclusion at the time which was she – my ex-wife – was making multiple false allegations about me, and their warning back then to her about possible charges for wasting police time. These two detectives clearly knew nothing about this. My final sentence stated that I had made no threats to my ex-wife about damaging her car, or any threats towards her about anything at all.

Now, the CID officers seemed to instantly give up with any investigation about my ex's claims, the sole matter I was in custody for. The questioning immediately went into my growing protest group called DADS. I was asked about the address books, asked one by one about most of the members who were written into my address book, comments in my address book about the two 'live together' gay social workers who had previously caused such havoc in my case and how I'd found their address. Each question I replied to with the simple phrase, "No comment!"

Then my address book containing various judges' home addresses was shown to me. The eldest detective then went through each judge listed, asking on each occasion how I got that address. Again, all I replied was, "No comment!"

Miss Hodge piped up after a few minutes of this and asked the officers about the relevance of their questioning in regard to what I was arrested for. One of the officers, a DC Gilroy, got angry with her for butting in, but failed to give any explanation whatsoever to her question – and they just continued asking about DADS members and the judges' addresses.

It became clear to me the entire arrest and search was nothing to do with whatever my ex-wife may or may not have alleged, but her latest false allegation was simply an excuse to enter my house and find out about the DADS protest group.

The interview concluded with my continuing of the 'No comment' answer to all questions, and a request for the return of my property, namely the address books and newspaper clippings. I was told, in Miss Hodge's presence, that I would receive my property "soon, but not today."

I was then released without charge at about 4 pm.

Now, Miss Hodge and I had a conversation about what had happened to me outside Plymouth's Charles Cross Police Station. She told me the entire police behaviour towards me appeared completely unlawful and looked to her as an excuse for the police to search my house on a 'fishing trip' to investigate the DADS protest group. I told her I wanted to take a civil action against the police for compensation for this clearly unlawful behaviour to me, to which she replied such an action would "probably succeed."

I asked if she could represent me in bringing such an action, but she told me that was a very specialist area of law that she was just not qualified in. However, Miss Hodge promised to send me the Law Society's contact address where she knew a solicitor of the appropriate expertise could be found.

Two days later the very professional Miss Hodge sent me the promised contact details of the Law Society who advised me to see a solicitor in Bristol called Stephanie Price, whose speciality was bringing civil actions against the police in such cases.

Miss Price was immediately contacted, an appointment for an interview at her offices was soon made, where Stephanie Price agreed with Miss Hodge's opinion that the Devon and Cornwall police had behaved unlawfully towards me.

As the letter below shows, Devon and Cornwall Police, over one year later and only after proceedings against them were commenced, paid £1000 in compensation for my unlawful arrest, unlawful detention and unlawful search of my house, plus Miss Price's costs (which I understand well exceeded the figure I got).

They never said sorry for what they put me through and they never prosecuted my ex-wife for wasting their time once again.

Price Watkins Solicitors

21 St Georges Road
Bristol, BS1 5UU
Tel: 0117 949 4144
Fax: 0117 949 4148

Mr M Harris

Partners: Beverley Watkins
Stephanie Price

Our Ref: SP/HAR/039/01
20 August, 2001

Dear Mr Harris

You will be pleased to hear that I have now received the cheque in settlement of your claim from Devon and Cornwall Constabulary. As the cheque was made payable to this firm inclusive of the costs, I now enclose my firm's cheque in the sum of £1,000 in full and final settlement of your claim against Devon and Cornwall Constabulary. Please acknowledge safe receipt.

I am pleased that this has been such a satisfactory outcome.

I shall now be closing your file and it will remain in storage for 6 years, following which it will be destroyed. As far as I am aware, I do not have any of your original documents.

If I can assist you with anything further in the future, please do not hesitate to let me know.

May I take this opportunity to remind you of the range of services this firm offers, which includes help with all family and matrimonial problems, education problems, all accident and injury problems including criminal injuries compensation claims, and complaints against the Police.

Best wishes.

Yours sincerely

STEPHANIE PRICE
PRICE WATKINS SOLICITORS
Enc

Devon & Cornwall police finally conceded that they wrongfully arrested the father & paid him £1000 compensation when faced with legal action.

Mark Harris, October 2000, leaves his banner outside the Royal Courts of Justice, sadly, no one took any notice; the case went before seven more Judges over another 22 hearings for 2 1/2 years

CHAPTER 5

Expert Witness Admits Misleading the Court but *Dad* Goes off to Prison Again

Ever the optimist (again!) I thought, well, yet another new judge, fresh eyes, fresh approach, let's hope this all gets sorted out. The nonsense and farce was stacked so high now, surely we were due for someone to put their hand on the dispensation of justice and at least try a new approach?

As always, on the run-up to any hearing, child psychiatrist Dr Hamish Cameron arrived at my house again to write yet another report for the court just after Christmas 2000. Now, completely mistrusting this individual, I set up covert taping of our meeting. I concealed a tape recorder behind a curtain next to the chair I intend him sitting in. I planned how I was going to ensure he could only sit there on arrival. I was totally convinced then, rightly or wrongly, that he was simply out to keep his privately fee paid involvement in the case going on and on. I viewed him as the enemy and a man not to be trusted.

Luckily, I did tape Dr Cameron without him being aware of what I was doing. To summarise, when I saw Dr Cameron arrive outside my house that afternoon by taxi, I switched the tape recorder onto record. I met him at my front door. When he entered my house, I 'invited' Dr Cameron to sit in the only available-by-design chair next to my taping machine hidden behind the curtain. Dr Cameron, unaware of the covert taping, immediately got his notepad out from his briefcase and soon asked me about what was recently described in the local press as 'The A38 bomb hoax'.

This now had been linked to the rapidly expanding DADS protest group. During the 'interview', Dr Cameron busily scribed notes of his questions and my answers while carefully shielding what he was writing from my view. Throughout the entire interview, Dr Cameron asked nothing about the contact issues soon before the court, despite that being his highly paid role, but only asked about the A38 bomb hoax and the now ever growing DADS protest movement that had quickly gathered pace and was spreading around the country. The protest movement and its expansion clearly concerned Dr Cameron well beyond any role as expert witness engaged to help resolve the children matters.

The A38 bomb hoax. This had happened a few weeks after a protest that took place outside the president of the Family Division's Devon home, Dame Butler-Sloss. Someone had stupidly planted a fake bomb on the A38 trunk road near Plymouth, less than a mile from my home, claiming to be a member of DADS. The hoaxer was reported to have told the press they wanted to 'up the stakes' in our battle for open family courts and equal parenting. The bomb hoax closed the main road in and out of Plymouth and caused a whole day of city-wide traffic disruption. If a father did do this, it was a completely stupid and wrong thing to do. But, as I detail later in this book, I now do not believe at all any father planted this hoax bomb, or the others that quickly spread around Devon during this period of time that was attributed to the fast establishing protest group called DADS. I believe these hoax bombs were deliberately planted by persons with a vested interest in the divorce industry who tried to turn the huge public support that DADS was getting at the time.

I was puzzled by the fact that Dr Cameron did not live in Devon; he lives in leafy Richmond, Surrey, about 200 miles away, but knew all about this bomb hoax. The publicity surrounding these hoax bombs (two more in Devon quickly followed the Plymouth hoax; one near Exeter and one in Newton Abbot) only stayed in the county. *It was never national news.* I immediately wondered just who had tipped him off about this. I told him, as the covert taping later proved, I did not think *any* member of DADS was involved in this at all, but if the press wanted to link it to us so be it, I was not that bothered. I also told him that at one point the police suspected I had some involvement with the bomb hoax, but this was just not the case at all.

Dr Cameron continued to write, concluded his interview with me, and left by his pre-arranged taxi.

Three weeks later, Dr Cameron's 64-page report arrived by post the day before our five day 'trial' before Judge Munby started. Dr Cameron's reports, attached to the Official Solicitor's reports, always seemed to arrive at the very last possible moment before a court case, making detailed examination of the content 'against the clock'. The combined reports usually exceed 100 pages, often nearer the 200-page mark. Dr Cameron reported that at this last interview in my house I told him 'I did it, I planted the A38 bomb'. My immediate anger was instantly replaced with relief as I had the tape recording of what I had truly said. I was quite prepared to accept by now that this 'well past retirement age' doctor may simply be incapable of writing anything accurately, and I could now, beyond any doubt whatsoever, *prove* it in the court.

For this hearing I managed, after appeal, to obtain legal aid for professional representation. I had a very good barrister from Devon called Miss Gina Small. I instructed Miss Small to expose Dr Cameron for what he was – a liar. Miss Small warned me that she was quite happy to 'wipe the floor' with Dr Cameron over what he had done, not only in 1999 before Judge Kirkwood, but also with the taped evidence of his falsely reporting to the court I admitted planting the A38 bomb hoax, but she said she didn't think it would help me much! However, I told her to do her best and expose him so we could get rid of him.

Gina Small did not disappoint, and it was quite something to see take place in the court. Miss Small is a very petite woman of about 4 ft 11 who wore thick glasses and spoke very quietly, in almost a whisper. Dr Cameron is a very large man, 6 ft 3 +, with a booming, well spoken voice. Dr Cameron started off with his usual bluster and arrogance from the witness box, demonising me, the father, from the outset. But Gina got to work, asking him questions about his misreporting, and Dr Cameron started to visibly rock – he clearly never expected anyone from the divorce industry dare to ask him about this. He fidgeted, he drank plenty of the water provided for the witnesses and, unbelievably, started stuttering.

Eventually, Gina Small cornered him over his false reports that he filed before Judge Kirkwood where he said two previously involved professionals in this case – a probation officer and a child psychotherapist – told him I had a personality disorder that affected my relationship with my children.

After what must have been the longest pause in giving an answer to have ever been made in a British court, Dr Cameron unbelievably admitted neither of them had ever said this at all, apologised, and said he had gone a leap too far in saying they had, whatever that meant.

Miss Small then went for his blood, and asked him about me telling him I was the A38 hoax bomber. At first, Dr Cameron stated on oath, yes, Mark Harris admitted to planting this hoax bomb to him. Then Miss Small produced the cassette tape of our interview. Dr Cameron's jaw dropped to the ground. Miss Small then told Dr Cameron that I had covertly taped our last interview, and having listened to what was said, confirmed that I had never said any such thing at all. Dr Cameron then paused for an even longer time, and asked the judge if he could refer to his notes taken at our interview. Judge Munby agreed, and Dr Cameron went through his notepad very slowly.

After what seemed several minutes of Dr Cameron staring into his notepad, Dr Cameron read out his notes at the time, that being I did admit to planting the hoax bomb on the A38. Miss Small, knowing this was false, offered to play him the cassette tape of the interview, to which Dr Cameron then completely discredited and ridiculed himself – he immediately 'recalled' the conversation and stated that I actually did not admit to planting a bomb hoax at any time!

Miss Small immediately asked for his explanation as to why this false misrepresentation was not only in his expert witness report, but also given by way of oral evidence under oath just a minute before. Dr Cameron, after a short pause, placed both hands up in the air and incredibly replied, "perhaps I was just being very economical with the truth!" He then hung his head in shame, and once again the courtroom was completely stunned with what had once again taken place in this absurd case.

Judge Munby made many motes, thanked Dr Cameron for his time in the case, and Dr Cameron left the courtroom immediately afterwards. The court then adjourned, and I thanked Miss Small for what she did. She was great, a true professional at her job, she destroyed Dr Cameron and had him admitting he had lied. Miss Small said to me she thought we would get a new expert appointed at some point, and thought that I had a very good chance of getting at least some contact back, as the only professional in the case opposing me could not sensibly be relied upon.

Anyway, at the end of the five days before Munby in January 2001, with now over 20 care worker, Social Services and court welfare reports now before him dating between 1993 and 2000, each detailing happy children coming to and leaving contact with me, Judge Munby reserved his judgement until March 2001. We all had to go to the Royal Courts of Justice in London on March 23rd to hear what he had decided.

In March, at the Royal Courts of Justice, London, Judge Munby delivered his 192-page private judgement. Like with most other court orders made in this matter by now, the mother simply did not even bother to turn up.

Unbelievably, Munby chose to combine the very last care worker report (of the children on the mother's doorstep saying they did not want to go and see Dad) with Dr Hamish Cameron's second fatally flawed opinion that they didn't want to see me ever again. Munby ordered all contact with my children was to end, and I could only send one birthday card and one Christmas card per year to each child – enclosing one banknote if I wished, to which he unbelievably added that I could be "generous" with that gift. Munby also enlarged the exclusion zone around the children's home – because he believed the children never wanted to see me – and handed me down a map of the locality with his adjustments marker penned in.

This madman was serious too. Despite the expert witness, Dr Cameron, admitting to lying in the court as well as in his previous reports, Judge Munby ludicrously still followed his recommendations. This insanity surpassed everything else that had taken place before, and after this debacle, Munby ordered me to the Royal Courts of Justice the next day for sentencing over the mother's latest committal application. I was no longer optimistic about any sanity taking place in that either, so that night I alerted London based DADS members to come and see what was about to unfold, as sentencing was in open court.

As (what had now become the norm in this case) the mother, fully legally aided throughout, had sought another committal order upon me to get me imprisoned for contempt of court, this was to be heard at the same time as my contact application in January. By intertwining both matters to run simultaneously, the whole committal hearing stayed in the secret court. With her solicitor, my ex-wife had applied for ten breaches of various court orders by me since her last committal application, which Munby had readily accepted as breaches.

Munby, for his part, made the fatal mistake of giving the children decisions on one day, and ordering me to the court for sentence the next day. He was an inexperienced judge. I really believe he thought no one else would turn up, and it could all be done *'à la Wilson'*, in secret. Besides, I was over 200 miles away from home; I believe he wondered by now just who could turn up anyway. So it was the next day and he had to 'sentence' me in open court.

Overnight, I managed to get a small number of very good people based in London who were DADS protesters to attend the Royal Courts in London to witness the sentencing. I suspected something extreme was to take place the day before. I had warned them that Munby would not disappoint – and he didn't. Within hours of what Munby then did, thanks to the DADS people in court that day and the Internet, fathers around the world heard about what Munby did to me. The touch paper was ignited. National protest and international campaigning for fathers' rights was conceived that day, 23rd March 2001.

With the mother and youngest children's identity removed, I can legally reproduce a full copy of the 'offences' from the committal order that Munby granted her against me below.

I only went to court before Judge Munby, which was now about our 118th occasion, to get a working contact order. The mother had again tactically cross-applied for my committal to prison, despite breaching the contact order herself. The unsupervised contact order of the time was failing because my ex-wife flouted it for years and my middle daughter asked me when I last saw her to do something about it. But Munby chose to leave the children matters unresolved, ignore the mother's contempt of court regarding contact and instead sent me to Pentonville prison for a total of ten months, together with a £500 fine for saying hello to my kids when I saw them in a shop. I have never paid that fine to this day, I still refuse to pay that fine. *I will never pay it.* The subsequent publicity surrounding all of this and the eventual outcome of the children matters probably ensures the Court Service will never pursue me for the payment either.

The offences, in bold, are as they appear on the committal order, which is a public record; the 'he' Munby refers to at each offence is me:

1) On 2nd April 2000 he approached the children Lisa Michelle HARRIS, [the middle child] and [the youngest child] outside Chaplins Superstore in Plymouth and talked to them thereby breaching paragraph (h) of the order.
FINED £250

2) Shortly before 20th April 2000 he sent to 'the mother' through the post a cheque for £900 post dated to 29th April 2000, with a note stating that the cheque could be cashed if Lisa attended the next session of contact and continued to attend contact, thereby breaching paragraphs…of the order.
6 MONTHS IMPRISONMENT

3) On 25th April 2000 he did enter Miller Way Plymouth in a car seeking contact or communication with the children and driving past the mother thereby breaching paragraphs…of the order.

6 MONTHS IMPRISONMENT

4) On 26th April 2000 he did hand presents to [middle child] and [youngest child] during the session of contact and without the presents first having been approved by Plymouth City Council thereby breaching paragraph…of the order.

EXTRA 4 MONTHS IMPRISONMENT ON TOP

5) On 27th June 2000 he left a note for [the youngest child] in one of [the youngest child's] books after attending an evening at [the youngest's primary school] to discuss her work and without the note first having been approved by Plymouth Council, thereby breaching paragraph…of the order.

4 MONTHS IMPRISONMENT

6) On 7th August 2000 he entered Miller Way Plymouth in a car seeking contact or communication with the children and driving past and waving to the mother and the children thereby breaching paragraphs…of the order.

6 MONTHS IMPRISONMENT

7) On 24th August 2000 he entered Miller Way Plymouth in a car seeking contact or communication with the children and driving past the mother and the children thereby breaching paragraphs…of the order.

6 MONTHS IMPRISONMENT

8) Shortly before 30th August 2000 he sent or caused to be sent through the post to Lisa an article from "Families need Fathers" and without the article first having been approved by Plymouth City council thereby breaching paragraphs…of the order.

4 MONTHS IMPRISONMENT

9) On 5th October 2000 he entered Miller way Plymouth in a car seeking contact or communication with the children thereby breaching paragraphs…of the order

6 MONTHS IMPRISONMENT

10) On 7th October 2000 he approached Lisa in New George Street in Plymouth and spoke to her, thereby breaching paragraph…of the order.

FINED A FURTHER £250

As you can see, I was imprisoned for the heinous crimes, amongst others, of trying to bribe my ex into complying with the contact order, giving the children birthday presents – non-birthday presents on these unsupervised monthly contacts were deemed fine – passing through the area near where they live hoping to see them and also fined for just speaking to them if I saw them in a shop anywhere. There was no 'something else' attached to this, these *were* the 'crimes' in their entirety as written by Judge Munby on the committal order.

The mother continually broke the contact order for almost two years without impunity.

Throughout this period of time between the Kirkwood order 1999 and this present case before Munby in 2001, I had an unsupervised contact order, even if it was only for once a month, later reduced to bi-monthly. On those six hourly visits, I could take the children where I liked: swimming, cycling, visit the zoo, cinema, go to the park, anywhere, buy them meals, give them gifts that were *not* birthday presents or just stay at home with them. Why would anyone see wrong in a father, clearly deemed fit to see his children after what was now well in excess of 100 court appearances, in his trying to see them a bit more?

Do these appalling people sitting in our family courts as judges seriously think it is 'in the child's best interests' for a father to totally ignore his own children if he sees them in a shop or not hand them their birthday presents when he's with them? Well clearly they do. Are contact orders a 'maximum allowed' time with your children?

And just what's the difference between birthday presents and no special occasion presents?

To completely round off this insanity, as dished out by Judge Munby, it came down to the inescapable fact that absolutely anyone could speak to my children if they saw them in a public place at any time *except me,* their father, unless, of course, it was during my allocated contact time, even though the mother wilfully obstructed it. And this is not an isolated piece of family court lunacy. When I set up the DADS protest movement, a science teacher at my daughter's school in Plymouth joined us. He was divorcing and having problems seeing his two children. He taught my daughters, he worked alone and unsupervised at their large comprehensive school. But he was on *supervised contact* with his own children. He was not allowed to see his own children without someone present at a contact centre. He worked full time as a school teacher without any concerns from the authorities in a school with 1000+ children, so just why on earth was he on supervised contact with his own two kids? It's insanity.

Now, neither of us were banned from speaking to or associating with any other children, anywhere, other than our own. To take this absurdness a small theoretical step further, if the science teacher had took up relationship with my ex-wife, and I did with his ex-wife, the ludicrous situation could have easily developed where both of us fathers could be living with the other's children, while restricted from seeing our own children, by orders of the court. I made this point to Judge Munby during the committal hearing, but he just got angry and told me I was 'missing the point'. He never explained that point, probably because there is none. I still cannot see the point to this day, I cannot see any point to this madness at all.

In my mind, the lunatics have not only taken over the asylum, they are now running amok in our lives and seriously harming people in the real world.

Only because there was a committal application caught up in the child proceedings was I able to get legal aid on this occasion. Despite strong representations made on my behalf by Miss Small when defending the committal application that the 'present giving' breaches were indeed a technicality and the court should never have overlooked the error of having two incompatible orders in place, Munby was having none of it.

This incompatibility of orders stemmed from the Wilson order of 1997, when he cut me off from the children, deeming I harassed my ex-wife. To enable me to get Christmas and birthday presents to my daughters, Wilson wrote into his order a facility where I could drop these presents off to my daughters at the local Social Services' office. They were ordered to then deliver them to the girls on my behalf. When Judge Kirkwood restored the monthly unsupervised contact almost two years later, he, like everyone in the court that day, totally overlooked the existence of the present giving order.

However, my ex-wife, with her legally aided barrister and solicitor team, found this technicality with others and went for it. But even they did not have the gall to claim harassment anymore, it was now simply 'breaches of orders'. Unfortunately, Judge Munby went for these technicalities too. As detailed here, he sentenced me to four months in prison for the birthday present giving and other similar offences. He then gave me an additional six months to run consecutively on top for trying to see my daughters in addition to times outside the contact order. Therefore, as the four month sentences finished, the next six month ones began, ten months in total.

During my 'stay' at Her Majesty's Prison, Pentonville, a few criminals I was housed with who had been convicted of street crime, burglary, taking and driving away and possession of low level drugs, arrived after me and were released before me. The family courts had made a mockery of the entire legal system.

Of course, nothing was ever done about the mother's continual breaches of the contact order (not sending any of the children out to the care workers for collection), which is what got us all into court before Munby. But my trying to 'bribe' her into compliance was punished. Nothing was ever investigated regarding the mother's boyfriend or if he still assaulted the kids. No one knew and no one wanted to know. Mother wanted Dad out of the picture and into prison, with the assistance of Dr Cameron's misreporting where applicable, and that's exactly what she got.

What Judge Munby found regarding Dr Cameron's inaccurate reporting of not just the bomb hoax, but his previous false claims degenerating me, altered the entire course of the case nearly two years prior in 1999 before Judge Kirkwood did make it into his public attack by way of his entry of our case into The Family Law Reports, it makes compelling reading.

The former QC Judge Munby recites Dr Cameron's very frank admissions over his own multiple inaccuracies in his report writing from the witness box which can only be described by the ordinary citizen as breathtaking. More unbelievable, and ultimately proving the eventual undoing of the years of injustices and orders that firstly restricted, then eventually prevented me being a father to my children, is that Judge Munby followed this man's dishonest reports and recommendations when deciding the outcome of the case in 2001 – this despite Dr Cameron's admissions about the wholly fault ridden quality and inaccuracy of his reports that was so blatantly exposed.

The public Judgement was handed down by Munby a month later on 24th April 2001. What follows is *word for word* what Munby said at the time about expert witness Dr Hamish Cameron and his credibility.

Unfortunately, paragraphs 195-285 *were then removed* by Judge Munby from the Family Law reports obtainable through Jordans Publishing Ltd, Bristol, *HARRIS V HARRIS, ATTORNEY GENERAL V HARRIS. 24 APRIL 2001, ref ; 2001 2FLR 89.*

The purchasable version simply 'jumps' from paragraph 179 to 286 on page 922, *but this is what Munby said*:

Para 244; Father does, however, as it seems to me, have three legitimate complaints against Dr Cameron which it is right I should deal with.

Para 245; The first, and most serious, is that in one of the documents annexed to his second report dated 30th September 1999, Dr Cameron wrote that Mr B [child psychotherapist] and another professional, a probation officer, had reluctantly reached the conclusion that father "had a disorder of personality which impairs all his personal relationships, including those with his children". Father was incensed on two grounds; first, that Dr Cameron should have made use in his report of the views of Mr B and the probation officer without first having obtained their permission, and secondly, Dr Cameron should have attributed to them views which they did not in fact hold.

Para 246; Pressed to justify himself in the witness box Dr Cameron had to accept that neither Mr B nor the probation officer had ever used the phrase that he attributed to them, that it was an extrapolation from what they had said to him, and that expressing himself in the way in which he had he [Dr Cameron] had gone "a leap too far."

Para 247; I have to say that it is most unfortunate that this should have happened and that Dr Cameron should have been as slow *(nearly two years – Mark Harris)* as I think he was, in acknowledging that father did have a real point of substance.

I say this because of a comment Dr Cameron made in the witness box to the effect that father does not need to stir it up every time he sees an error…

…by the end, Dr Cameron was prepared to acknowledge quite frankly that he had been quite sloppy…

…However, let me make it quite clear that this error on Dr Cameron's part – and it was, I think, a serious error of professional judgement – does not, as it seems to me, in any way affect the overall validity and weight of Dr Cameron's opinions in the case.

(**Para 343**; My second complaint regarding Dr Cameron writing false statements was dealt with by way of legitimate 'mistake' – Mark Harris.)

Para 249; The father's third complaint is more serious, and again, as it seems to me, well founded. In the course of preparing his fourth report dated 18 January 2001 Dr Cameron had a discussion with father in the course of which he asked him about the hoax bombs on the A38. Dr Cameron's report reads, "Bomb hoax, A38, Mr Mark Harris accepted responsibility for this as the publicity for DADS was good." Mr Harris denied having said any such thing to Dr Cameron. Dr Cameron produced his contemporaneous manuscript notes taken at the meeting with Mr Harris. The relevant part reads, "Bomb hoax on A38. Accepted. It's me, I'm being affected."

Para 250; Now Mr Harris had in fact tape recorded his meeting with Dr Cameron, so I was able both to listen to the tape and to read an agreed transcript of the relevant part of their conversation. Unfortunately at one crucial point the quality of the tape was too poor to enable one to be confident of the precise words used. However, it is fairly clear that Mr Harris was not telling Dr Cameron that he had either claimed or accepted responsibility for the hoax…

…Dr Cameron accepted that his language he had been "very economical."

It was worse than that. It was, albeit I am sure unintentionally, positively misleading.

Para 251; I have to say that this is a matter of concern to me that this is the second time in just a few months on which it has been demonstrated to my satisfaction that a very eminent expert witness in the Family Division has mis-reported in a report for the court – I am sure entirely innocently – an important conversation with one of the adults involved.

Munby concludes **Para 251** with this frank admission, "Only comparatively rarely does the judge ever have the opportunity to go behind the written report in order to examine the underlying materials on which it was based. Very often it will be impossible or impracticable for him to do so. It is therefore vital that nothing should be done to impair judicial confidence in the scrupulous accuracy of such reports."

But since Munby's 'going public' with his findings over Dr Cameron's admissions over being very economical with the truth, Munby *himself* appears to have sanctioned the editing out of his own findings on Dr Cameron to the wider public when the purchasable public version does not include what he said. He seems to have attempted since to protect Dr Cameron's dishonesty by going into private again! Jordan's publishing of Bristol are the only organisation that I know of selling these law reports to the general public, but part of what was said had gone missing from the purchasable copies. Yet this judge at the time had the gall to make a point of going public, telling the press and DADS members "everyone needs to know the truth" about the dad.

But by Munby simply accepting such horrendously defective and positively misleading reports anyway, he was declaring that 'anything goes' in the secret family courts. For any judge to accept or follow the findings of an expert witness whose reports are found to contain "serious" and "positively misleading" defects (Munby's words) is farcical, especially when the judge states such defects are "near impossible" to detect or expose in the first place. When the expert witness himself admits, as Dr Cameron did, to being "very economical" with the truth, then the entire family legal system is a sham.

Judge Munby, when arriving in this case, had only been a family court judge for just three months, and for well over a month of that time he had been away on Christmas vacation. However, the entire can of worms regarding these court players started to get kicked over when he admitted it was "the second occasion" it had happened in a court of his during his very brief tenure (weeks) as a judge that an eminent expert witness had filed this sort of flawed material.

Again, even this admission 'disappeared' from true public consumption when the nationwide law reports got 'doctored' – by the judge!

One logical way to stop this misreporting and court sham involving these expert witnesses, if you must have them at all, and in particular the eminent ones, would be to only pay them their huge fees if they *actually resolve* contact disputes such as in this case. Let them look at the files by all means, let them see the kids and adults involved, and pay them up to that point. But only then if they want any further involvement in the case, and make no mistake these people are paid handsomely by the hour, then further payments should only be made upon *resolution* of the problem, namely a working contact order. And no payments whatsoever should be made whenever 'near impossible to detect inaccuracies' are discovered in their reports. They should also have to compensate the wronged parents and fund the replacement expert. If that was the case, flawed and wrongful reports would in all probability never happen as these people are very money motivated.

Only then could anyone have confidence in any of these reports being compiled with the care and diligence expected.

In Chapter 6, I detail how the protest movement mushroomed and took off at the very moment I was escorted off to London's infamous Pentonville prison in a secure van. I was housed for most of my time there on the prison's notorious A Wing with convicted murderers, terrorists, gun runners and drug dealers. I served a total of 84 days there for non-criminal 'offences'. I also reveal how on the 23rd March 2003, two years to the *very day* Munby criminalized fatherhood how this whole abuse of me and my daughters ended, by my children having to take the law into their own hands to get what they always wanted and where I then became a full time father to them once again. Then the family courts simply went away.

Although there is no doubt that the information about your involvement in a bomb hoax in Dr Cameron's report of 18 January 2001 was incorrect the screeners did not take the view that the doctor had deliberately set out to mislead the court. They have asked me to explain that given this they did not believe that formal action was warranted against Dr Cameron.

Nevertheless, the members have seen fit to advise Dr Cameron of the importance of being trustworthy and of satisfying himself, before providing evidence in formal enquiries, that he has taken all reasonable steps to verify any statements he may make.

178 Great Portland Street London W1W 5JE Telephone 020 7580 7642 Fax 020 7915 3641
email gmc@gmc-uk.org www.gmc-uk.org

Extract from General Medical Council letter dated 04.04.2002 signed by Tina Uhrynowycz. Despite Dr Cameron's frank admissions in Court to being 'very economical' with the truth in his reports and evidence, the Doctor's regulatory body, the General Medical Council, after nearly a year of deliberations, only saw fit to advise him of the importance of being trustworthy.

CHAPTER 6

The National Protests Begin, The Campaign Goes Global, Judge Munby Launches His Public Attack

When Judge Munby jailed me on 23rd March 2001, certainly part of his agenda was to put down the fast growing protests against his judicial colleagues that I had started. But this backfired on him, and in spectacular fashion. And the bigger the hole he started to dig for himself, the quicker he appeared to want to dig.

During 2000, our small but poignant protests outside the Plymouth and other family courts grabbed press attention, and DADS membership started to steadily grow in number. Members of organisations such as Families Need Fathers, the United Kingdom Men's Movement, Live Beat Dads and others clamoured to join in. The protests in July 2000 expanded from outside the Devon court buildings to the home of the top family court judge of that time, Dame Elizabeth Butler-Sloss, who had been recently promoted to president of the Family Division some months earlier. When reading of Dame Elizabeth's reported reaction to the first protest outside her country home, we expanded the home protests to other judges around the South of England. This first protest at Butler-Sloss' home is believed to have been the first ever fathers' rights protest to make the national press when it appeared in the Sunday Observer on 16th July 2000, and was certainly the first to ever take place on a judge's driveway.

Tracing this prominent judge was simplicity itself. A quick search of the Who's Who directory at the local library revealed that Dame Elizabeth Butler-Sloss was an active member of various hunting, blood sport and agricultural organisations in East Devon. It was quite obvious that she either lived in that locality, or at least maintained a home there. A simple check of the East Devon phone book revealed the address of only one Butler-Sloss in that entire area, a Mr J Butler-Sloss, to an address in the leafy village of Marsh Green, near Honiton, Devon.

Now, one of the DADS protesters said he recalled reading in the News of the World some years before about Dame Butler-Sloss' husband, Joseph, a former High Court judge, admitting to using the services of young prostitutes in Nairobi, Kenya, while his wife headed the Cleveland child abuse enquiry in 1988. A quick check at the local library of East Devon's electoral role revealed the occupants of the same Marsh Green farmhouse as Elizabeth & Joseph Butler-Sloss. With such a surname, we knew we must have found our judge.

Following the national press attention from the first protest at Butler-Sloss' home came floods of enquiries from all around Britain that arrived by phone, fax, post and e-mail to DADS campaigners from people now queuing to join up. Fathers frustrated by the farcical and corrupt family courts across Britain wanted to get involved, they wanted to protest and air their grievances in public. They wanted to engage in positive action against the injustices dished out by the secret family courts to them. And not just fathers joined up. Grandfathers and grandmothers, deprived through their son's inability to see their grandchildren through the farcical UK family courts joined up too. Even a 34-year-old mother from Exeter, Alex Newman, joined up. Alex never had any recollection of her father as the family courts, over thirty years before, had cut her off from her father when her parents split and she was aged just two. The pain of being deprived of a father she never knew cut deep with Alex. Alex became a very active member.*

Footnote; *DADS are proud to declare that through our tracing activities, DADS reunited Alex with her long lost Dad within weeks.

CLEVELAND JUDGE SEX SCANDAL

THE husband of Cleveland inquiry judge Dame Elizabeth Butler-Sloss cheats on her with young black prostitutes.

While SHE was in Cleveland, HE was picking up tarts in one of the world's highest-risk AIDS areas.

Joseph Butler-Sloss, a High Court judge working in Nairobi, Kenya, has confessed that he regularly pays for sex with local hookers.

His Honour, 61, who has been married to Dame Elizabeth for 30 years, admitted: "I rather like prostitutes. I like them in England and I like them here.

"You pay your money and you get what you want. There is no humbug. They are some of the most honest people you meet.

"They are very nice. They treat you well."

Butler-Sloss, a former Midlands circuit judge, was appointed to the Kenya High Court in 1984.

"I don't get lonely for my

EXCLUSIVE

Dame's randy spouse frolics with vice girls

By JOHN LISNERS in Nairobi, Kenya

wife," he said. "She comes here on holiday at Christmas and Easter.

"I'll go on until I'm rumbled. I love the weather and the lifestyle."

His wife Dame Elizabeth, 54, is Britain's first and only woman Appeal Court judge.

She is the sister of former Attorney General Lord Havers, TV cad Nigel's father.

She was appointed to head the Cleveland probe by Health Minister Tony Newton with the full

THE Butler-Slosses: He's cheating on her

backing of Mrs Thatcher. *The Premier is one of her greatest admirers.*

Dame Elizabeth lives at the marital home, a farmhouse in six acres near Exeter, where her hunting husband served as joint master of the East Devon Foxhounds.

The couple—who have two grown-up sons and a

daughter—also own a London flat.

Over a curried-chicken lunch in the Kenyan capital, the white-haired judge admitted paying for sex at Nairobi's notorious Starlight Club.

He confessed in a taped conversation:

● "It's not really the done thing for judges to be seen in **TURN TO PAGE 2**

Despite the actions of the Family Court Judges' husband, who was also a judge, his unlawful acts and infidelity did not bar him from being a father & Grandfather-or a High Court Judge - while his wife sat in judgment of other fathers in family courts. Reproduced by kind permission of N I Syndication Ltd from the 1988 News of the World article.

Spurred on by Dame Butler-Sloss' published complaints about the inconvenience of the home protests during family time in the Sunday Observer and to her local press, it became abundantly clear DADS campaigners had hit a raw nerve and had attracted the attention of the judiciary, at last!

During the remainder of 2000, protests outside courthouses, judge's homes and in city centres escalated throughout Southern England and

Wales. Amongst others, Lord Justice Matthew Thorpe received the first of a number of protests at his home in Seend, near Melksham in Wiltshire. Judge Joy-Anne Bracewell was targeted more than once at her country hotel in Somerton, Somerset, a Judge Tyrer experienced DADS campaigners on his front lawn at his home in Princes Risborough, Buckingham, and Judge Wigmore of East Devon experienced DADS protesters on his front garden on numerous occasions.

This new approach to lawful protest soon spread across Southern England. His Honour Judge Timothy Milligan, of Hampshire, was also targeted by a mass protest at his country home by fathers from the Southampton family court area. His Honour Judge Milligan is understood to have suffered first hand family tragedy as brother to the late Conservative MP Stephen Milligan, who tragically died in 1994, allegedly as reported in the press at the time during a sexual experiment involving an orange and some rope. Despite this tragic personal loss to Judge Milligan involving his close family, Timothy Milligan has a fierce reputation for marginalising fathers from their children's lives.

December 2000, and DADS mass in Bristol City Centre for a march on the Bristol family court. January, February, March 2001, Butler-Sloss, Thorpe, Bracewell and others see repeated and co-ordinated protests on their front lawns, protests spread to South Wales. Protests became more co-ordinated. Then word came through via the media that the Lord Chancellor's Department had commissioned a consultation paper, to complete within a year or so, headed up by Mr Justice Wall, called 'Making Contact Work'. At last, the authorities, for the first time in history, were now accepting that the family courts, as they were, *did not work*.

The judiciary were now rocking. The pressure had to stay on and intensify. In March 2001, I organised in advance, another protest at the home of Lord Justice Thorpe, the UK's most senior Family Division appeal court judge. The protest was well published on various websites and local media outlets in Wiltshire. A simultaneous protest was planned on the same day in Southampton city centre by other activists. Unfortunately, I was not able to attend either, as Judge Munby had jailed me for the contempt of court a couple of days before the planned demos.

However, the momentum was with us; it could and did go on without me. DADS campaigners were now fired up and had the bit between their teeth, they simply took over and developed the protests while I was incarcerated at Pentonville. The protests at Thorpe's Wiltshire mansion and Southampton city centre went ahead with renewed vigour. (It is understood Lord Justice Thorpe was not amused.)

DADS campaigners, starting to gather in protest outside the Country home of the then President of the Family Division, Dame Elizabeth Butler-Sloss in Marsh Green, East Devon, April 2001.

However, while Munby's jailing of me suspended my personal involvement, Munby's actions took the attention of the protests from national to global, thanks to the determination of the growing DADS campaigners and the Internet. The small handful of DADS who witnessed my sentencing by Munby in court got word out via the Internet to various fathers' rights' websites around the world. USA, Canada, New Zealand, and more – e-mail's were flying everywhere. Debate was now up and running, and it was not about to stop. Every day, from my very first during my time at HMP Pentonville, streams of fathers visited me, often people I never even knew. As a civil prisoner (meaning jailed for a *non*-criminal offences during civil proceedings) I was automatically entitled to extra privileges, one of these extra privileges being unlimited visitation rights, unlike the convicted criminal inmates, or even fathers with contact orders from the family courts. Mail started to arrive at the prison from around the world by the sack load.

Men I had never met or even heard of before obtained visiting orders by phone and just turned up, daily, to the visiting room. Each wanted to join in the protests and find out what they could do. Each had their own story of family court woe to tell. Pentonville prison visitors centre became the best public recruiting centre for the DADS protest movement imaginable. One such visitor was Matt O'Connor, who later took over the protests, reshaped the structure of the campaign, turning the protests into a far more professional affair, and re-launched the ongoing campaign under Fathers 4 Justice.

My first ever meeting with Matt was in early April 2001. He told me he had recently separated from his wife. Matt was quite frank with his admission that he was to blame for his marital breakdown. He was quite unusual in the fathers I was meeting in that he harboured no malice or grudges at all towards his estranged wife. However, like so many other fathers he found himself, after separation, on supervised contact with his two sons at a contact centre and could not understand why. Like so many fathers seeing children they once lived with under such strict supervision, Matt could not understand why this supervision at a contact centre was happening at all. No one had ever questioned his fathering in any way, the only complaint about him was from his estranged wife who considered him not to be a very good husband, which by coincidence he seemed to have no argument with.

Matt told me all about his thriving marketing business, his success at promotional work and his publicity campaigns and his past involvement years ago with CND when a student. He wanted to put fathers' rights on both the national and political map. This was a man clearly capable of promoting the case for open courts and equal parenting far more professionally that I ever could. Matt admitted he had 'a little cash' he could risk in getting something launched. He clearly had great vision and imagination. He was on a research mission when visiting me. I knew he could take the movement to new heights.

In the next chapter, I detail the first, and other protests Matt O'Connor put together and developed under the Fathers 4 Justice banner. I was glad someone with Matt's imagination and drive was considering a friendly take over of the protest campaign, as I must confess, I never really felt comfortable leading these campaigns, despite being totally committed to the cause. I would always rather have followed than lead!

Meanwhile DADS activists, spurned on with support now arriving throughout the world, traced both homes of Judge James Munby. The latest Who's Who was published and this newly appointed judge was featured. The now well established method of cross referencing from the Who's Who directory to the 192.com service on the Internet bore fruit once again. DADS members quickly found Judge Munby had two homes, one in Kennington, South East London, and another in Manningford Bruce, Wiltshire.

So, on April 21st 2001, over 60 DADS activists converged outside the London home of Judge James Munby. They were met by large numbers of police in riot vans lying in wait at Munby's London abode as the 1 pm march from Kennington tube station converged at his residence. The police, as always, were very sympathetic to the cause. Even a couple of separated police officers had joined DADS by now. One Met officer standing guard outside Munby's house told a DADS member that the judge had been monitoring various websites for weeks and saw for himself the planned demo coming his way. Munby, of course, made sure he was not at this home, but ordered the police in numbers to be there instead.

That afternoon, after the protest, two of the protesters came to visit me in Pentonville on their way home. They produced some photos of the Munby demo, which gave me some amusement and told me of the whip-round organised to help pay my mortgage and household bills while inside. Just a week before, a South Wales businessman called Pat Lyons of Port Talbot, a divorced father, whom I never met, sympathised with my plight, came forward and put me on his staff payroll for the duration of my imprisonment. My home was at least now financially secure until my return.

Like Munby's attempts to avoid his duty in dispensing justice in my case, and getting contact between me and my daughters restored or even resolving anything, his attempts to strangle the protest movement had exploded in his face, and quite dramatically. He became the core of ridicule and the popular target of most of the protest. He apparently received mail and phone calls to his homes. But his absolute panic reaction to the protest outside his London home just three days later propelled the protest movement far further into the media than any DADS member could have possibly hoped for, and opened the public door very slightly to the routine farces and injustices taking place in the UK family courts.

On 24th April 2001, I was suddenly woken up by the prison guards in Pentonville. It was early, about 7 am. I was told to get my kit together as I was off to the Royal Courts of Justice that morning. This was totally unexpected. I had no court applications up. I was awaiting an appeal of all matters, but that was not due for weeks. It did cross my mind that perhaps I might be up for an early release, who knew, but I refused to build my hopes up. I really did not know what to expect. But pack my kit I did, boarded the prison van and off to the Royal Courts of Justice I was taken.

Moments before my escort put me in the secure van to the court, I managed to get to a prison phone and call out to a DADS member nearby in London and I told him about this unexpected hearing at the Royal Courts. Luckily, his phone number was easy to remember, there was just no time to look anything up, I had seconds to make the call. I got word out to where I was going. Upon my arrival at the court, fully handcuffed and escorted by three guards, I was sat in Munby's court. A stream of press were there, but strangely for the first time, no sign of my ex-wife's legal team or anyone else from the family proceedings. But again, as word got round, a handful of DADS members had made it.

After a very short wait, Munby entered the court. He appeared an angry and a somewhat shaken man. He carried into the court a huge pile of paper that easily exceeded 12" in height. Judge Munby sat, then started to explain, in a slightly agitated voice, that because of the 'events' outside his house the previous Saturday, he was 'going public' about his reasons to stop me seeing my children. This statement of the judge struck me as just simply not true at all. I thought to myself, my ex-wife was the one who had stopped me seeing my children by breaking the court order. Munby simply took the court order away afterwards!

Now, this pile of paper he brought into the court transpired to be a number of edited-down (by nearly 80 pages) versions of the private judgement he gave out the month before in the family matters. The mother and children's identities were removed from the edited versions, together with all the information regarding the 20+ care worker and court welfare reports of the children loving contact with me, and all the police evidence of the mother's false claims of harassment, the photo of her waving to me and her boyfriend's past documented assaults on my children.

Munby immediately passed copies of this edited-down judgement to the Daily Telegraph reporter, who he had obviously arranged to be in the court for this 'public humiliation' of me, as well as a number of TV and newspaper reporters from my West Country area he almost certainly invited too. He then declared he was to put 'in the post' to the various father groups copies of his 'public judgement'. He recited each of the groups he was to mail this too. Also, for the first time ever, we had the official law reporters in the court. We were now about to make history with a permanent – but later on incomplete and quietly edited-down by 105 paragraphs – article in the family law reports *(Harris v Harris, Attorney General v Harris, ref 2001 2 FLR, 895)*.

I had to sit there, handcuffed up and surrounded by these security guards while this man, protected by the court staff and entire legal system, abused me publicly as much as he could, without me able to have any form of redress or defence. His intended aim, as could be seen in the opening paragraphs of his judgement, was clearly to turn DADS protesters against me and turn the rising tide of public vilification coming his way.

However, this very well educated but extremely 'out of touch with the real world' judge clearly missed the obvious yet again when embarking on this mission of public humiliation; each and every member of all the various protest groups had *themselves* been degenerated, ridiculed, humiliated, unjustly treated and attacked by people like himself in the family courts in varying degrees for years. Most had been in the past or were currently suffering unjustly restricted access to their children for no good reason. They simply saw through him and his excuses straight away. No one who had *not* been through the family court farces would had been interested in becoming involved with the DADS actions anyway, or interested in what this judge had to say. He was trying to preach to the unconvertible. It was just water off of a duck's back to them, as it was to me.

Not many, but some certain sections of the popular press in the UK have a long standing but unfortunate habit of building people up, be it the famous or infamous, sportsmen or sportswomen, people in authority, even a maverick Fathers 4 Justice member such as 'Batman' on Buckingham Palace in 2004 as heroes one day, then producing a second 'scoop' of demolition on the character of yesterday's hero or campaigner the next. One logic to this maybe is it sells two papers, rather than just the one, who knows.

Of course, the Daily Telegraph and my local papers immediately put Munby's words of attack of me into print after weeks of very supportive press. 'Charlatan Father', was one headline from the Telegraph. 'In an Extraordinary Move, Fed Up High Court Judge Says Everyone Has Right To Know 'Truth' About Jailed Dad' was another, with 'Dad's pig-headed fight has blighted his girls' lives' sub headed to that on a two-page centre spread in my regional paper.

I might have been embarrassed had I been living at home, but I wasn't, I was locked up over 200 miles away. All of this at the time did not really bother me at all. As they say, today's news is tomorrow's chip wrapper…and I was not going home to buy chips for months!

Munby set out, in this very edited-down version of what he had said in private just four weeks previously, only the facts he wanted public. He accused me of giving "tendentious accounts of what was happening in his children case…" when in fact he was doing exactly that. He did however, quite surprisingly, recite in public my views about the cohabiting lesbian social workers from the now distant past and their hidden agendas, but predictably left out the concerns I documented in that very same statement the assaults to my children commited in their mother's home by her boyfriend – which was the very thing that brought these two social workers into the case.

Munby, rather surprisingly, also publicly detailed my concerns – and his own findings – about Dr Cameron's repeated misreporting to the court, and my claims of his dishonesty attached on the note with my brick put through the doctor's window. Munby goes on to publicly say, "the children really now do not want to see him…and it's all Mr Harris' own fault." However, as the story concludes, this proved every bit as inaccurate and wrong as most of what took place in this absurd court fiasco. Yet, no public apology was ever forthcoming from Judge James Munby to me…or to my children.

In Munby's mind, with this extraordinary public attack of vilification of me, he clearly attempted to drive DADS members away from wanting to be associated with me. When he said, "The remedy for Mr Harris' antics…is publicity for the truth which at present lies concealed behind unfounded complaints," that was his feeble attempt to try and justify his absurd jailing of me. But he never explained *why* giving my daughters presents, or trying to see them more, justified prison. He never answered or explained that question at any point. He probably still cannot.

Secondly, after much more of the attack on me (and the protest outside his house a few days prior still obviously at the forefront of his mind) his real motives became transparent when he concluded with, "One wonders whether the members of DADS appreciate just how cynically they are being abused and manipulated by Mr Harris." This was simply another doomed attempt of his to smash the now spreading protests against the family court judiciary and him in particular, but support for me too. But like everything else Judge Munby did to me and my family, not only did it fail, it had the complete opposite effect to his intentions and not too much later came crashing down with the most enormous bang to haunt him.

Now, despite this public lampooning, the now international

ridicule of Munby jailing me for the matters as birthday present giving and saying hello in a shop mushroomed and become a cause to unite fathers worldwide. His actions and reactions reverberated throughout various father groups and on the Internet. Munby's public judgement was being dissected and scrutinised by people also victims of the injustices of the family courts. Facts that could not previously be exposed because of the secret family court rules, in my case now could. People continually asked why was it the judge never explained in his public judgement, anywhere, how any of these 'offences', as he saw them, warranted prison? Another question even more frequently posed and debated was, "The judge says the children liked seeing their dad in the past. But nowhere does he explain *why* contact with the children stopped."

But the most common observation of all that ridiculed Munby for what he was up to, and was debated on various forums around the World Wide Web was, "Just how can this judge be serious when he describes the mother as 'encouraging the children to continue seeing their father' when the family have been to the courts well in excess of 100 times in the last eight years over contact?"

Munby, ex-public schoolboy and appointed Queen's Counsel, was never able to grasp the reality that the ordinary man in the street, in particular the ones that had experienced the secret family courts of the United Kingdom, would ask questions of him and his judgement.

I believe Munby seriously thought everyone would take on face value what he'd said, because he was a judge and he was telling them something, and just walk away. But fathers, having been through the family court farce, are the only people likely to have any interest at all in what he had to say anyway and they would never just accept his word without total explanation and investigation of all the facts because of their own past bad experiences in the secret courts. Fathers hardened to the failures of the family courts are well on their guard against farce and injustice by natural reflex to their own experiences. It's almost like a radar that senses farce and injustice if you are exposed to enough of it. And they immediately spotted it.

One of the best points to come from what Judge Munby did with his public attack on me three days after the DADS protest outside his home was to remove all logical reasons as to why *any* family proceedings are not held in open court. Munby's actions – and the eventual outcome of my case – go to prove it would be most dangerous and unjust to allow only piecemeal proceedings into the public view. It must be everything in its entirety, not just selective material at the judge's discretion or the process will continue to be skewed. The nonsense that the children's identities must be protected becomes a joke as in my case – my children still to the day share my surname – only their mother's name is different. as she later married Wayne Taylor!

Justice not only has to be done, it has to be fully *seen* to be done, nothing else will do.

CHAPTER 7

Judge Munby Caves In, Protests Go Global and Fathers 4 Justice Arrives

As always, I went through the farce of appealing all of what Munby did, my first appeal heard at the Court of Appeal was against the committal and sentences. I obtained further legal aid and had very good representation. As always, the appeal against all the sentences including the giving of the birthday presents, saying hello in a shop, etc. all failed in May 2001. Therefore, the three Court of Appeal judges simply endorsed all what had taken place several weeks earlier.

However, the court was full of DADS campaigners. One of the appeal court judges, Lady Justice Brenda Hale, now a Law Lord at the House of Lords, was promptly traced to her nearby North London home and responded to the DADS protest on her doorstep days later with an emergency call to the police.

No matter what the judiciary did to me, it only made matters worse for them. They are all very educated people, but they just could not fathom this. The more they tried to bury or justify their wrongful collective actions, they simply expanded the DADS campaign. More judges became targeted, more courts picketed, the membership grew, and other tales of injustice and farce surfaced. I was due to remain incarcerated until the end of August 2001, the half way point of sentence.

In June 2001, amongst my almost daily correspondence with Munby's lady clerk, I was surprisingly 'booked in' to another hearing before him to hear my third successive application to purge my contempt. As soon as one application was refused, I simply filed another. There was not much else to do on A Wing in Pentonville Prison.

But the attitude of Munby in his letter via his clerk changed dramatically overnight. Instead of the usual terse reply with just a time and date of hearing, I was invited by letter to 'find' an expert witness of my choosing to bring into my children's case and to obtain confirmation from my employers, at the time AA Driving School. So I still had a job to go to and I could fund my own expert, something I offered to do in court the year before when I asked for Dr Cameron's removal. Munby asked me to post him the correspondences. It was obvious the will of Munby had been broken, and release was imminent.

So, on 14th June 2001 I was yet again escorted in handcuffs to the Royal Courts of Justice in a secure van from Pentonville. I was taken swiftly into Munby's court after being given lunch. DADS campaigners, tipped off by myself the day before, had arrived at his court in numbers, as was now becoming the norm. Upon being seated in the court, Munby's usually frosty-to-me lady clerk greeted me with a 'hello Mr Harris', which quite frankly stunned me somewhat. It was clear I was going home, *he really was surrendering.*

Minutes later, out comes Munby, all smiles and with civility beyond words. It was hard to believe this was the same man who saw such 'crime' in me giving birthday presents to my children almost three months prior...

He explained, as always for him by using far more words than necessary, that he was now going to release me from my sentence, remainder suspended, so I could get this work with the expert of my choice, a Dr Nigel Blagg, of Taunton, Somerset underway. Munby even had the gall to tell me that I *should* be seeing my children after all of this, and that he was sanctioning my choice of expert, Dr Blagg, to come in and try sorting the case out for 'us'. One condition Munby imposed was that I had to undertake a psychological assessment with my expert, but if that came back OK, then onwards to sort out the children matters we would go. Well, so he promised. My late mother, Sheila Harris, who lived at Hornchurch, Essex, turned up at the court, as always, and within minutes I was with her and the DADS campaigners, a free man, for a celebration drink at the bar opposite the Royal Courts.

After the celebratory drink, I boarded the tube train with my mother and brother back to her home in Hornchurch and spent that evening and overnight with them both. My brother had kindly looked after my car while I was away, as I had driven up to Hornchurch in March for the verdict on all the matters. Before setting off home to Plymouth the next day, home I had not seen now for almost three months, my mother and I attended a DADS protest outside the Cambridge court. Never more vital than now, with the judiciary caving in, was it to keep the pressure up upon these individuals. DADS had arranged numerous protests outside various UK courts that day.

I arrived back in Plymouth that evening. The phone never stopped ringing for days, with people wanting to wish me luck, ask how I was – and how they could become involved in the DADS protests.

I immediately engaged my expert, Dr Blagg, and funded his appointment in the main by credit cards, which took years to clear. I sent Dr Blagg the court papers Munby had sanctioned.

But still the protests went on. Outside Butler-Sloss', Thorpe's, and other Judges homes across the UK. I attended and organised some, others organised operations in other areas. One we held at Lord Justice Thorpe's started with an equal parenting meeting in his village at the function rooms of his local pub. I wrote to him inviting him to attend and hear our concerns, but, as expected, that request was ignored, so we simply took our meeting to him. He refused to come to the door, but several police officers were lying in wait upon our obviously expected arrival. TV and press, all awaited our arrival, too, and interviewed DADS members who wished to speak about their grievances with the family courts. Lord Justice Thorpe never surfaced.

Of course, my appeal against the denial of contact was, as always, rejected out of hand in July 2002.

My expert witness, Dr Nigel Blagg, was now available to start work. At my first meeting with Dr Blagg, he informally told me, after reading the court material, he had never seen a contact case so badly handled in his many years of experience in such cases. Dr Blagg indicated that it shone through to him the children probably did want to still see me, and he would work to try and resolve matters as expediently as he could.

In September 2001, DADS protested outside the world congress on family law that was held in Britain that year at the Forum, Bath, Somerset. This is basically a bit of a bun fight and mutual back slapping meeting held in various cities around the world, bi-annually, where family court judges meet to tell each other how well they are doing. We even managed to get a DADS member into the audience (by way of a ticket costing many hundreds of pounds) to ask questions. However, once the flavour of his questions became clear and somewhat embarrassing to the UK judiciary, he found he was becoming ignored. The congress was attended by many of the top UK judges who DADS members recognised from earlier protests at their homes; amongst others, Butler-Sloss, Thorpe, Wilson (he of the wine drinking episode in Plymouth years before), Holman and, quite unexpectedly, the child psychiatrist from my case, Dr Hamish Cameron.

These people were indeed heckled by the protesters as they entered. DADS made the top regional news story on TV in Somerset and Bristol that night and the front pages of all the local press with the protest. Matt O'Connor attended the protest and explained at length to me about how the plans he was formulating were taking shape, with the intent to put the issue of family courts not just into the press, but on the political map too. And his plans sounded good.

Now, at my next and last meeting with Dr Blagg, he made it quite clear that he had been 'told', through the grapevine, to let me know that if I were to cease the protesting, contact with my children would return. Now Dr Blagg never actually *said* he had been told this, but the clear insinuation was someone, somewhere had spoken to him in these terms.

Dads protest outside law conference

By Kate Tarling

ANGRY fathers disrupted a major conference on family law in Bath yesterday in their fight for parental rights.

Top lawyers and judges from around the world were picketed by protesters outside the conference who chanted: "Children need both parents".

The protesters gathered outside The Forum in St James' Parade to call for changes in the way courts handle custody battles.

They handed out leaflets to professionals attending the 2001 World Congress on Family Law and the Rights of Children and Youth and held up banners saying: "Family courts are creating 150,000 divorce orphans every year", and "The best parent is both parents".

The protesters had planned

CONTINUED ON PAGE 3

ANGRY FATHERS: protesters outside The Forum in Bath yesterday

Mark Harris, foreground, leads a DADs protest outside the World congress on family law, Sept 2001, Bath, Somerset, UK. Reproduced by kind permission of The Bath Chronicle.

I was appalled that I had to abandon what was becoming a national cause if I ever wanted to see my children again, but knowing Matt O'Connor was waiting to take off, and some of the things he was planning, I agreed to what can only be described as blackmail sent down through the grapevine by the judiciary. My paramount concern was, as always, to see my children again.

So I agreed to end the protests, well, at least my involvement in them. Dr Blagg sent Judge Munby his psychological assessment that I was OK, which included my agreement to end protesting, and recommended it was time to start the process of contact again. In November 2001, word came from the court to Dr Blagg that he was to see the mother and the children.

Well, Judge Munby, who had assigned himself in 2000 to the case for 'at least' two years, simply left Dr Blagg to arrange with the mother a time for him to see her and the children. That unrealistic expectation of co-operation from the girls' mother immediately ran into resistance; she simply refused to co-operate or communicate from day one with Dr Blagg. This was in November 2001.

Meanwhile, the next month (December 2001) was the inaugural launch that Matt O'Connor had planned for Fathers 4 Justice.

Despite having to agree to withdraw my involvement from all future protesting if I was to ever see my kids again, the operation that was planned was to be done wearing full Santa suits complete with full facial beard as well. So, despite the threats from the court, I knew I could still take part quite safely as this time I was the one in secret. I made sure I was there for the launch spectacular that was to take place.

So, like 100 other fathers that day, I donned my Santa suit and boarded one of the two battle buses at South Mimms' services on the M25 for the storming of the government department.

At Hyde Park Corner, another 100 Santas boarded what were now becoming seriously overloaded open top buses. But we didn't care, we were on a mission for our children, and it felt good. Of course, the almost sole topic of conversation generally on those busses was what everyone had suffered in the courts, the disbelief as to what each individual had suffered, and the growing realisation from all the passengers that our own injustices were in fact just par for the course in the corrupt family courts. It soon became apparent that every father in the family courts, up against a mother opposed to him seeing his children, was being picked off as an isolated troublemaker, that they were each told they were entirely to blame for the fact they were not seeing their children, and, quite unbelievably, most of our exes, so the courts were often trying to indoctrinate us with, actually wanted us to see our kids! It was production line farce, and the game was now up. And most of us had to go for psychological assessments, under direction of a variety of judges from the various courts if we ever wanted to return to make any further applications to see our children. By amazing coincidence, every single father on those buses who had an ex-wife or partner refusing access to the children, and who had therefore been made to undertake such an assessment, had all come back with a clean bill of health – absolutely nothing wrong.

Amongst that crew of fathers on the buses, a number of grandfathers and grandmothers were there too, all desperate to see their lost grandchildren. It's not just the fathers being shafted when the courts unjustly cut Dad off from his children, his wider family are shafted too. And let's not forget these children, who may well never see these grandparents again if they are cut off from the father's family for too long. There was anger, resentment and disbelief at what was routinely passing for justice in the secret family courts. However, *one clear consistency emerged on the bus that day*: if any father had a contact order that was broken by the mother, applying to a court for enforcement upon the mother almost always led, after a number of hearings, to psychological assessments on the father being ordered – assessments that usually put him in the clear. Then the inevitable delay would cause the father to lose his contact order or the order would be replaced with an 'indirect contact' order.

An indirect contact order. This invention of the secret family courts means a father can write a letter to his child or children a specified amount times a month or year. Often the length of the letter is limited not just by frequency, but by length of pages. Unbelievably, one father had his day-long, once-a-week unsupervised contact order with his two-year-old-son reduced to an indirect contact order after the mother wanted the father removed from the child's life. The mother's change of position coincided with her moving in her new boyfriend. The court refused to enforce the father's contact order upon the mother, despite it working well until the mother simply refused to comply. Astonishingly, but quite in keeping with how ludicrously the secret family courts operate, that particular county court ordered the mother to read the father's letters to him on the day it arrived. The father, in place of spending a weekend day each week with his son, had to write the letter, of no more than two pages, by order, addressed to his son, aged just two. It's the law of the madhouse, but nonsense like this was and still is routinely being dished out every working day in these secret courts.

A quick show of hands on the buses revealed over 100 of the Santas on the buses that day had court orders for contact taken away after they dared to ask the family courts to enforce the current contact orders upon the children's mothers. In other words, no court anywhere was prepared to enforce any order upon any mother.

So what was done to me and my children over the years by Judges Sander, Wigmore, Wilson, Bracewell and Munby was actually taking place, quite routinely, the length and breadth of the country, and had been for years. The only difference was it happened to me and my little girls a lot more.

Mark Harris centre, directly behind the Santa taking the photo, suitably disguised after the Court threats for him to stop protesting if he wanted to see his children again. London, December 2001, for the first ever Fathers 4 Justice protest - the storming of the Lord Chancellor's department.

But the protests were then taken over by Matt O'Connor. No more hand painted banners and ad hoc arrangements. Things were going professional. With 'Captain' Matt O'Connor leading the charge, organised and focused, the buses drove off to the target. Press, TV and London Radio were tipped off at the very last moment, and the 200 Santas headed off to the Lord Chancellor's Department. The buses raced up, stopped outside the tall building, and behind Matt, we all piled in through the revolving door. I was about the fourth or fifth one in. The three security guards looked totally bewildered at this endless mass of red-suited Father Christmases coming through the rotary door, blowing whistles and sounding claxons. One tried to get to what appeared to be the locking mechanism of the revolving door, but two of us managed to obstruct him.

The Guard said to me he was going to call the police, so I offered him my mobile phone to make the call. And still the Santas piled in. He declined to use my phone but sauntered off to find one. But it was made clear as he walked away that we *were* coming in, they could call the police if they wished, but we had a message for the Lord Chancellor and his Department, and we would not be leaving until it was delivered.

Moments later the police arrived, about 20 or so in a number of vehicles. The purpose of the storming was to deliver a huge Christmas card with various messages to the Lord Chancellor that his family courts were not working and Fathers 4 Justice had arrived. Matt O'Connor had clearly done his homework by finding out that the Department's most senior civil servant, Amanda Finlay MBE, was there on that day. It was decided she should receive the card for onward transmission to the Lord Chancellor.

Inevitably, Ms Finlay refused to come down and receive the card at first so the Santas simply refused to leave until she did. The police were powerless to eject such a large number of protesters, especially through that revolving door. One officer to arrive that day told one West Country Santa that he too would not be seeing his child that Christmas either, and as long as we kept it lawful, which was our only intention, he thought what we were doing was actually a very good idea.

The senior officer who took charge of the incident then spoke to Ms Finlay up in her office. One can only speculate just what was said, but within minutes, Ms Finlay appeared in person and collected the card with the 'advice' from Matt and others that this was just the first, not last, mass protest against the family courts by the group Fathers 4 Justice.

After some time to pose for questions from the media and a photo call, the Santas left on the buses. Despite the authorities promptly issuing a 'D' Notice to suppress further publicity, what took place, a perfectly lawful and peaceful protest, got some welcome publicity. Fathers 4 Justice was born.

Throughout 2002 more protests mocking the family courts took off under the Fathers 4 Justice banner. There were a number of 'Elvis Presleys' who carried a huge inflatable broken heart to the Royal Courts of Justice proclaiming it 'heartbreak hotel'. Lord Justice Thorpe saw more campaigners on his front lawn, as did other top judges. Fathers scaled bridges and cranes with banners and generally fathers' rights became the popular topic in every national newspaper.

As 2002 progressed, protests spread around the western world. The USA, Canada, Germany, New Zealand, South Africa, amongst others, saw fathers on the streets waving banners and asking questions of the authorities. Fathers 4 Justice became an international name. But what was the British government's response; well, it was to infiltrate, subvert and eventually destroy everything.

Meanwhile, my case to see my children crawled along, despite the recommendations of the expert witness I was allowed to bring in, Dr Blagg, stressing the importance of speedier resolution for the children's sake and well being.

Dr Blagg made no progress from December 2001 to April 2002 in regard to getting the mother's co-operation for him to see the children, so I returned the matter to Judge Munby, for when he was sitting in the West Country next, at Exeter court in May 2002.

Munby had by then painted himself into a corner, and not for the first time either. He agreed with this expert witness who'd made it clear the children would suffer significant harm if things drifted along without resolution any longer. Munby made public his stance that court orders must be obeyed no matter what when he dealt with me, and now the mother was simply refusing to co-operate with the court system that she sought her petty retributions against me through for years.

By now the mother's legal aid had expired. She had also now married her boyfriend, he of the many assaults on my children and the threats to kill me from the witness box. So now his earnings were taken into account with her public funding application, which meant she no longer qualified without having to make a significant contribution. So she attended Exeter court in person. For over one hour, Judge James Munby tried every single way of getting her to agree to bring the children to a meeting with Dr Blagg so he could get on and report their views on seeing me, their father. All the mother would constantly say, like a worn out gramophone record, was, "But they don't want to see him, *and that's what they will say...*"

Now, Munby knew he had to act. Persuasion of this mother, whom he had said publicly just over 12 months before was "not opposed to contact", was not getting him anywhere at all. She still made clear she wanted all the court orders banning me from the children maintained, but was not prepared in any way to agree or co-operate with anything that did not suit her, even if it was what the same court wanted.

When push came to shove, and he clearly was making no headway at all with persuasion, Munby eventually said he was going to make an order anyway for Dr Blagg to see the children. The mother promptly, but unbelievably, interrupted him before he could even finish his sentence and said, "I'm sorry, your Honour, *but I will not comply with the order.*" Munby was stunned and his eyes went straight to me. Here was a woman (having previously raked though every technical breach of any court orders she could find that I had breached, such as giving the children birthday presents or saying hello to them in a shop) with her solicitor of the time, having asked this same judge to send me to prison, now telling him basically to get stuffed, that none of this applied to her – she really believed by then she was above the law.

Munby, but far more me and my children, were now paying the price for what he and his judicial mates had allowed her to do in ways that had mocked the authority of the law for years. Munby was bright red. Here was open defiance of the court – by someone who had caused international condemnation of him and his courts for his enforcement of orders on me. You could see he wanted to run away and hide, but he dare not. I really believed he sensed just what I would be getting up to if he did...

But then he uttered, in the most unconvincing manner I have ever seen in a court by any judge anywhere, the magical words that should be said in every court when anyone (in particular a mother obstructing a father's relationship with his children) refuses to comply with its orders, "If you do not comply with my order to let the children see Dr Blagg, anywhere of your choosing, of course, by the end of this month, I will bring enforcement upon you when I'm next sitting in the West Country, which is next month…"

It worked, and it worked a treat. The mother instantly backed down and agreed, through somewhat gritted teeth, to let Dr Blagg see the children. To this day, I'm totally unconvinced Munby would ever have followed up that threat to enforce, I really believe he simply would have bottled it and just never listed the enforcement hearing. But she swallowed his threat, hook, line and sinker. Dr Blagg was in court and instantly arranged an appointment in front of Munby to see the children, the order was wrote out and we all went home.

Of course, when Dr Blagg saw the children at his Taunton surgery a few days later, each child recited exactly what their mother had said in court they would, word for word. Lisa, who I had not seen for five years, admitted to Dr Blagg she had quite recently phoned me up behind her mother's back to have a chat, but still maintained she did not want to see me. The other two children also gave Dr Blagg the speech the mother had said they would: "We don't want to see him now," although the middle daughter, then 13, was reported to have cried throughout the interview.

Dr Blagg, a divorced father himself, and a man I found of the utmost professional integrity, told me about how the meeting with the children had gone when I phoned him as soon as his practice opened the very next day.

Although he said the children's views on contact with me had now suddenly appeared hostile, and with no stated reason, he said he was totally unconvinced each or any of the children actually meant anything what they had said about not wanting to see me. Dr Blagg went on to tell me it was perfectly normal if any child goes long enough without seeing one parent and has to live in an environment hostile to that missing parent – and he was clear after meeting the mother and her former boyfriend, now husband, on the previous day that the adults in the children's home were very hostile towards me – to expect the child or children to eventually adopt the carer's hostility as if it was their own, especially when the child couldn't get proper access to that missing parent to maintain his or her own independent views.

Dr Blagg wrote a very detailed report within days to Munby, copied to each of us parents, spelling out in clear terms the lasting emotional damage that would bestow these girls if this position they were now in was not quickly resolved. Dr Blagg recommended the only resolution was to get the father and his daughters together to see just what the true feelings of the children were. As stated earlier, Judge Munby, having previously relied upon the untrue reporting of Dr Cameron, had gone public just over a year before saying this mother did *not* oppose contact. Now the new expert witness, that Munby himself sanctioned coming into the case just 84 days later, said that her opposition to contact was so severe it was going to damage the children permanently. Munby was now in a corner, all caused by his failure to deal with the problems caused by lies in his courtroom that he had let just slide by.

But did Munby now try to act in the children's best interests? Or even just try to put right his glaring mistakes? Or even apologise? No, of course not, he bottled it. He sat on this report for over six months, despite endless correspondences and applications from me to him to just get on with matters. Then he handed the case over to a Mr Justice Coleridge just before the Christmas vacation in December 2002, and walked away from the case.

CHAPTER 8

More Judicial Nonsense, But the Kids Take on the Judges - and Win!

In December 2002, just before the entire Family Division was due to close for its six-week Christmas holiday, Judge James Coleridge suddenly listed a hearing to consider Dr Blagg's report about restoring contact with my three daughters.

Now this was a very quick listing indeed for any High Court judge sitting at a West Country court. Was Judge Coleridge, having read Dr Blagg's report, concerned about the permanent damage to my children if things were left any longer? Or could it be that he was more concerned that he had been traced by Fathers 4 Justice to his South West London home on the first day he was appointed to our case? I must admit, I wondered.

I'd sensed he felt uncomfortable with my case when we'd first met him in court. He appeared from the start to be pussy-footing around my ex-wife, unwilling to grasp the nettle and force her to allow access. But being 'found' at his home so quickly and the high-profile protests that Fathers 4 Justice were pulling off probably didn't help his frame of mind when approaching our case once more.

Legal aid had been refused for this hearing and so, as a result, I was now acting in person and so was my ex-wife.

I sensed from the start Judge Coleridge might try a different approach to that of Judge Munby. I was sure that, in the true tradition of Family Division High Court judges, he was never going to challenge any mother's hostility head on, but I got the impression he was likely to be a bit more in touch with the 'real world' than previous judges I had encountered.

I was right. With a combination of veiled threats and sheer persistence over about two hours, he eventually persuaded my ex to allow a meeting between me and the children, with Dr Blagg to supervise. It was a pleasure to witness him slowly chipping away at her arguments. He was always pleasant but very determined. What clinched it was his suggestion to her that just one meeting with me could put the lid on everything – if the girls refused to see me again the meeting would act as a sort of closure to the case. I honestly don't think he was acting in my best interests or the children's – I think he simply wanted to break the deadlock and get this troublesome family out of court and out of his life.

So, to get her co-operation, he made it clear that if the girls were hostile to me in front of Dr Blagg, the matter would never return to court ever again. I am sure she went ahead with the meeting believing that all she had to do was hype the children up to be hostile to me and she would win her argument, permanently – and I'm pretty sure Judge Coleridge believed the same. However, things did not quite work out the way they had planned.

Judge Coleridge then turned to me and tried to persuade me to agree to this meeting which he said should take place some time in the spring, in three or four months' time. Well, that was just nonsense and I was having none of it. Luckily I had foreseen this would be a stumbling block. After all, by then, I was an old hand at the stalling and delaying tactics of the family legal system.

I pointed out to Judge Coleridge that everything he had just said to my ex, appeared to me, to be an invitation for her to sabotage and destroy any success of this meeting. I also added that Dr Blagg had identified "serious permanent damage" was taking place to my daughters by them not seeing me. I suggested in the strongest possible terms that the time for this meeting should not be months away and that the very next day Dr Blagg could get to Plymouth.

I said all this knowing I had an ace up my sleeve. I'd expected more delay to be a possible outcome and so I had previously checked with Dr Blagg that he could be available in the first few days of the New Year. I'd also guessed that Judge Coleridge, like every judge I'd ever come across, would be allergic to doing anything in a hurry. I also predicted that he would then inevitably throw up the next problem of a suitable venue. So, the day before the hearing I had contacted my nearest Social Services' office – the very one I staged the rooftop protest on way back in 1996 – to see if they would provide a facility for a meeting. But – as it was me – they refused to answer or co-operate in any way, despite numerous phone calls. However, the local court welfare service (now renamed CAFCASS) did respond to my enquiries and said they would provide a suitable room for this meeting. "But only if the court requested it," I was told by one of the staff.

Back in court, Dr Blagg piped up and told Judge Coleridge that he was available on the first working day after New Year's Day. So when Judge Coleridge threw up the predicted obstacle of the venue, I was able to see that one off. Now the decks were clear; he simply had to act.

And so it was that Judge Coleridge made an order for my ex to bring all three girls to the CAFCASS office in early January. She was ordered to leave them with Dr Blagg at a set time and I was told to arrive shortly afterwards.

Now, this all took place just a couple of days into January 2003. Dr Blagg came to Plymouth and awaited the children's arrival. But when my ex turned up, she had brought only our youngest daughter to the meeting. She told Dr Blagg the older two girls had refused to come but that she had persuaded the youngest to attend. She left my little girl, 11, there and I arrived minutes later.

Dr Blagg came to tell me upon my arrival in the nearby waiting room that only my youngest daughter had arrived. "Just make the most of seeing her," said Dr Blagg, "We'll deal with the non-appearance of the others at a later date." It was good advice.

My daughter, he said, was nervous and in tears. "I don't know how this is going to go," he said, warning me to not expect too much. So my priority was to cheer my youngest girl up. It was likely to be no easy task – the room we were given was 12 ft square with no windows, a shabby carpet and a couple of boxes of battered toys for toddlers. But it did not matter; as soon as my youngest daughter saw me, the tears stopped and the smiles and cuddles started. My daughter and I spent two wonderful hours together. The fact the place we had to reunite at was more like a prison visiting room did not matter to either of us – we were together again.

It was initially quite a shock to see my youngest daughter after another gap of two long years. She had just started secondary school and was about eight inches taller than before. From the first moment it was clear that she had grown up both mentally too, with lots of questions to ask me about what I had been doing since we had last met. As her tears dried and I managed to make her laugh with some daft jokes, I soon saw that her affection for me was as strong as ever.

Afterwards and in his report, Dr Blagg said he found it hard to believe that my youngest daughter and I had not seen each other for over two years. He wrote there was instant love and affection both ways and no sign of the estrangement that he had read about in all the court documents.

All too soon my ex arrived, collected our daughter and left. I sent my youngest daughter home with pocket money for her and her sisters. I knew it would almost certainly annoy my ex but I was beyond caring about that by then, I just wanted the older two to know I was thinking of them and that there were no hard feelings about their no-show. As for my youngest daughter, her parting words to Dr Blagg as she left were that she really did want to meet up again with me soon. He promised to do what he could.

It was very difficult to part with her. Despite the years apart, our relationship was totally intact. I was on a high because the meeting had gone so wonderfully but terrified of what would happen next. How would my ex sabotage this – as I knew she would try. I later discovered that when she got home my youngest daughter had been sent to bed by her now stepfather at 4.30 pm without any food as a punishment for daring to come and see me. Apparently, my ex was in the house at the time and tacitly allowed him to do this.

Not knowing what the poor girl was about to go through, Dr Blagg and I now had a very lengthy conversation. Dr Blagg freely admitted he really had not expected the meeting to go anything like as well as it had. It was amazing to hear this experienced psychologist, who had done much of this sort of work in the past, telling me that he was shocked by just how much my daughter was attached to me despite the years of enforced absence and the open hostility towards me in her home.

We then turned to the absence of my middle and eldest daughters. Dr Blagg said he would be recommending that we should progress to a series of meetings and that he would seek court enforcement to ensure the older two girls came too. He told me that he would contact Judge Coleridge's clerk the very next day about this.

So the next afternoon I phoned Dr Blagg to see how this phone call had gone. Dr Blagg said to me Judge Coleridge had spoken to him in person and had seemed genuinely pleased to hear how well things had gone with my youngest daughter. He had immediately ordered two more meetings with the three girls. I was thrilled but immediately cast down by the rest of Dr Blagg's news; he rather gloomily told me that Judge Coleridge had point-blank refused to enforce any attendance by the older two girls upon the mother.

The next order arrived in the post a day or so later detailing two more meetings with Dr Blagg in attendance. Judge Coleridge held back from calling these occasions 'contact' or even 'access'. He seemed far more comfortable trying to appease the mother by calling it just a 'meeting'; something – in appearance at least – of lesser importance.

For me, I didn't care what these get-togethers were called. At least there were now two more dates and times set, one each for the next two months, with all my daughters named in the order.

But I was bitterly disappointed – although not surprised – to see that, as with all previous High Court Family Division judges, Judge Coleridge had buckled to the mother's refusal to abide by court orders when I saw he wrote on this order: '...it is hoped and expected [the eldest] and [the middle daughter] will attend too'.

I didn't know whether to laugh or cry. This was supposed to be a court order, that's what it said at the top in black and white. 'Hoped and expected' was hardly giving an order, was it? I remembered back to my days in prison. Nothing was 'hoped and expected' when I gave my daughters' birthday presents directly, nothing 'hoped and expected' when I said hello to them in a shop.

No – my court orders did exactly what they said on the tin. They stated what I could and could not do, swiftly followed by prison and hefty fines when I disobeyed them in the slightest detail, no matter how absurd the order. Dr Blagg was very disappointed too and, like me, predicted this left the girls' mother free to wreck my chances of seeing my children once again.

A month later, the next meeting took place. Sure enough, only my youngest daughter arrived. What's more, she freely told me in front of Dr Blagg that she wanted to see me "lots" and hated all the breaks between visits. She also said that her sisters wanted to come too, but that they couldn't because the situation at home was too difficult for them to. Dr Blagg again relayed all of this to the judge afterwards, but again this 'hoped and expected' nonsense remained on this piece of paper for the third meeting the following month.

At the third meeting my youngest again was the only one to arrive. This time, she told Dr Blagg and me yet again that both Lisa, my eldest daughter, and her middle sister wanted to come and see me too, but, "It's just too difficult at home." During this meeting, Dr Blagg used his discretion to allow my daughter and I to go out into Plymouth together, eat lunch and visit various shops. Remember, these were *supervised visits*, by order of the court. Like every child her age, my daughter was desperate for her own mobile phone. I had very little money at that time, especially after paying £10,000 in fees to Dr Blagg to date. He was costing me over £100 an hour, plus VAT.

But like so many estranged and part-time dads, I couldn't refuse her anything. I was just so pleased to be seeing her. I was putty in her hands and the phone that she wanted – top of the range and costing more than £100 –was soon bought for her. I put lots of credit on it, she programmed my number in and asked me to keep in touch. Little did I know just how momentous that decision to buy her the phone was shortly to prove to be.

During the visit, Dr Blagg asked my daughter how she would like the situation to develop. My youngest daughter said, "I want to stay with Dad every other weekend and half of all the school holidays. Oh, and I'd like to come round for a couple of teatimes in the week." If only, I thought to myself, but was delighted she'd asked for it, at least.

She also told him she would like it more if her sisters could be there too – and could he help them? Dr Blagg said he would report her requests to court for her. "Hopefully, things will sort themselves out," he said, smiling, clearly captivated by her optimism in the face of so much opposition.

Well, things did sort themselves out just 24 hours later and in the most dramatic fashion imaginable.

At precisely 11 am the next morning, Sunday 23rd March 2003, my daughters rescued me – and themselves – from our ten-year nightmare at the hands of the family courts.

I was reversing up my driveway, having just popped out for a Sunday paper. My mobile rang and a young woman's voice I barely recognized said, "Dad. It's Lisa." I was perplexed – my mobile was a new one. In a flash I guessed she must have got the number from the new phone I had bought her youngest sister the day before.

Up to now, I had had only one brief phone call to my house with Lisa in the past six years and seen her once, in passing, in Plymouth when she was out with friends – for which Judge Munby fined me £250! Aside from that, we had been totally estranged. I couldn't believe it was really my little girl, sounding so grown up and with such a strong Plymouth accent too.

"I've had enough, Dad," she said, remarkably calmly. "I'm 16 and I can do what I like. I'm coming to live with you."

She seemed as cool as a cucumber but I was absolutely gobsmacked to hear her voice, let alone get my head round the idea that she might actually be coming to live with me. My eyes swam and

I literally could feel myself reeling. I grabbed onto the steering wheel with my free hand and leant my head against the car window.

Meanwhile, Lisa was explaining herself. There had, apparently, been a huge row the previous night when my youngest daughter had come home from seeing me. The final straw had been my ex-wife's decision to take the new mobile phone, my present, away from my youngest daughter. She had been devastated and Lisa, too, felt the injustice of the whole situation.

"I'm just fed up with it all, Dad. I've had enough of all the court people coming to the house and never really listening to us, never helping us. I just want out, Dad, can I come to live at your house?"

I thought how fortunate it was that Lisa had managed to get my number from the phone before it was confiscated. It later turned out days prior to this, Lisa had done some detective work of her own to get my mobile number, which she explains for herself in the next chapter. I later discovered that the accounts from my youngest daughter of our meetings, plus her evident happiness, had swayed Lisa and made her admit how much she had missed me. And if her sister enjoyed seeing me so much, I couldn't be all bad, could I?

"I just want to leave Mum and come and live with you, Dad," she said. "I've really missed you." I was shocked to the core, but ecstatic. It was a good job I had just arrived home as I was shaking like a leaf, adrenaline pounding through my body. I was certainly completely unable to drive and could only just totter to the house with the phone to my ear.

Next, Lisa asked what time that day could she move in – that very day! I couldn't believe my ears. She said she wanted to wait until her mother had gone out later that morning. "If she finds out I intend moving to your house, she'll throw a wobbler," Lisa said, "and she'll never let me take all my stuff." Oh, yes [youngest daughter] wants to come too!" By this stage I was clinging to the doorway for support. Two out of the three daughters coming to my house that very day. It was unbelievable! "She's so fed up with being told off by Mum and Wayne for coming to see you. And she's really mad 'cos Mum's nicked her phone off her. We're going to pack and ring you later to tell you where to meet us."

As I stood there, my heart racing, I realised to my astonishment that it was exactly 11 am on March 23rd. That meant it was two years to the very minute since Judge Munby had sent me to Pentonville jail, because he believed that my kids did not want to ever see me again. How incredibly ironic. I made myself a cup of tea with shaking hands and waited to see if this was all a dream, or really happening.

And it was indeed real. Within an hour Lisa called again to say she'd got all her stuff into bin liners with help from her boyfriend. Boyfriend? My little girl had a boyfriend? I certainly had some catching up to do.

Lisa sounded incredibly cool and organized. She'd hidden all the possessions she wanted to take at home ready for the escape, she told me. But she wanted me to meet her first in the town centre, about four miles away. Then we could collect her belongings from her mother's house later, when the coast was clear.

And so I met Lisa, after being kept apart from my daughter for six long years, at 1 pm that day. I smiled to myself to remember the miserable day exactly two years before. At about 1 pm that time two years prior, prison staff at the Royal Courts' holding cells were giving me lunch just before I was taken off to be incarcerated in Pentonville prison for trying to see these very same children.

My thoughts were racing round my head. I couldn't believe I was now meeting my daughter, entirely through her own endeavours and in spite of the court orders still in place banning me from seeing her and her sisters anywhere outside of Judge Coleridge's 'hoped and expected' nonsense.

As she approached, I hardly recognised her. The last time I saw Lisa she was just ten, still at primary school and very young-looking for her age. Now she walked up to me as a fully-grown young woman, hardly recognisable, in make-up, high heels and with a 6 ft + boyfriend in tow. It was shock – but a very happy shock.

We fell into each others arms in the street and of course we both cried. Lisa said she missed me and wished we had not lost each other. Through the tears, I said pretty much the same too. Lisa introduced me to her boyfriend, who was a few months older than her and hanging around looking slightly embarrassed. Finally Lisa and I pulled ourselves together (much to the boyfriend's relief) and made our way to the car.

We drove back to my house to wait for a call from my youngest to say that the coast was clear. Meanwhile my middle daughter was out for the day with friends and had no idea of the drama unfolding. Upon arrival, Lisa walked around my house. She said she had always remembered it to herself and could clearly recall every detail of the place despite not having been there for six years.

She was amazed to see her bedroom still had all her childhood things in it from all those years before. It had been a point of stubbornness for me never to clear the girls' bedrooms out. They had instead become something of a shrine. I'd kept everything clean and dust-free, but exactly as they'd left them.

This clearly amused Lisa. For me, the sight of her in my home, in her old bedroom, was bitter-sweet. As I looked at her laughing at her long-lost possessions in her fashionable clothes, I realised ruefully that the days of colouring books, soft toys and sparkly ornaments had passed her by. I had missed so much of her childhood, all stolen by the insanity of the family courts, days which could never be given back either.

But my melancholy did not last for long. Soon enough Lisa got a call on her mobile phone. It was her youngest sister ringing up to tell Lisa that my ex had gone out and it was all systems go – and the breakout was on. Lisa could pick her stuff up – and what's more, my youngest had packed all her things too and was on her way. To me, it was like all my Christmases had come at once.

We set off to collect my youngest daughter and both the girls' belongings. There was an atmosphere of hilarity and nerves in the car as we drove towards her mother's house. Lisa told me to stop at the nearby bus stop just around the corner. We had to be very quick as my ex was expected back home from her mother's house within the hour. Lisa and her boyfriend got out of my car and raced towards the house. I simply had to wait – praying there would be no last-minute disasters.

While I sat there, the absurdity of Judge Munby and his 'exclusion zone' nonsense that was still in place came back to haunt me. Since

2001 he had banned me from coming within a mile's radius of the children's home. I wasn't even allowed to go shopping at the nearby Asda. Munby even issued me with a map of the locality, with a red line defining his exclusion zone! But here I now was, parked up in the middle of this hideous exclusion zone drawn up by the insane family courts who had found my children did not want see me. Now, by my children's request, I had just taken one daughter into this exclusion zone to collect their belongings and picked up her youngest sister. Did I care at that moment about the banning orders or the exclusion zone? Not one bit; the law had ridiculed me for years, now it was time to ridicule it back – and the kids were joining in with me. I realised I was grinning from ear to ear.

I sat in my car at the bus stop, desperately hoping my ex would not return early, recognise my car and scupper all their plans. But fortune at last smiled on us and minutes later a seemingly endless pile of bin liners of belongings started to be lowered over the garden wall. It was just like something out of *The Great Escape* – I jumped out of my car and start loading up. The car I had then was large – and good job too. The kids' things filled the boot and much of the front passenger seat. But we squeezed it all in somehow and finally Lisa and my youngest climbed in the back with Lisa's very helpful boyfriend – who was certainly growing on me. Off we went, out of the Munby's ridiculous exclusion zone and back to their new home with me.

My youngest daughter was absolutely hyper – still angry that her mother had stolen the mobile phone off her that I had bought her the day before, but so clearly excited she had empowered herself – not only against her mother, but the army of court officials who had frustrated her wish to be with her dad for years. She asked me, "What will happen now?" clearly mindful of the injustices that she had suffered by these people for years. I assured her that I thought, that as she and Lisa had stuck two fingers up to the courts and its people, things would have to change.

Youngest, only 11, seemed slightly confused by my reference to the two fingers, but Lisa soon explained what I meant!

My thoughts now turned to my middle daughter and I wondered what her reaction to the flit would be. She had always been something of a different character to the other two, who despite the age gap were very similar personalities to each other. But my middle daughter had always been quieter and more inward thinking. I hoped she would not witness too many upsetting histrionics when her sisters' escape was noticed and I hoped she would not feel too left out. I also hoped that she would soon follow them too, if only for a visit.

But now that we'd done it, and sprung the trap as it were, my mind started buzzing with the implications of my actions. I was still totally banned from seeing these children, apart from the monthly supervised meetings with Dr Blagg. I'd been into Munby's mad exclusion zone with one daughter to collect another. It was a Sunday – what on earth could I do to legitimise the situation? I needed to make the authorities see that this was all done at my daughters' instigation. If I wasn't careful, my ex could call the police, brandish her court order and the children could be dragged back to custody with her. All too easily I could end up, once again, in prison.

So, upon arrival at my house, my first action was to phone the Royal Courts of Justice in London. I'd once rung up at the weekend before and remembered the answerphone had mentioned that there was an out of hours clerk who could be contacted in emergencies – and this was an emergency.

So I phoned the Royal Courts' main line and, eventually, a security guard answered the phone. I asked for the out of hours clerk and I was put straight through. I explained that Judge Coleridge needed to be told urgently about the situation.

I said to this clerk, "I'm currently banned from not only seeing my children, but even speaking to them because the courts decided my children did not want to ever see me, but my children are actually in my house right now with all their belongings and they are refusing to leave."

"Please, I need Judge Coleridge's attention right now and I need the banning orders lifted today."

Already, I had it in mind if the court did not help, I would just go with my daughters on the run. Perhaps a couple of Fathers 4 Justice members who I knew would help us, I reasoned. I could even just 'disappear' for a few days with my daughters if all else failed. I pictured us as outlaws – it might even be fun for a while, but these kids were going to get their wish now, no matter what.

Meanwhile, the girls were busily unpacking their enormous quantities of crop tops, glitter pens and the rest of the paraphernalia into their new – old – bedrooms. Laughter filled the upstairs rooms and my house felt like a home for the first time in ten years.

There was just no way I was going to have them taken away from me again. The children had at last escaped the imprisonment of the family courts and they had broken free. My job was now to keep them free.

Within ten minutes Judge Coleridge himself telephoned my house. He asked to speak to my two daughters. First, Lisa came to the phone. She told him she had decided to take action because the courts had not help her when she was a child. Now she was 16 and not a child any more she was going to live with her dad, end of story. He did not seem to argue that point with her, in all probability because he could sense her determination.

Then he asked for my youngest, still 11, to talk to him. Standing nearby, I clearly heard Judge Coleridge trying gentle persuasion on her to return to her mother, but she was having none of it. She told him in no uncertain terms that she hated living with her mother's new husband, and that although they had just split up there was in her mind clear danger that he might come back. She started to tell Judge Coleridge about the punishments heaped upon her for coming to see me with Dr Blagg, and the phone I had bought her being taken from her by Mum. Without hearing just what he said, Judge Coleridge seemed to immediately head her off from talking any further about the punishments for visiting Dad. This of course would not fit with the 'good mum, bad dad' agenda of the UK family courts in difficult cases. She went on to say she was sick of no one listening to her about wanting to see her dad and she was staying with me.

Her final words were, "If you make me go back to Mum I will just run away in the middle of the night to my dad." That final statement from the 11-year-old caused Judge Coleridge to crumble, and he asked her to put me on the phone.

I now came to the phone, determined either to get common sense from him or simply pile the kids into the car and set off for who knew where. There was no room for any compromise on my part; at last I held some winning cards and felt, at last, a real sense of power to determine the best interests of at least two of my three daughters.

But to my delight and relief, Judge Coleridge said he was going to grant me a temporary residence order for the two escapee children. He asked me if I had a fax, which fortunately I did. He then added that he was ordering all of us – me, all three girls and my ex-wife – to appear at Bournemouth court, where he was sitting, on the following Tuesday, in 48 hours' time. He said the mother would be getting a copy of the order in the morning post.

I agreed, and put the phone down to await the fax, which arrived a couple of minutes later. I had a sense of total triumph and vindication. I hugged the girls and we all jumped around the hallway and they were shouting, "We're staying! We're staying!"

But just as my two daughters and I watched the fax machine churning out the court order, two policemen could be seen walking towards my front door, just visible through the frosted glass. As they knocked on the door, the fax finished unfurling. It was a properly typed and stamped residence order, signed by Judge Coleridge. I hurriedly read through it, copied a second edition on my fax machine and then took it to the front door, with my two daughters proudly walking either side of me.

I opened the door. Before the policemen spoke, I said, "I take it their mother has sent you?" indicating with a nod of the head in the direction of the girls. The younger of the officers said, "Yes…" but before he had the opportunity to say anything more I passed him the fax. "Please, read this to her," I said, as politely as possible, "because these girls now live with me, by order of the court."

He read it carefully, then said, "That's good enough, we only need the bit of paper." They turned, walked away and I closed the door. It was now official. After ten years of courtroom farce and injustice of having these highly-paid individuals trampling all over my children's hearts and minds, I was a dad again. Where it took 33 different family court judges ten years to reduce me from loving full time father to nothing, it took 16-year-old Lisa just a two minute phone call to put all this right. Zero to hero in 120 seconds.

So, the two girls seemed completely relaxed and relieved. And so did I. They finished the unpacking of their belongings and started to make plans on how they wanted the decor of their respective bedrooms updated. Realising I only had food for one in my house, my mind started to turn to feeding them something, but what? They were getting hungry, having made the great escape across lunchtime, so off we went into town to find a restaurant, with Lisa's boyfriend tagging along.

We ate, we talked, smiled a lot at each other and we went home, bellies full. My middle daughter dominated a large part of our conversation. Both girls were clear she too wanted to see me and would have almost certainly have come along as well, even if she would have returned to Mum's house in a few days. I made it clear though that we would meet up with her at the court on Tuesday, and I said it would almost certainly all get sorted out once and for all. I felt optimistic.

That night, the disbelief of the day's events still had me somewhat stunned. I could hear my children's chatter in the upstairs of the house, something I had not properly experienced for years. Both girls went about their evening getting ready for school the next day, and for the first time in ten years, I would be taking them there.

So, then it was Monday morning and off we went by car across Plymouth to their school, situated just yards from their mother's home, through Judge Munby's absurd and now obsolete exclusion zone. Knowing the school had been given copies of the banning order – and the map highlighting in red the exclusion area – previously by the mother, I took my copied Coleridge's faxed court order from the day before and went to the school reception desk.

I asked to see the headmaster, someone who, by influence of the mother I believe, had been quite hostile to me for many years. As always, he was not available, but another teacher, I think a head of year, soon arrived, obviously aware of the family history but clearly wondering just why this banned father was in his school.

I explained what had happened, asked if a message could be relayed to the head that now the two children on the court order lived with me, their records should be amended so. I gave him my other copy of the faxed order. The head of year just nodded in compliance with all I said. I recall my parting comment was that I hoped now that all the staff would stop treating me as some leper, as they had done for years, and start treating me just for what I was, the children's parent. He didn't say anything to that and I left.

I was just so excited all day about the simple prospect of collecting my daughters from school, a simple chore that I was wrongly denied for nearly a decade. I got there 20 minutes early, but I actually enjoyed the act of parking up at the school to fetch my children. Out they came, one at a time, and home we went. By now I had food for all in my house, and we enjoyed a simple night in watching television and preparing for the trip to Bournemouth court to meet Judge Coleridge on the following day, Tuesday.

Although I was still missing my middle daughter, it was clear that now she too would be back in my life before very long. And she was.

So, on the Tuesday afternoon, I arrived with Lisa and my youngest daughter at the Bournemouth court where Coleridge was sitting. The mother arrived in her car together with my middle daughter and her mother as escort. I immediately approached my middle daughter in the Bournemouth court waiting area and I told my middle daughter just how much I'd missed her and that all this nonsense we'd been put through for so long was about to end. With her mother nearby, she could not say very much, but whispered that she loved me and asked whether we would see each other soon. I said I loved her too and told her we would be seeing each other properly, very, very soon.

Then Coleridge at first saw all the children together, away from us parents for about ten minutes. The children soon emerged all smiles. Us parents were called back into Coleridge's court. Neither of us had legal representation. We simply didn't need it, and the children had clearly represented themselves too.

Judge Coleridge explained that each child had made it very clear to him what they wanted, that being Lisa and the youngest wanted to live with their dad and see their mother when they liked, the middle child wanted to remain living with her mother and see her dad when she liked. So that was what he was ordering, end of story. Coleridge then removed all the banning orders upon me *except* the one allowing me to disclose what I saw in the Official Solicitor's barrister's files (Miss Wood) from the Wilson case in 1997 to anyone. Although I am at present on a lifetime ban from speaking about what I read in Miss Wood's files by the injunction imposed by Wilson and carried over by every single judge after him, the notes of Mr Szulc from the Official Solicitor's office were not included in the banning order [probably by accidental omission of Judge Wilson while he was panicking about what I read that day]. So although I can reveal Wilson's wine drinking session from Mr Szulc's briefer notes as described in chapter 4, I simply cannot ever reveal the additional detail that I saw in Miss Wood's files regarding herself, Judge Wilson and Mr Szulc, otherwise this book would inevitably be banned. So much for freedom of speech!

Anyway, Coleridge ordered a review that was to be heard by him on June 13th 2003 in Plymouth, to which each parent and child was to attend, to see how the new arrangements were working out

By now, Fathers 4 Justice were not now just up and running, but well established as a group with a legitimate aim and growing international support. My case, the case that led to the conception of the organisation, had gone the full circle and highlighted the ills of what routinely took place. My children had made a complete mockery of what the secret family courts do and our case was in the public domain. Munby took it public in 2001, and no one could now take it back into private. The tabloids queued up for stories from us and they had a field day. The Daily Mail, The Observer, the local and regional press, various women's magazines and regional TV all ran stories. This was now time to ram home the message: the secret family courts of the UK were simply not working in the interests of any child. They were a sham, they only operated to line the pockets of all their players – the barristers, the solicitors, the child psychiatrists and their like. This corrupt industry actually harmed the children it pretended to act in the interests of.

Within weeks, Fathers 4 Justice sought to disrupt and close a family court down, and the obvious choice in the light of what it did to my children and I, was Plymouth's farcical family court. The press dubbed my difficulties of seeing my children as 'Britain's worst access case ever', so it was somewhat fitting that two Fathers 4 Justice members climbed above the Plymouth court entrance and hung a banner above proclaiming it the UK's worst family court. I was most certainly not the only Fathers 4 Justice member who experienced judicial farce and nonsense in Plymouth, I just received much more of it than most. The Sunday Express amongst others covered the protest. The two members who braved the wind and rain that May day high upon the Plymouth court roof, after being brought down by the police with the aid of Devon Fire and Rescue Services were arrested, but were later released without charge when they simply did not accept that they had done anything wrong.

Oppostite, two Fathers 4 Justice members climb upon the Plymouth family court roof and attach a banner proclaiming it the UK's worst family court.. Above, Mark Harris outside the Plymouth court where he went 133 times just to see his children. May 2003,

Now public opinion was with Fathers 4 Justice, and the acknowledged statistic from the Lord Chancellor's Department that 50% of all marriages these days end in failure means that almost everyone seems to know of someone who has experienced trouble seeing their children post divorce or separation at some time. Almost everyone I have ever spoken to anywhere seemed to have knowledge of someone getting nowhere in the family courts with access to a much-loved child – in my work as a driving instructor, sometimes the very person I am in conversation with can turn out to be a young adult cut off at some point in the past from a father they wanted to see.

But my case, as summarized in this book, is unique. It's unique because it's almost certainly the only case in family law ever where a father has been identified (and publicly lambasted on such a personal basis) by a judge when the children were all under 18 – then for those same kids to subsequently end up living with their dad, while still being well under 18.

I really do not believe Judge James Munby, like so many of the other judges who blighted our lives, having had a public school education prior to becoming a barrister before his appointment as a High Court judge, possessed any 'real world' perceptions – or even experiences – at all. He never contemplated the farces and injustices he personally heaped upon us and the past wrongs in our case would ever surface. I sensed in my appearances before him he knew full well most of what had previously taken place was very wrong, but he just did not want to go against any of it, it would be easier to just carry it on with more of the same. Munby's public attack in 2001 was clearly intended not just to fragment the rising protests against the judiciary, but also to make me just crawl away from my children and not come back; to basically 'kill off' the father. But, as I told judges Wilson, Kirkwood and Bracewell before him, I was *not* going to go away, ever. Unfortunately, like his predecessors, he chose not to listen...

However, because Munby took my case public, I, and anyone else, can always now legally talk all about what happened, we can say what we like about the proceedings and how it all ended, so long as the mother and children's identities – while they are all under 18 at least – remain concealed. Because of this, I gave Matt O'Connor and other activists within Fathers 4 Justice free reign to use our experiences to benefit the cause, and they did.

Now, Judge Coleridge was due in Plymouth on 13th June 2003 to review our situation regarding the children. The girls were then 12, 14 and 16. Coleridge clearly just wanted to get out of the case. But prior to his arrival in Plymouth, various members of Fathers 4 Justice very ingeniously let a story slip out that the Plymouth court was to be targeted with a sit-down protest inside the entrance area on the same day we were all to appear before Coleridge. Now, that day outside the Plymouth family court, police riot vans were parked directly outside the front entrance, police officers were standing outside the main doors, more officers were positioned around the sides and rear of the building and more officers patrolled the adjacent side streets. I had never before even seen any police in the vicinity of the Plymouth court on any of my many forays there. The rouse obviously worked beautifully. I knew full well nothing at all was going to happen in or near Plymouth court, but I knew all about the Fathers 4 Justice operation that was assembling elsewhere…

Now, by this court case in June 2003, my youngest daughter had chosen to go and live back with her mother again, after a month with me and Lisa. She returned to her mother on the proviso with Mum that she would come and see her eldest sister and me whenever she wanted. The mother now agreed to this with her, so the youngest child, after establishing this point with the mother, went back to live with her in the May. I had no problem with this at all.

So, I arrived at the Plymouth court with my daughter Lisa, passing the police stood on guard outside. When we sat in the upstairs waiting area, the court's security staff came and sat alongside us. I then popped to the toilets, where I was followed inside by another security guard, while the others stood over Lisa. They had clearly taken the bait, and expected some mass protest to take place at any moment. Now I was trying to keep a straight face through all of this, because I knew nothing at all was going to happen in Plymouth. So when I got back to the waiting area to sit with Lisa, I made a huge point of looking at my watch then looking out of the window as if I was expecting something to happen. It was quite amusing, the security guards were scurrying around trying to see what I was actually looking at. So, unable to resist after so many years of mistreatment in this place, I then waved through the window as if giving some kind of signal to someone on the outside below, which caused them all to panic and one immediately radioed out. They were now upstairs in numbers trying to see from this window just what I was looking at and who I'd signalled to. But there was simply nothing to see and I was waving at no one and nothing was going to happen. Well, not in Plymouth…

At this point of ridicule, Lord Justice Thorpe's words on June 2000 to me come flooding back to me at this point, "This is a very simple contact dispute…"

However, while we were waiting to go in before Judge Coleridge in Plymouth that June day in 2003, 200 Fathers 4 Justice members were swinging into action with their planned storming of a court. But not in Plymouth – over 200 miles away at the Principle Registry in Holborn, London, instead. They successfully stormed court number one at the Principle Registry while the authorities' eyes were transfixed on the Plymouth court. Fathers 4 Justice occupied court number one at the Principle Registry and held the protest inside that court for two hours. No one was threatened, hurt or assaulted, no property was damaged. Likewise, no one was arrested or ejected but much national news was made.

Meanwhile, back in Plymouth, under one of the most well manned of security operations probably ever seen in Plymouth, myself, my ex-wife and three daughters were called into Judge Coleridge's courtroom.

Firstly, Judge Coleridge saw all of the children together in private once more. He saw them for about ten minutes again. When Coleridge emerged, he came back into the court and the children sat between both myself and their mother. Coleridge then said he believed the best course of action to take was to remove all court orders, and let the children, then 16, 14 and 12 just go wherever they wanted. The mother, again acting in person, protested strongly. She wanted residence orders to her for the youngest two, with my time restricted, and she also wanted the exclusion zone restored. The strongest excuse she gave was that she was now in the middle of another divorce from her second husband and wanted her first husband's restrictions restored while she sorted her latest divorce out! She also argued that if the two children living with her could just go to their dad's house any time they wanted, it would disrupt her life. Coleridge quickly made the point to her that while he was truly sorry to hear about her second divorce, he immediately pointed out that although I had broken various court orders for years, to which she had brought successful committal applications upon me, she was at that moment in time breaking his court order made in Bournemouth just three months before in retaking residence of the youngest child without applying to the court first. She could not really answer that.

Coleridge then followed that broadside up by saying to her that he saw no point in any more court orders as no one in this family, including the children now, complied with them. Therefore, he said he was removing all orders except, of course, the barring order preventing me discussing the contents of Miss Wood's files that I saw during the Wilson hearing in 1997.

We left the court that day, on our 133rd appearance, never to return to fight over access to our daughters. I have never had to take my ex-wife to court again, I have never had any trouble seeing any of my children and, of course, my ex-wife has been unable to bring any committal applications upon me. I understand my ex-wife's second divorce went smoothly, and I hear she is now busy planning for her third marriage to her latest man. In early 2005, my youngest daughter came back to live with me again as she was unable to get on with her mother's latest intended, and has settled here with both my eldest daughter, Lisa, and I. I have also just taught my middle daughter, now 17 and who's always lived with her mother and her past and future husbands, to drive.

The secret family court has wronged my children and I for years. In the wider picture, although these various judges pleasured the mother somewhat by mistreating and abusing me for what was a decade, in this pleasuring of her they did not actually do the mother any real favours with the children, as they grew to resent her for what she was allowed to do.

Each of my children, now between 15 and 20, are affected by all that went on. Each of my daughters are damaged by the years of my enforced absence from their lives and the uncertainty regarding if they would ever get to see me again. Each of my girls are angry that for years no one took any account of what they said to the stream of welfare officers, child psychiatrists and social workers that interviewed them about what they wanted, or when they spoke out about the physical abuse they had suffered in their home from the mother's boyfriend, later husband number two. The family courts claim that they – and their players – always act in the best interests of the child. The phrase often recited is, "the best interests of the child are paramount." But that has proved to be a downright lie in my case and in so many others.

How can it be in the interests of any child to routinely deny that child the love and time of one of its parents just because the other parent does not want that parent around?

How can it be in the interests of any child to be asked, as is routine, do they want to see their father again, when that child knows the parent they live with does not want to see the other parent themselves? Yet this putting of children, often very young children, in this terrible position of divided loyalties routinely happens virtually every time across the country when a welfare report is prepared for a court.

And just what interests of any child are served when the mother can bring home any – or even many – different partners, as often as she wants to where the children live when these various men never have to be assessed by anyone or checked out for their suitability to share a home with children? The 'new man' who moves in or stays in the children's home is presumed fine while natural Dad has to go off and make court applications and undergo assessments by hostile and usually not very impartial court officials.

To take this point further into the absurd, let's explore the result of what the courts routinely do. Assume the mother successfully persuades a court that her previous choice of man to have children with is now 'not suitable' to see the very children she chose to make with him, and the court [as often] agrees. Surely it should follow that her next choice, or choices of men, she takes home to meet or even live with the children be open to automatic legal scrutiny regarding new man's suitability for contact with the children?

The mother in this scenario is as much admitting she got it wrong first time if the father, in her mind, is unsuitable to carry on seeing their children. If so, then the question that should surely follow must be; how can she be trusted to not get it wrong a second or subsequent time?

Britain today checks the background and suitability of anyone working with or near children, be it a lollypop patrol working in a public place seeing children across a busy road, driving a bus, or even cutting the grass or sweeping up at a school. But an active or potential paedophile can move straight into a separated mother's home with her children while the father of those same children gets cut off from them through the courts. Nothing exists to pick this up. Any man, by becoming the lover of the mother, gets presumption he is fine with the kids, end of story, while natural Dad has to go through the absurd hoops in the secret family courts, often without success. The best interests of the child? No, sorry, they are having a laugh, the lunatics really have now taken over the asylum.

So, unless any parent has actually done something that presents a danger to a child – like a criminal conviction for an offence involving or against a child, proven uncontrolled drink or drug taking, then that parent – mother or father – *must* be considered fit or good enough to remain being a parent, whether the parents are together or not.

Of course, when the mother does not object to the father's presence in their child's life, as in the vast majority of cases that never go to a family court, and the parents agree between themselves arrangements over their children, then the father in each of those families *is* presumed fine to be with his children, no questions asked.

Only when the mother objects to the dad in the children's lives do questions over his continuing to be a parent ever arise.

The children's best interests are paramount? No, in the UK secret family courts, that's just nonsense. It's a lie and they should be prosecuted under trade descriptions. Or, as the leading child expert witness, Dr Hamish Cameron, confessed to in my case, perhaps they are just being "very economical with the truth!"

CHAPTER 9

Lisa's Story

Although I have little recollection of my parents living together, what stands out in my – and my two sisters' –minds most throughout our childhood was the constant uncertainty over seeing our father.

What has stayed with me most, though, is the constant flow of court officials, social workers, welfare officers, child psychiatrists and psychologists, all questioning us all, over and over again, to see if we still really wanted to see our father again. But what a ridiculous question! Of course, every child wants to see both their mother and their father, so why do these people ask any child this question?

Not only did we each find this a stupid question anyway, but being put on the spot, repeatedly, for years, to have to declare our wishes to see our dad often made our situation with Mum, and in particular her boyfriend, Wayne, difficult for us. Looking back, these court people clearly never wanted to hear us say we wanted to see or be with our father anyway.

Whatever our parents themselves did to each other, or how they fell out with each other, was nothing to do with us children. Of course, what every child anywhere deep down wants is their parents to live together with them in one house. But if this cannot happen, the next best thing all children want is to be able to see and be with each parent as much as possible, and to know seeing both parents would never be in jeopardy.

But unfortunately what happens, especially when you are younger and your parents split up, is this: you live with your mum and you get to hear that Dad is taking her to court so he can see you. Mum gets all in a stress about it all, and starts complaining to us children and everyone about what he's doing for us. Then there's this big build up to the 'visit' of the court welfare officer, social worker or whoever, who's going to ask you lots of questions. Mum, the other relatives, and in particular for us the mum's boyfriend, all try and tell you what to say. But that's just not fair. We all wanted to see our father, and for years we wanted to go and live with him because Mum's boyfriend, Wayne, was so cruel to us three. We reasoned it would be better to live with Dad if Wayne was to be around, and visit Mum lots when he was simply not there. If it was not for Wayne, then living with Mum was fine provided we could see our dad often, of course.

Now these court people do not try to make a child's position very easy at all. They certainly never made any effort to make life easy for my sisters and I. Often, you get taken to their office, by Mum, usually hearing all her complaints about having to do all this on the way there, and it's all Dad's fault. This started when I was nearly seven, and lasted until I was about 15. Then Mum would sit just outside the court welfare officer's room where we would try and tell a complete stranger that we really did want to see our dad, knowing that Mum did not want us to say that at all. But this always put us in the position of having to upset one parent to see the other, which is truly terrible for any child. As soon as we reasoned to these people as to why we wanted to see our dad – or even more so why we did not like Wayne in our house – we would always be headed off from expanding on our complaints by being told that anything said would be written in the report, which *both* parents would read! The impression these people gave – and we were seen by what must have been dozens of these people over the years – is that anything said about our dad would be analysed, raked over and questioned, whereas any comment about our mother, or complaints about Wayne, her boyfriend, were just not welcome at all. Eventually, after our wishes to be with our father got ignored time and time again, it just seemed an easier option after years of being ignored to just go with what our mother and Wayne wanted. Besides, whenever we stood our ground and said we wanted to see and be with our dad, no one from the courts wanted to listen to us anyway.

However, because we each really wanted to see our father, we did persist with this intolerable situation of upsetting our mum – who we all deeply love and still do – by telling these people we wanted to see our dad. But they just kept asking the same old questions, every single time. Eventually, with Wayne making our lives so miserable we started to tell these people that we wanted to go and *live* with our dad and visit Mum lots when Wayne was not there. But this seemed to upset these people even more, especially the social workers who used to come around after Wayne had hurt one of us, which was a fairly frequent occurrence. I can clearly recall *trying to* make a stand when I was about ten on behalf of myself and my two younger sisters to a court welfare officer and a social worker about where we wanted to live – with Dad – and why. However, the result of me making this stand for all three of us not only made life with our mother difficult for ages, but it effectively ended all of us all seeing our dad for years.

At the time, being cut off from Dad after saying this really felt like we were being punished for speaking out about our true wishes and feelings, even though these people kept saying they had come to speak to us to hear what we really felt and wanted. It was a truly dreadful time in all of our lives.

Some months after I made this stand, I recall my mum having to go to the court every day for about a week. Just before this court case, though, we had a very strange, large man come and interview us individually in our bedrooms at Mum's house (summer 1997). I'm told since that he was a child psychiatrist called Dr Boothroyd-Brooks. This man brought a tape recorder with him, and we were 'interviewed' individually, on tape, by this complete stranger, alone in our bedrooms. Looking back, in my interview by Dr Boothroyd-Brooks, once he established that I wanted to see my father, the entire conversation revolved around him trying to run my dad down and make an issue out of him waving to us when we went to school each day. My two sisters, much younger at the time, about eight and six, felt the same too. We never minded Dad waving to us at all, but we all would have far rather gone over to his house to see him like we used to, and told Dr Boothroyd-Brooks this. But it turned out he did not want to hear this either. Anyway, as far as we knew what we all said went on the tape, and he left.

Then, days later, another man called Mr Szulc came to see us, bringing a leaflet for each of us. I recall to this day the leaflet having some kind of cartoon character on the front of it. Mr Szulc then explained to us, with Mum and Wayne in the room, that he was from some place in London (the Official Solicitor's office) and was involved to 'represent' us all in court. He explained what representation meant, as none of us really knew. Then he wrote down everything we said, and we were all still very clear to him about what we wanted – we want to see our father. With Mum and Wayne present, we reasoned that it was best not to mention what Wayne did, the smacking and hitting of us all, the shouting and unhappiness he caused us, and we hoped that if we just kept quiet about what he did these people would stop coming to see us and we could see our dad again.

But no, it all went to court and we lost our dad for years, and Wayne still continued to hurt my sisters and me. It became clear at that time that no one cared about what we wanted, or what we said – or what was happening to us. It started to become obvious no one was in any way interested in what we wanted, no matter how much we said so.

One thing that does stick in my mind to this day was, just after this big court case (before Judge Wilson in 1997) two of the social workers came around to see us girls once again. Looking back, they could hardly contain themselves. They gleefully explained to us three together that our dad had been sent to prison for trying to see us and that he was bad and mad, and we should just live our lives with Mum and Wayne. They told us all that Dad would write to us sometimes, but we did not have to write back to him. I recall my youngest sister, aged six, started to shout back at them in tears, trying to persuade them to allow us all to see Daddy. They just kept saying it was 'the court' that decided this, not them. Social workers tried to calm us by telling us we would get letters from Dad every now and then. But all we wanted was to see him, and we had been telling them and everyone else this, but it was clear now no one wanted to listen to us. Our views and wishes were worthless. I remember the social workers having a cup of tea and a friendly chat with Mum, and I don't recall ever seeing these particular two appalling people ever again.

The feeling of frustration and confusion I felt back then still lives with me now to this day. We knew all along that Mum wanted our dad out of our lives from an early age, *but we never wanted that at all*. Each of us made it very clear to all these people that we wanted to not only see our Dad, but eventually go live with him to because Wayne was so cruel to us all. But saying we wanted to live with Dad and telling about the abuse of us by Wayne seemed to upset them more. This never ending stream of court welfare officers, social workers, child psychiatrists, psychologists and representatives from the Official Solicitor's office all started off the same way; explaining that they were seeing us to get our wishes and feelings for the next court case, but in reality they never wanted to hear us say anything nice or positive about our dad at all. Looking back, it's now clear they contrived situations to question us in (like when Mum and Wayne were nearby) about our dad, making huge issues out of him waving to us when we went to school, and trying to persuade us to fall in line with our mum's viewpoint. And besides, just how can you say you don't like living with Mum's boyfriend in the house with him and her nearby? We had already told some of these people this when we were seen in the privacy of their offices, but he always got to find out shortly afterwards what we had said – and we still had to live in a house with him.

On reflection, no one *ever* asked us at all about our feelings towards Wayne, or how he treated us, or what we thought about him living in our home. If we just came out and said, our views were simply brushed aside. All the questions were always all about our father; dissecting visits to him in the most pathetic detail, trying to get us to say something negative about him or that we did not want to see him, and of course, trying to turn his waving to us in the street into something really terrible, which it simply was not. *We loved seeing him, he was our dad*!

Just after Christmas 1998, the beginning of the year I was due to move up to secondary school, we heard Dad was now out of prison for this waving to us. We thought prison was for bad people who hurt others or stole things, we could never work out why our dad went to prison for waving to us; we liked seeing him and waved back, despite Mum telling us to ignore him. We lived very close to where Dad's house was, we could even see part of his street from our living room window. We always hoped to see him somewhere every day, and we hoped he never blamed us because we did not see each other anymore. Within days of Dad being out of jail, we bumped into him in a shop nearby. He smiled, he waved, and I recall him telling us that he loved us all, despite Mum hurrying us away. It was very reassuring indeed, and lifted our day, although we now worried about what might happen to him again.

Within weeks, we became aware that Dad was taking Mum back to court yet again to see us. This pleased us, knowing he was still fighting to see us all, but the dread of these awful court officials coming to see us again filled us with horror and confusion. Are they just going to ask the same daft questions again, and if so, just what's the point? No matter what we said, no matter how much we were prepared to go against our mum's feelings, what *we* really wanted was always ignored and disregarded for what had now become years. And by now, Wayne, more than Mum, used to pressurise us all with threats and punishments if we told these people we still wanted to see our dad. So just what could we do?

Sure enough, as summer 1998 approached, these court people once again arrived to question us. Each of us now aged about seven, nine and eleven, tried to just withdraw from the process. As much as we all had a burning need by now to see our father and be with him, there became no point at all in saying so. We felt totally helpless. We had been telling these people now for years what we wanted and all they did was ignore us and it felt to us like it was our fault that our dad was sent to prison. None of us could ever understand the fact that our father, who had never wronged us in any way, was banned from seeing us, and the only man alive who did wrong by all of us, time and time again, continued to live in our home. As much as it hurt so deeply to say so, we started to say we did not want to see Dad just now; in saying this we hoped that he would not get sent to prison ever again. Us saying this made Mum and Wayne happy, for a little while anyway, but having to say this cut very deep with all three of us. It was not what we wanted at all, and we wondered just what Dad would think if he got to know what we had said. We hoped he would understand though.

What I recall now of this period of time was Mum being taken to court time and again by Dad, and us bumping into him occasionally in various places. I remember that by now (mid 1998) Nan wanted her second house back and we moved with Wayne and Mum into a council house in another part of Plymouth. We each had to change schools and make new friends once again, and I wondered just why we had now moved twice into worse and worse homes. We were also frightened that now we had moved we would never see our dad again. But somehow Dad found out where we were and Dad used to make a point of bumping into us around the town. We knew full well he had probably made this 'accidental' bumping into us on purpose. Mum proudly told us after we moved that she had got a banning order from the court on Dad from ever seeing us on the way to our new schools. We all hoped he would never wave to us on the way to school again, not because we did not want to see him, but just because we did not want him going to prison ever again for trying to see us.

For years, Dad used to write to us every fortnight. We never understood why these letters were first read by the Official Solicitor's representative, then posted on to Mum in one of his envelopes. Mum then read them first, then if she approved of them, she would pass them to us a couple of weeks later, when she 'remembered' to give them to us. But at least we all knew he still cared.

In early 1999, about March or April, a new child psychiatrist turned up at our new home, Dr Hamish Cameron. None of us could bring ourselves to tell him we did not want to see our father, because we all really did. Luckily, Dr Cameron never actually asked this question, unlike Dr Boothroyd-Brooks and the others, who always did. We also sensed that something good might happen in the next court hearing too. He talked about Dad, asking if the waving upset us, and lots about what we could remember about him and his home. We also overheard Dr Cameron talking to Mum in the kitchen before he left, and from how that conversation was going, he seemed to be preparing Mum for us seeing Dad again in light of what was found out in court last time. *(This being the results of the police covert observations from late 1998 on the mother that established she made multiple false complaints to them that I was Harassing her – Mark Harris.)*

Now I remember Mum getting all stressed out about all this when she had to go to court for a couple of days after Dr Cameron's visit and when she got home we found out the court had made an order for us all to see Dad. We were so happy. None of us had seen our dad for well over two years, apart from the odd occasion of bumping into him in a shop or whatever. Mum and Wayne were so angry that he got this court order. Each of them kept going on at us not to go with the new social workers to see him, so I said I would not go on the first visit, which pleased Mum and Wayne, but my youngest two sisters did. I remember feeling really sad that day when they left without me, I really wanted to see my father, but it kept the peace at home with Mum and Wayne.

When my sisters returned that day from Dad's, they were almost hyperactive, they were so happy. They kept going on about how I should have come too, and gave me some pocket money Dad passed to them to give to me. Mum and Wayne made it clear they approved of my staying at home with them, and my sisters felt their disapproval of going to see Dad for days, but they didn't seem to care. I planned on going the next time, which was to be in one month's time.

The next visit came around (May 1999), my sisters were both really excited about seeing Dad again, but I was being pressed, especially by Wayne, not to go. He promised me treats if I stayed at home on this occasion, so I did. Again, my younger sisters went, and they came home happy and excited. I confess, I felt very jealous of them. Later that day, I started to ask them about Dad when Mum and Wayne were not around, all they said simply was I should have come along too and found out for myself.

I then remember another court case came along, and we had Dr Hamish Cameron visit us yet again. I remember hoping he might talk to Mum and Wayne about not making it all so difficult for me to go and him perhaps persuading them to give me their blessing to go with my sisters and see my dad. But no, all he did was talk to me about *not* having to go and see him! I just got more and more confused by it all, and I just wanted to withdraw from the whole process. Dr Cameron certainly seemed to approve of me not going too. I do recall Dr Cameron talking to my sisters as well, and all he seemed to do was try and find fault with my dad to my sisters on their visits to him. Like all the others, he was in no way interested in what we wanted, or making life easier for us to each see our father. To me, there seemed no point to his existence at all. I tried to have as little to do with Dr Cameron on each of his next visits too.

This all went on for about another year, Social workers arriving in a car once a month, picking up my sisters, dropping them off at Dad's for the day with Mum and Wayne expecting me to stay behind. Each time this really hurt me. Just why was it being made so difficult for me to see my dad? I started to feel so torn. After all this time, I often asked myself could Dad still love me? Would he even recognize me? Every month, my sisters came home from Dad's house, taxied by the social workers, happy, and with pocket money for me sent by Dad. By now the visits to Dad's were unsupervised visits, as if our father needed supervising anyway! Each time I got to hear about all the exciting things he did with my sisters on these day visits. One, which I recall, was to the Sparkwell Wildlife Park on the edge of Dartmoor, where tigers and seals were kept.

Then we had another visit by Dr Cameron. We were all seen together. I remember telling him I would like to go and see Dad soon, but it was all a bit too difficult at the moment. He seemed to brush over my concerns of feeling 'difficult' about seeing Dad, and clearly gave the impression it was probably best not to go 'until I was ready'. He was far more interested in talking to my sisters about their visits to Dad though. I was about 13 then, and I remember Dr Cameron's questions to them which all seemed to have all sorts of 'traps' in them. He went on and on about what they did at Dad's on the day visits every month, but more in a fault-finding way than anything nice. I particularly recall him asking all about what Dad *asked them* on visits, time and again. My sisters freely told him all about Dad asking how school was, what they had done since the last time they went to his house, their friends, and other general things. Dad always asked them how I was, and asked them to pass me the message that he really wanted to see me as soon as possible. I remember this brought much 'note taking' from Dr Cameron and I sensed he, like all the others, was out to invent a bad picture of our dad from nothing at all.

Well, yet another court case passed, and despite my sisters telling Dr Cameron in front of me they really loved seeing Dad and wanting to see him more, the visits got cut down to just once every other month. Then, just six afternoons a year! Nothing changed. Different faces arrived over the years with different titles, but they still disregarding everything we said as worthless. Mum and Wayne now put pressure upon my younger sisters to stop going to see our father, and by then it was expected that I should never go. I still clearly recall the sheer hopelessness of it all, I still wanted to see my father, but what could I do? It was now expected that I should not see my father by not only Mum and Wayne, but Dr Cameron too, who seemed only concerned for supporting Mum and Wayne's views.

Anyway, a few weeks later (April 2000) I was doing my homework in the dining room at Mum's house when the local news came on the television, and a story about a fathers' protest outside the family court in Plymouth caught my attention. I instantly stopped what I was doing. Mum, my sisters and Wayne were in the room too, and it all went silent. Then a group of protesters were featured in the story, and there was my dad leading the protest. I could not believe what I was seeing; there's my father on the television. Then my dad was interviewed. He had not changed much from when I saw him last, which was about four years previous. His hair was a bit longer than I remembered and he had different glasses on. It was so strange to see him on TV, with his name captioned beneath his picture. He sounded the same as I remembered, but I recall thinking it was strange as he had a tie on, and I never saw him wearing a tie before. The story was over in seconds, and something else was on. When Dad was on, he was explaining how the family courts treated fathers unjustly, and only seemed interested in what the mothers wanted. Mum and Wayne were furious. Mum said she would be phoning her solicitor in the morning and she would try and get an injunction to stop him protesting.

A few weeks later, I had my radio on while I was getting ready for school. It was the local station, Plymouth Sound. One of the stories was about another fathers' protest outside the Plymouth court scheduled for that afternoon. I turned the volume up, and once again Dad was mentioned and interviewed. It was great. I'm hearing my Dad speak in my room, and in what he says he seems to know how the courts were ignoring what us sisters had been saying for years. My mother shortly entered my room, and asked if I had heard what had been on the radio. I said yes, and tried to brush it off as nothing important. Mum said she was going to phone the local radio station and complain about it. I carried on getting ready for school, happy to have at least heard my father's voice that day. None of us were allowed to watch the news that night.

My sisters went on the next, now bi-monthly visit to Dad's. I found it easier to just stay at home again, especially witnessing the pressure now being applied to them, mainly by Wayne, not to go. Both returned happy, bringing my pocket money from Dad once again, but complaining that despite asking Dr Cameron to see Dad more, they now had to go two months without a visit.

The two months passed, Dad was getting more and more on television and radio talking about the now growing fathers' protest movement he had started locally. It started to dawn on me that perhaps it was not just us that were being ignored by the family courts as so many other dads were saying the same thing too. It occurred to me that other children must have been in our situation too, wanted to see their father, but no one listening. I remember my dad, looking quite pleased with himself in the latest interview, explaining that he was leading a march to a judge's home in Devon that coming weekend over access rights and he would be carrying a banner proclaiming: 'I would rather be seeing my kids on a Saturday than doing this!' That made me really laugh inside, and it was nice to see he still cared.

There was now over two months between visits to my father's home. Wayne, especially, put endless pressure upon my youngest sister not to go, making lots of fuss about 'him' (Dad) always on television. My youngest sister eventually caved into Wayne's demands, and stayed at home with me on that visit. Only our middle sister went. That day, my middle sister came home to endless anger by Wayne in particular, who told her she was the difficult one for going to see 'him' (our dad). However, she said to me she was pleased to have gone and brought pocket money back from Dad's for both of us.

Now, there was a change in my youngest sister at this time. Whereas up to now she had been doing well at school (she was now nine), the school started reporting various tantrums from her and difficulties with other classmates and teachers. It was clear to me this feeling of being so torn between having to refuse seeing our father to please the adults, the one I felt for so long, was to blame for her growing misbehaviour. But I sensed straight away no one would be bothered or cared, as they never ever cared about what we wanted anyway.

Another visit to Dad's came, (about September 2000) but only our middle sister went. By now Wayne in particular made her life an utter misery days before going to see our dad and for days afterwards too. And he would be especially nice to me and my youngest sister for promising not to go. We just did not want the hard time our middle sister was now getting.

Again, our middle sister went, enjoyed herself, brought us back pocket money, and tried to shrug off the flack for going from Wayne and Mum. However, after days and days of grief for going to see our father, she eventually promised them she would not go on the next visit, and things at home settled down.

By now we had heard Dad had applied to court once again to

force Mum to allow us to see him. Once again Dr Cameron visited us, and rather strangely spoke to Mum first, rather than us, like he usually did. When Dr Cameron saw us, he started to question us about Dad's protesting outside the courts, his TV and radio appearances, and he suggested to us he might have planted a hoax bomb on the main A38 out of Plymouth. He had lots of newspaper articles on all of this, and showed us some of it.

Nowhere on this visit did he ask about us seeing Dad more, or even at all. The clear suggestion from Dr Cameron was that our dad was a troublemaker, who should stop all of this fuss if he ever wanted us all to see him again. He seemed to rather cleverly put it into our minds that we should not see him *until* the fuss died down. Dr Cameron's position was certainly don't go and see Dad until he stops protesting! But why? What on earth was that to do with us? Although it struck me straight away Dad was probably only making a fuss so he could see us properly, it was obviously not something Dr Cameron wanted to hear, so I simply said nothing. Dr Cameron, like all of the others, arrived with his own agenda against my father going on. But at least Dad waving to us – as he still did whenever he saw us in passing – was no longer an issue!

Anyway, the social workers, about November 2000, arrived to collect whoever was going to see Dad. Mum took all three of us to the door after Wayne had lectured us into refusing to go. Although no actual threats were made, the point by Wayne was clear: life would be far worse for any of us who went to see our dad. What could we do? We all reluctantly told the social workers we wouldn't be going to Dad's, and went upstairs. Within seconds the front door closed and they were gone, and Mum and Wayne seemed so happy. I wondered how we had actually said the words they wanted to hear, "We don't want to see our Dad." Perhaps they would all do the opposite in the court, just like they had done for years, and help us to see him soon. It was a very slim hope, but hope to a child nevertheless. But no, that proved yet another false dawn.

Now Mum had another week in court in January 2001. I had not seen my father – other than on television or in passing in the street – for what was now four years. Dad was still writing these fortnightly letters, via the Official Solicitor, and Mum passed these on to us, or so we were led to believe. Christmas presents from Dad arrived via the latest social workers, and Wayne still hurt us children and made us very unhappy. Mum and Wayne announced their engagement, which was something none of us were happy about at all.

THE DAY I MET THE JUDGE

On one of the days Mum was in court, she came home rather concerned that this judge, Mr Justice Munby, wanted to see me and was planning to ask me if I wanted to see my father. That was the touch paper for Wayne to be right in my face that night. I was lectured, to the point of bullied, in what to say to the judge. I was told to refuse all further contact with my father. By now, I almost felt like I knew the drill of what I was expected to say anyway. Deep down, I hoped that the judge might see through what I was going to say and insist that I was to see my father. I also hoped my father might be at the court when I arrived too.

So, the next day, Mum drives me to Plymouth court. I recognised the building from the TV where I first saw my father protesting. As I entered, Mum and I hardly spoke. I looked around everywhere to see if I could spot my dad, but he was nowhere to be seen. Then someone from the court staff met us and I was taken into this rather posh but small room with lots of books on shelves to meet this rather funny looking short fat man with very greasy hair in a sort of comb-over style, who introduced himself as Judge James Munby. He also introduced his clerk called Mary, who was in the room too but did not say anything apart from hello.

I was not there very long. He did not question me much at all, unlike the other people we had to see over the years. He explained that Dad was in court that week trying to persuade him to let Dad see my sisters and me. He had read what I had told Dr Cameron and the two social workers at the door the previous month and wanted to know if that was still my position, that I did not want to see my father at that moment. No possible opportunity was there in what he said to do much other than agree with what he suggested. Like the others, going with what was said was the obvious line he wanted to hear, so what else could I do, now aged just 14? Also, I had to face Wayne that night too. Within minutes, I was led out of this room, back to my waiting mother, who asked me in detail once outside what I had said before taking me off to school.

The hopelessness of it all depressed me for weeks. The social workers, court welfare officers, the child psychiatrists and psychologists, the Official Solicitor's people and now even the judge all pretend to be so interested in what we had to say, but none of them wanted to hear it – unless, of course, we went with the flow and agreed with Mum and Wayne. My sisters, when they came home from school and asked what had happened, like me, despaired of the utter hopelessness of it all. We started to wonder if we would *ever* see our dad again.

The court hearing ended after a week. Mum arrived home annoyed that the judge was not going to order anything for several weeks while he decided what to do. Apparently, Mum's solicitor reassured her in court that it all went well and she should look forward to the verdict.

The weeks went by, and then in March I remember coming home from school to seeing Mum and Wayne really happy about something. My first thoughts were that perhaps they had won the lottery or something. But no, Mum's solicitor had called her with the verdict and explained that the judge had stopped all contact with our dad, even stopped his letters to us, and sent him to prison for ten months. This was devastation. Each time our dad tried to see us through the proper channels, he got punished and sent to prison. And we still didn't see him. No matter whether we said we wanted to see him or not, he went to prison for trying to see us. Mum and Wayne both thought that was the end of it, and him. I just hoped that he would be OK in prison, and we would be able to find him when we were old enough to take the law into our own hands.

However, that was not the end of it all. Within days, Dad's protesting friends were on the television in numbers talking about what Judge Munby had done to him. On one banner there was a picture of my dad being held up. The local Sunday Independent paper, which Wayne bought, had pictures and stories about my dad and what had happened to him. One story talked of 60 fathers protesting outside Judge Munby's London home. When the papers were thrown out, I sneaked into the rubbish bin and retrieved the stories and the pictures of my dad. I read them time and again. All the stories were so supportive of my dad and so against the mad judge for doing what he did. One headline sticks in my mind to this day: 'Wave Dad Banged Up With Murderers'. I was so worried about my dad in prison, with murderers, hundreds of miles away (Pentonville, London) all because he wanted to see us. My sisters and I felt almost guilty; should we have stood up to Mum and Wayne and gone and seen him anyway? Should we have run away to Dad to make them listen? All of these thoughts ran through my mind.

Then a couple of weeks later, after my Dad's story had ran each week, the judge got a story into the paper, complete with his picture of his greasy comb-over, bad mouthing our father. The judge, who tried to make our dad sound so bad, now attacked all the good everyone had said about our dad for weeks. It was so unfair; all we ever really wanted was to be with our dad, like we had years ago. We knew all our father wanted was to be with us. I hated this judge, and vowed never again to bother seeing one of these awful people.

But the story still ran on and on and once the judge had gone public, the TV stations covered the story in graphic detail, and father protest groups became national news. Mum and Wayne were angry the judge's attack on Dad seemed to increase the public support for our dad, which in my mind confirmed no one believed what the judge said about him at all. Mum was worried now the judge had gone public she would be identified and we would have fathers protesting outside our house.

Now, we had no letters or contact with our father anymore, who remained in jail as 'The Wave Dad' for three months. Meanwhile, the fathers' protests got bigger, and my father's name and picture started to get more known. Internet searches under my father's full name had endless stories of support for him from around the world, which gave me some comfort. He seemed to have triggered an international movement, which I got some comfort from too.

We heard he was released from Pentonville prison in June 2001. Mum and Wayne were unhappy about this, yet more stories followed my father upon release and he returned straight to protest. In what seemed like just weeks, but was actually about six months, Mum was back in court as Dad had applied yet again to see us all. We really did not want him jailed again, we thought it best if he waited until we were old enough to leave Mum and see him ourselves. But another, then another, followed by other court hearings took place. Meanwhile Mum and Wayne got married. Then one day Mum came home very upset. She said Judge Munby had ordered her to take all three of us to see a Dr Nigel Blagg, who was a clinical psychologist in Taunton that my dad was privately paying to help sort the case out.

We all viewed this with dread. Yet another person from the courts asking us the same old questions and what would happen if it all went wrong for Dad and he ended up in jail again? Wayne did his usual coaching of what we were to say, and the appointment was booked.

Now, I had kept my dad's home phone number all this time, about four years, so I phoned him and had a chat with him when Mum and Wayne had popped out. He seemed so excited that I had called him. I had a brief chat with him, without my sisters knowing, about school, my first boyfriend and football, which I recalled Dad liked. I told him that I had been to Manchester United's Old Trafford ground with my boyfriend. Dad said he had been to many football grounds, but could never get a ticket for Old Trafford, and wondered how I'd got one! I told him my boyfriend's father was a member of the supporters' club and we'd got them that way.

However, sensing Mum or Wayne might come back soon, I got to the point of my call to Dad. I told him that we would all see him soon and we still wanted to, but not yet. I asked him to not keep going to court, as I did not want him to get into trouble again. He chatted about this to me and said that this judge had started the process with this Dr Blagg, and I should not worry about seeing this man, as he was different from what had been before. Dad told me he loved me, and that I should not worry about anything from now on. Anyway, despite Dad wanting to chat loads more, I finished the call and that was that.

A few weeks later, we all got dragged up to Dr Blagg's office, which was about an hour's drive away in Taunton, to see him. All the way there in the car, Wayne told us over and over again that this Dr Blagg was bad, that we could not trust him and that we were to say we did not want to see our father. So at the office, we told Dr Blagg what we had to say. Dr Blagg asked me about the phone call to Dad, which Dad had obviously told him about and I told him that, yes, I did make the call. I did at first ask, though, if it made any difference to what would happen and he said definitely not. My main concern was I did not want Dad in trouble because he had talked to me. My middle sister, now 13, cried throughout her meeting with Dr Blagg, as she had to say she did not want to see Dad, when in her heart she really did. We left Dr Blagg's office after he spoke to Mum and Wayne and we all went home.

Nothing much seemed to happen for quite some time after, but then we heard that there were more court cases coming up which Mum had to go too. It was near Christmas 2002. Mum came back from court on one occasion very angry. She said the court was making her take all three of us to the CAFCASS (Children and Family Court Advisory and Support Service) office in Plymouth after Christmas to meet our father, with Dr Blagg to supervise. Wayne was very angry with this, far more than Mother ever was. He said having this coming up would spoil our Christmas. Almost immediately and throughout the Christmas holiday he started to tell us what to say and do. Both my middle sister and myself once again did not fancy the utter grief of going to see Dad – and then suffering the consequences of going afterwards.

Then on the local news one night, there was a brief story of 200 Santas storming the Lord Chancellor's Department in London that day in a protest over child access rights just before Christmas. The story was that many West Country fathers had gone up to London for this and I guessed my father was probably there too. I later found out he was.

Anyway, Christmas passed, and the meeting with Dad at the CAFCASS office approached. Daily, Wayne would lecture and threaten us about even going, let alone what we had to say. Under this pressure, my middle sister and I simply chose not to go that time because of the consequences we would suffer, not so much from our mother, but Wayne. Our youngest sister, now 11, said she would go anyway, and just take whatever Wayne was going to do to her. She was very brave indeed.

Anyway, the visit took place on the first working day of January 2003. Wayne told my youngest sister that if she dared to see our father, she would 'pay for it' when she got back home. Although scared, she was determined to see Dad anyway, so Mum had to drop her off at the CAFCASS office. The visit lasted about two hours. That afternoon, after she got home, about 4 pm, Wayne sent her straight to bed with no tea, drink or anything. Our youngest sister was upset about this, but told us it was all worth it, as she loved seeing our dad again, which was once again after another two-year break for her.

Both my middle sister and I admired her bravery, and envied her seeing Dad, even if it was only for a couple of hours. We both sneaked up to her room with biscuits and food, together with some drink, as we guessed she would be very hungry. Wayne never found out we did this, but I think our mother suspected we did, but thankfully she said nothing.

Another month passed and our youngest sister went once again to see Dad. This time she organised some snacks to hide in her bedroom so when Wayne inevitably sent her straight to bed after the visit, she could at least have something to eat. My middle sister and me discussed that we too must make a stand soon, but we had to weigh up the consequences that would surely follow.

Another month passed (March 2003) and our youngest sister went to see Dad again with Dr Blagg. I asked her to tell Dad that I would be seeing him soon, and I would get in touch as by now Mum and Wayne had just split up and it looked promising that Wayne would not be coming back. My youngest sister said she was going ask Dr Blagg to tell the court all about what was going on as he seemed so different to all the others who we had seen in the past. We knew Dad was paying for Dr Blagg's services, so we guessed if Dad was paying this man himself, he must be OK.

Anyway, youngest sister came home that day so happy. Not only because there was no Wayne in our house, but also for her a lovely day spent with our dad. She arrived home with a mobile phone that Dad bought her while he was with her, and excitedly showed it to us all. Dad had programmed his mobile and home numbers in and our youngest sister was so proud of her first mobile phone, which was a top of the range model for its time.

Unfortunately, Mum was livid about the phone gift and took our youngest sister's phone away from her because she was worried that Dad, having her number, would call her. My youngest sister was enraged, she was angry the phone she wanted for months was now taken away. She was so angry and tearful. This was all on a Saturday. My middle sister was out, so I tried to console my youngest sister myself. Youngest sister asked me tearfully just what could we do? I told her I didn't know, but everything would be OK in the end.

As the months and years of this hell of not being able to see our dad went by, I argued increasingly with my mum. Each argument got worse and worse and now with Wayne out of the picture, my nan (my mum's mum) started to get involved and cause more dispute between my mum and I. On this particular Saturday evening, I wanted to stay out camping with friends not far from my mum's house, but she told me I wasn't allowed. I told her I thought she was being unfair and we started to argue. The next minute there was a knock at the door and it was my nan. Great, I thought, come to cause more problems, has she? We all argued un-controllably, which resulted in my nan trying to block me into a room and agree with what they were saying. Next, a fight began, which was started by my nan, and I ran out of the house crying. How can these people love me, if all they do is hurt me and make my life so sad and depressing, I thought.

All night I cried with my boyfriend comforting me. He knew how upset I was living at Mum's because I longed with my sister's to see my dad. He told me he knew a lad in his year was having driving lessons with my dad and that he could give me my dad's number.

He then rang him and asked for his number and within a couple of minutes I had a piece of paper with my dad's mobile number on it. My heart was racing. I really wanted to talk to and see my dad again. I hadn't seen him for six years and it broke my heart. I decided to sleep on it and make a decision in the morning. I was so scared to ring him because I knew I would be in so much trouble with my mum and her family if I did.

The next morning came. I had hardly slept all night because I was thinking about my dad. I then made the decision to ring him.

As I started to dial the number on my mobile, I was trembling with nerves and excitement. When he answered I paused. It was so nice to hear his voice after all these years. I then replied, "Hi, Dad, it's Lisa." He paused for a second, I could tell he was so shocked to hear my voice and as we started talking he started crying because he had missed me so much. We spoke for a few minutes and I told him I missed him so much and I wanted to see him and even live with him! I had had enough of telling social workers, court welfare officers and child psychiatrists that we wanted to see our dad and no one listened – not one single person. All of these 'professionals' were supposed to be helping us children and having our best interests at heart, but they didn't care – no one did. I knew if I lived with my dad there was nothing anyone could do and it would put an end to this ridiculous heart-breaking mess. We arranged to meet up in town in a couple of hours' time, with my boyfriend.

When I met him it was so strange. I was so happy to be in the arms of my dad again, I loved and missed him terribly. We couldn't stop crying for a few minutes because it seemed so surreal to see each other again. I was then filled with hatred towards all the people who had stopped me from seeing my dad. How could all these people stop three young children, now teenagers, from seeing their loving father? Who would be so cruel to do such a thing?

We went back to his house where I tried to get hold of my sisters. It was strange being in Dad's house after all these years. It was almost as if time had stood still. Nearly all his furnishings were still the same, although they looked a bit more worn than I remembered. But the single most surreal thing was going into my bedroom I used to stay in at Dad's; everything was exactly as I had left it six years before, when I was just ten. Teddy bears on my bed, my CD player, colouring pictures still on the bookshelf and even a pack of chalk I had Dad buy me, for reasons I could not now even remember all these years on, were still on my bedside cabinet. It was obvious he had kept it all clean and tidy, but he had left everything just as it was waiting for our return.

Outside, my black bike I kept at Dad's was still in his garage, although by then I would never have dreamt of riding a bike anyway! It was comforting to know that despite all the courts had done to him, he was always there waiting for us, no matter what.

My middle sister was staying at her friend's house, so I couldn't get hold of her, but I managed to get hold of my youngest sister. When I told her I was at Dad's house with him, she was ecstatic! She told me Mum had packed my stuff, but I didn't care because I was going to live with Dad and she jumped at the chance and said she wanted to as well. So Dad drove us over to my mum's to collect our stuff.

When we arrived at my mum's, my boyfriend and I leapt out of Dad's car and went into Mum's house. My youngest sister was very excited and we both took all the packed bin liners up to the wall behind the bus stop where my dad was waiting and lowered the bags over the wall to him, whilst he filled the car with them. Both my youngest sister and I then slammed shut Mum's front door, leapt into Dad's car with my boyfriend, and set off to live at Dad's.

As far as we were concerned, that was that. But Dad reasoned with us that Mum would take steps to get us dragged back, so he said he would have to take action to stop this. He told us not to answer his front door to anyone while he made some phone calls. Us sisters both protested that if he was phoning the court for help he should not bother, as they had never helped us before. But Dad said that he should call the emergency court line and if he got nowhere there, we could all just disappear for a few days on a short holiday while it was all sorted out. We were all also concerned about our middle sister being left behind, so we both agreed that he should make the phone call after all.

Minutes later, Dad said he was waiting for a call back which would decide what we were going to do. Sure enough, the phone rang and he had a judge on the phone who wanted to talk to us children. Both of our initial reactions were to resist this, as these people would just ignore us. But Dad said that as we'd taken such action or were simply running away, things would change. He reassured us that if it did not, we would still take the short holiday. He asked us to please talk to this man just for a moment. So I went to the phone first.

The man on the phone introduced himself as Judge Coleridge and asked us to tell him about what we had done, and why. He made it clear that now I was sixteen, I could go and live wherever I wanted. So I told him all about what life with Mum and Wayne had been like, and that I was fed up not seeing my father, so I was going to live with him and my youngest sister. The judge said to me that would be fine and he then asked to speak to my youngest sister.

So she then went to the phone and he started to talk to her. Youngest sister then started to raise her voice to him; it seemed as if he was trying to persuade her to return to Mum's. However, I recall clearly my sister shouting down the phone to the judge, "If you make me go back, I'll run away back to Dad's in the middle of the night." It appeared to have the desired effect and he then seemed to let her have what she wanted immediately. I then heard her say, in her parting comment, "That's great, I'll pass you back to Dad now..."

Dad went to the phone, and whatever the judge said to Dad seemed to please him. Dad put the phone down, told us we could all live with him, and we all started cheering and shouting.

Minutes later, a fax started to arrive at Dad's just as two policemen arrived at the door. Dad told us not to answer the door until he'd read the fax. Dad read through it quickly and took it to the door. We went with our dad. Although I really cannot remember the conversation between Dad and the policemen much, I remember Dad telling them, "...better give this to her!" and he passed them the fax. I remember the policeman saying "We only need the bit of paper, mate," and they left.

At last, we were now with our dad. We both went with Dad and my boyfriend to a restaurant for a meal as a family, minus my middle sister. It was great, first time for me in six long years and something I'll never forget, but I wished my middle sister were there to experience it with us.

Now we all had to go to Bournemouth court two days later and meet Judge Coleridge. Dad said we would almost certainly get the middle daughter's situation sorted out there, too, as Mum was ordered to take her there as well. I asked Dad what would happen and he said to both of us we should just say to Coleridge what we both wanted. So we both did, and Judge Coleridge assured all three of us at the court we could come and go as we pleased between our parents, and he would see us all back in Plymouth in three months' time to see how things worked out.

By June 2003, my youngest sister had gone back to live with Mum on the condition she could come and see Dad and me whenever she liked. My mum, although feeling betrayed by me for moving to Dad's, got over it pretty quickly. She also divorced Wayne that summer while Dad took all three of us on holiday to Dorset. My middle sister to this day lives with our mum but comes over to Dad's house lots, and my youngest sister came back to live with me and Dad in March 2005, where she remains to this day, nearly two years later. We all see our mum often too.

I am now 20 years of age. I still feel very bitter and betrayed by the family court system. For years, we all asked these people to help us see our father, but none of them wanted to listen. I've since found out that the ascertainable wishes of the child is supposed to be the first consideration in these cases, but it was clear over the years of hell that the family courts were in our lives that they only want to hear a child's view if it is the same as the mother's.

Wayne mistreated all three of us girls for years, Mum's boyfriend, and then husband. No one was interested in that either. We all really resent what was done to us for all those years by these so-called childcare and welfare people. If a child's mother can bring home any man without asking what the kids think, then why on earth do children get put in the dreadful position of being asked if they 'really' want to see their father when Mum chooses to leave him? Every child really wants to see a father they love.

CHAPTER 10

The Authorities' Move to Stop the Growing Protest and Destroy Fathers 4 Justice

By 2002, the authorities, backed by the divorce industry, started sinister moves to destabilise and destroy the growing protest. The first really well executed mass protest took place just before Christmas 2001 with the storming of the Lord Chancellor's office by the 200 Santas.

Press and TV were there to witness the protest, and some coverage did get out. However, a journalist, friendly to the aims of Fathers 4 Justice, told its leadership that later that day a 'D' Notice had been issued against them, so most of the planned coverage already not out was instantly halted. (A 'D' Notice is a government directive to the press, usually issued in times of national emergency, where a news blackout is ordered.) Various London radio stations put the story out for a couple of hours prior to the 'D' notice, and the story managed to seep out to a few regional branches of the press and TV too.

Further protests throughout 2002 included dozens of fathers dressed as Elvis Presley carrying an inflatable broken heart to The Royal Courts of Justice, London, where the protesters renamed the place 'heartbreak hotel'. National coverage was not stopped this time, and the protests started to escalate. There was a protest at the home of Mrs Justice Bracewell's Somerset retreat, further protests at

Lord Justice Thorpe's Wiltshire Mansion and various courts around the UK had fathers dressed as super-heroes, either manning protests outside the main entrances or even up on the rooftops.

But the authorities did not want to look at the legitimate complaints of these fathers; they instead started to follow key members around, infiltrate Fathers-4-Justice meetings, feed dishonest or one sided stories to the press and got involved with active members in a variety of ways.

A ploy most of us completely fell for during this period was to take part in a number of phoney 'documentaries' that were supposedly being produced, but never materialised. I personally had three so-called journalists contact me under the guise of making a documentary about the Fathers-4-Justice campaign during 2002-2003. My first particular female 'researcher' who called herself Joanne Summers, a very attractive 30-something, contacted me via a withheld phone line and arranged to come to my Plymouth home to film an interview with me in the autumn of 2002.

Joanne, maybe her real name or not, I still don't know, arrived with a rather antiquated camera, lighting, recording equipment and lots of well prepared notes. She was very plausible. I made her a cup of tea in my kitchen while she set up her filming equipment in my lounge. I then gave her a full one-hour interview on film for her documentary project. Of course, believing she was genuine, I talked openly and very candidly about the aims of the protests. I elaborated about the future plans of Fathers 4 Justice and I named certain members and mentioned their plans and, of course, I mentioned my own grievances surrounding my access problems, that were, still unbeknown to me at the time, many months from resolution.

Many of the higher profile protesters and members also had visits from a number of these people making documentaries on the fathers' protest movement. Strangely, none of us had the same people call. Usual MO though; attractive woman interviewer contacts via a withheld number, arrives with filming and recording equipment plus lots of well prepared notes, gets the interviewee talking all about what's going to take place, naming names – then leaving, never to be heard from ever again. Coincidentally, most of our home phones started having very suspicious 'clicking' sounds when we made calls or received them around this time too…

The suspicion my phone was being bugged from around 2002 was confirmed a couple of years later, long after the last phoney researcher had come to interview me on camera. In 2004 my home phone line developed a fault. The phone engineer was called, who then dismantled the connection box in my lounge to not only discover the fault, a loose wire, but a tiny 'non-BT part' connected to the line in the connection box. Now I confirmed to the engineer that I had never opened the connection box in my lounge, therefore if anything irregular was connected to my phone line, the previous owner of the house may have been able to explain it.

Anyway, the engineer removed the non-BT part, fixed the loose wire and left me with a fault free phone line. Slightly puzzled but not really concerned by this object, a few hours later the penny dropped. 'Joanne' had been fiddling around in that very corner when she was setting up her camera in my lounge. I saw her with a screwdriver in that corner where she was shielding what she was up to when I came into the room. I presumed 'Joanne' was just connecting her filming equipment up – she had loads of wires, plugs and equipment to connect together. The power point connection she needed for her camera was there too, right next to the phone line connection box. I suspected nothing at the time. Now I believe while I was out of the room making her a cup of tea, 'Joanne' removed the connection box and fitted this device, whatever it was, to my phone line. This certainly coincided with the clicking noises that accompanied every incoming and outgoing call from that day onwards. The clicking also ceased after the phone engineer rectified the fault that had developed and removed the foreign part.

Other activists and Fathers 4 Justice members had similar visits to their homes by people claiming to be researchers doing documentaries on the protest movement. In all, about 60 of these 'researchers' made home calls around the country to various well-involved members, but, surprisingly at the time, not a single one of these documentaries ever got broadcast, anywhere.

Fathers 4 Justice meetings had started to spring up around the country. Their founder, Matt O'Connor organised meetings to plan action across the UK. Fathers 4 Justice became a household name, and membership blossomed. In the spring of 2003, a purple painting of the doors of CAFCASS offices happened in nightly Fathers 4 Justice operations across the UK (purple being the colour of equality) and in May 2003 Fathers 4 Justice successfully closed the Plymouth County Court down for two hours when two members donning Tony Blair masks scaled the front of the building and draped a banner high over the top of its entrance proclaiming it Britain's worst family court. Both were arrested, but soon released without charge.

In June 2003, with public opinion riding high with them, Fathers 4 Justice took on more and more daring, but always non-violent, direct action stunts. On 13th June 2003, 100 'Men in Black' stormed the Principle Registry in London and held a sit-down protest for two hours in court number one. As explained in Chapter 8, I took part in a rouse that led the authorities to believe the Plymouth court was to be the target of the court takeover while I was before Mr Justice Coleridge on my very last ever family hearing, and they took the bait. We had beaten the infiltrators and their bugging devices once more. Again, no arrests were made, but much national coverage – and sympathy to the separated fathers' plight – was again forthcoming. Another Fathers 4 Justice protest saw 'Batman' on Tower Bridge, and a breakaway individual, Dave Chick, AKA Spiderman, started his own one-man protests, fully supported of course by the members of Fathers 4 Justice.

Dave Chick, a father who had not seen his four-year-old daughter for 18 months, carried out a week-long vigil on top of a 200 ft crane overlooking Tower Bridge. Dressed in his comic Spiderman costume, his one-man protest in late 2003 brought London to a standstill for six days and headlines around the world. When Dave Chick finally came down, he was of course arrested and charged with being a public nuisance. It was then the underhand activities of the authorities first started to surface at Dave Chick's trial at Southwark Crown Court six months later.

It became apparent at Dave Chick's nine-day trial that both the police and government had been party to a conspiracy to discredit his Spiderman protest and turn public opinion against him – and the growing fathers' protests around the country. The log of the police superintendent who ordered the closing of the roads around Tower Bridge, which subsequently caused a huge ten-mile gridlock in the Capital and cost London business an estimated £9 million was read out in court and revealed:

1) Chick had not asked for the roads to be closed.
2) He posed no threat whatsoever.
3) That he was mentally stable.

This was the police's own opinions and judgement that they recorded during the protest in their own records. The chief superintendent signed the log off 'My decision…leave the roads closed'.

Now Dave Chick was simply up 200 ft on a crane with a banner. No one ever saw fit to close any roads off when the builders had been operating the same crane in the same location, even when the crane was shifting heavy building materials from one place to another. But the police tried to use this inconveniencing of the public at large as a bargaining tool to shame Chick into calling off his protest – and turn public opinion against.

The completely unnecessary closure of the roads around Tower Bridge also had the full backing of Ken Livingstone, the controversial left-wing Mayor of London. Speaking to the media during Dave Chick's protest, 'Red Ken' (as he was known during his days leading the now disbanded Greater London Council –GLC – in the 70s and early 80s) said, "He [Chick] is amply demonstrating why some men should not have access to their children. The idea that an individual can hold London to ransom is completely unacceptable. We would not put up with it if it were Osama Bin Laden. I don't see why anyone would expect us to put up with it for this man. He is putting his own life at risk, police officers at risk, and other Londoners who may be passing along the road at risk."

Those comments of Red Ken regarding terrorist Osama Bin

Laden struck a particular chord with us who lived in London and are old enough to remember his tenure as leader of the GLC. Red Ken back then caused outrage amongst ordinary Londoners when, after an IRA bombing campaign in the 70s killed and maimed scores of Londoners, he very controversially invited a number of IRA supporters to a party at the GLC headquarters – at London taxpayers' expense. The Conservative government of that time, led by Margaret Thatcher, shortly after disbanded the GLC.

Dave Chick's protests came after two years of legal fighting to see his daughter. All his efforts through the courts, like in so many other cases, failed because the mother of his child simply opposed him. He tried the system, it failed him and his daughter. He could have then tried the well worn and futile path so many fathers over the years have tried and failed on too: letters to the editor of the daily papers, visits to his MP etc. But none of that has succeeded over the last 40 years for anyone else, Dave reasoned, so why would it work for him? So Chick tried this new approach and he immediately received much public support.

At his high profile trial for causing a public nuisance, Dave Chick was subsequently found not guilty by the 12-man jury in a case that won widespread coverage around the world, including being voted by the Men's Coalition of New Zealand as 'inspiration of the year', but 'Red' Ken Livingstone still chose to compare him to a terrorist.

Just days after Spiderman's protest on the crane in November 2003 had ended, 'Batman' and 'Robin' appeared on the overhead gantry at the Royal Courts of Justice, by coincidence on the very day Fathers 4 Justice held another protest outside that very court. Again, despite their arrest, Batman and Robin were soon released, without charge.

However, 2004 was the year Fathers 4 Justice became an international brand in all the western world countries that model their failing family court systems on the British one. And 2004 was the year the authorities infiltrated the movement and fed carefully seeded stories to the press to discredit individuals in the protest movement who were quickly becoming international household names. Meetings infiltrated by men claiming to be fathers denied access to much loved children became places of conflict and argument, even fights broke out all caused by these people who promptly melted away from the scene. The press were fed carefully seeded establishment views that the leaders of Fathers 4 Justice were a variety of drunks, wife beaters or sexual deviants. But still the protests grew, as did the public support.

In May 2004, two Fathers 4 Justice protesters obtained passes to enter the House of Commons and during the Prime Minister's question time lobbed condoms filled with purple flour at Tony Blair. Once again, public support for the non-violent direct action was huge, as was the international attention that inevitably followed. The 'hero' status afforded to the 'condom lobbers' that made all the nationals on the day it happened was soon followed with the establishment view of 'irresponsible dad' tag the very next.

Irresponsible father was the authorities' angle to try to discredit and destroy what had taken place. A father wore a superhero suit, climbed on a building or crane, or threw flour at an unpopular Prime Minister, and he was instantly deemed irresponsible, with the clear insinuation that followed being his irresponsibility was why he 'probably' did not see his kids.

Yet weeks after the flour throwing, violent protests took place outside the House of Commons by pro hunting activists who fought with police and caused numerous injuries. Yet the pro hunting rioters (and rioters can be the only term to describe mature adults who collectively hurl missiles, stones and crowd control barriers at our police) were seen as nothing more than aggrieved citizens who got a bit carried away in pursuit of their desire to continue to kill wildlife in the name of sport. That riot was followed by another pro hunting activist, Otis Ferry, breaking into parliament and fighting with security staff on live TV in the Commons' chamber simply to further their minority argument for the right to kill wildlife, which had just been outlawed.

Yet nowhere were these unlawful and violent acts by the pro hunting group deemed irresponsible, despite their open violence that could have proved fatal. Red Ken certainly never commented about their violence towards the police, or parliament's security staff. Blood sports had been outlawed; they did not like it and so resorted to gratuitous violence. Yet fathers, in their non-violent acts of attention seeking, were now immediately being branded with the 'irresponsibility' tag, despite them only wanting the intention of law in the Children Act – shared residence – to be implemented, along with the enforcement of contact orders upon mothers. But still the peaceful protests by fathers grew, while the pro hunting lobby openly declared it was going to just defy the law that forbade their blood-sports anyway.

So, in September 2004, probably the most headline grabbing Fathers 4 Justice protest ever took place. Once again, another Batman and Robin climbed in protest. The dynamic duo now scaled the perimeter wall of Buckingham Palace. Batman, alias, Fathers 4 Justice member Jason Hatch, ran across the wall that lead to a ledge adjacent to the royal balcony. Robin, alias Dave Pike, just behind Batman, was halted in his tracks by armed security marksmen pointing high powered machine guns at him as he made his way to the ledge too. Wisely, he did not follow Batman up to the royal balcony and retreated under the threat of being shot dead.

The international coverage was immense. Batman was on the front page of every paper worldwide. Every TV channel across the globe led with the story, and the quite ridiculous pictures of Batman on Buckingham Palace, watched by uniformed police officers, complete with his banner proclaiming 'Super dads of Fathers 4 Justice, fighting for your right to see your child' beamed out. The website address of Fathers 4 Justice was on the banner too, and the overwhelming surge in member applications to join caused the Fathers 4 Justice Internet server to crash. Fathers 4 Justice membership grew from thousands to hundreds of thousands in the UK alone, Fathers 4 Justice branches sprung up around the planet, and fathers' rights was now the number one issue discussed globally in every area of the media.

Once again, the first day's coverage was of the heroics of Batman. One national paper's headline was simply 'Batman', with his very heroic story, followed the very next day with the play on words to the opposite headline of 'Badman'. It transpired that while the hero Batman story filled one day's edition, the same reporter was out tracking down Batman's ex for a dirt digging story for the very next day's copy. And, of course, exes often have dirt to give.

Although newspapers may well see a commercial reason to try and make two stories out of one, which certainly seemed to have happened here, this practice can be hurtful to the victim of such actions.

Hero Jason was, on the first day at least, reported as the devoted father wanting access to his children from a past relationship. He, like so many others, simply could not get proper access to them through the courts. He happily lived with his new partner and his new child with her, but was unable to see his children from his previous relationship properly.

Jason Hatch, alias Batman, on Buckingham Palace, September 13th 2004. Reproduced by kind permission of Mirrorpix.

But no matter what corrupted angle of Badman was levelled at him next day by his ex through the papers, it surely follows that if he successfully lived with a child of his from his new relationship, there just cannot be any logical reason why he was prevented from seeing his kids from his past relationship, can there? Jason Hatch, like the tens of thousands of us other fathers who had been through this insane and corrupt family court process, did not have to be 'model citizen' to be a good enough father. If any of us drink, if any of us have not been model husbands or partners or even have criminal convictions for anything that in no way affects the safety of any child, then we must all be afforded the right to be fathers to our children if we part from their mother, surely?

But if not, and the establishment's angle is followed and separated fathers have to be model citizens, then why are none of the mothers' new boyfriends checked out before moving in with your children, to see if they have drink problems, criminal convictions or whatever? No one looks for these – or any – defects of character in the new man who arrives to live with your children, he simply moves in, no questions asked. It's never any issue. Neither does he have to make any residence or contact applications though the courts to live or be with your kids either. Even convictions for offences against children are not looked for.

Yet all of the press attacks on Jason and other campaigners avoided these points, either by choice or oversight. It was understood Jason's ex was paid a fortune for the 'dirt' story, and through her giving this story of 'Badman' from home, the identity and location of the children was immediately revealed to all. This broke all laws in Children Act cases regarding protecting the identity of the children and where they lived, but no one cared. Jason Hatch *had* to be demonised, no matter what. So it was stuff the law – and stuff the children..

Of course, the 'irresponsibility' tag was soon hoisted upon Jason, this time he was branded irresponsible for exposing the frailties of the security at Buckingham Palace by politicians. But, if an untrained, volunteer Fathers 4 Justice member in a comic outfit, complete with tights, can run a ladder up the perimeter wall of the home of the

Queen in broad daylight and make it all the way to the royal balcony carrying a banner and stay there for five whole hours, should not the authority responsible for security at the royal household be deemed somewhat irresponsible too?

Batman's scaling of Buckingham Palace in September 2004 now placed protest well and truly on the international map and it became clear change had to be to be forthcoming if this level of ridicule of the legal system continued. A white paper was pushed into parliament proposing changes to family law with a proposal for changes to take place in about 2006, but it's now 2007 and nothing has changed at all. The divorce industry, along with the authorities, were simply buying time while stepping up its efforts to cause Fathers 4 Justice to implode, and implode it did. But Fathers 4 Justice did not go down without a fight.

Within days, individual members of the high profile protests had their characters attacked in public one by one. The systematic way this was done was unprecedented. The law protecting the identities of people involved in family court proceedings was disregarded to suit the objective of the establishment. The very law in place to protect the identities of children related to these protesters was just ignored. Channel 4 promptly ran an hour long fly-on-the-wall documentary on Fathers 4 Justice, where its founder, Matt O'Connor, was portrayed as an alcoholic. Again, despite this portrayal by the TV, Matt was regularly seeing his two school-aged sons weekly, by consent of his ex-wife. Nowhere did the feelings of his two boys, the subject of family court proceedings at the time, ever get taken into account when the TV chose to publicly demonise their father. But demonise Matt they did, and unfortunately Matt started to rock under the intense pressure.

Other members were also treated to the same public vilification tactic that Mr Justice Munby did to me back in 2001. Programme after programme now appeared on the TV to degrade Fathers 4 Justice members, and the popular press had a field day. Eddie 'Goldtooth' Gorecki, an active protester throughout the 2002-2005 campaign, was exposed for having a past criminal record for robbery by an undercover agent at a Fathers 4 Justice meeting, who posed as a father denied access to his child.

But once again, Eddie saw and had his son stay regularly and the law on not identifying parties in Children Act cases was again ignored to serve the purpose of demonising the dad. Instead, Eddie's criminal record for a matter totally unrelated to his abilities as a father from his distant past was exposed to demonise him. His young son's feelings on this exposure were never an issue with the authorities.

Funnily enough, it never matters when a mother has a criminal record – crèches exist in women's prisons for mothers convicted of even the most heinous non-child related crimes for them to have their youngest children in prison with them. But if a father has, even a long since, spent conviction for anything totally irrelevant to his abilities as a father, when the mother objects to the dad's presence in the child's life it is considered relevant and the 'irresponsible dad' tag is applied once again.

Throughout 2004-2005 the nationwide protests continued. Fathers 4 Justice superheroes climbed bridges, courtrooms, public places and even Yorkminster Cathedral on an almost weekly basis. Fathers 4 Justice super-heroes appeared in protests worldwide. Change, by public pressure, was on the horizon. Judges unbelievably started coming out against the absurdities they themselves were passing as justice in our family courts. Mr Justice Munby, the man who had caused me and my children so much pain a couple of years before, even had the gall to go public with complaints on what he was told to dispense in the family courts. Coincidently by then, Munby had charge of 'Spiderman's' case – but he still refused to force the mother to facilitate access for Dave Chick and their daughter.

Meanwhile, Dave Chick had since climbed the London Eye, and stayed up in protest for 18 hours, an hour for each month he was denied access to his much loved daughter. Again, despite the now routine arrest, Dave Chick was never charged for his latest protest.

With every angle of the media pointing its artillery at Fathers 4 Justice protesters, meetings became flooded by government agents hell bent on disruption, with journalists secretly filming members during private conversations over a pint, and the final push to turn public opinion was launched. On the back of a one-sided documentary on ITV's *Tonight with Trevor McDonald* show, Special Branch infiltrators fed a story to The Sun newspaper in January 2006 that a couple of Fathers 4 Justice members were plotting to kidnap Tony Blair's young son, Leo. No members were named either by the Sun or the ITV programme. No members were named as this plot to kidnap simply never took place. It was simply a lie fed by the establishment to our media.

But this appalling lie, again designed to try and turn public opinion against Fathers 4 Justice, failed in essence, but succeeded in pushing the now beleaguered Matt O'Connor over the edge. Matt had simply had enough of what was now daily personal attacks upon him in public. The pressure this put upon his two children, who he saw plenty, and his new partner, who was now expecting their first child, lead him to just give up, exhausted and broken. He went on TV and announced he was to disband Fathers 4 Justice as at first he thought some element of truth may be in the kidnap plot. He reiterated Fathers 4 Justice was all about non-violent direct action to bring change, nothing more. But the press had a field day, Fathers 4 Justice was no more. The establishment had won and the divorce industry was free to ply its sordid trade as normal.

I recall a phone conversation I had with Matt, then a broken man, a day or so later. Together we explored the likely truth in this kidnap plot, if there was any plot at all. I asked him did he think the alleged plot to kidnap Leo Blair had any truth in it – the story immediately struck me as one of fantasy. Why did Special Branch not make any arrests (conspiracy to kidnap is a very serious offence carrying lengthy prison sentencing) but instead phone The Sun newspaper with a story? That was simply just not what the police would do if this plot had any plotters. I joked that Special Branch looked to me to have taken a leaf out of the Fathers 4 Justice style of rouse, like in June 2003 when they were misled into thinking the Plymouth court was being stormed while the Principle Registry, 200 miles away, was. Matt thought about this for a moment, laughed and agreed. The police would *never* tip off a newspaper in the middle of any serious undercover investigation involving anyone's safety, let alone the

Prime Minister's son. Unfortunately, though, Matt confided that the sustained attack he had endured for so long had taken its toll on him, his children and new partner before this phoney kidnap plot, so he was simply coming out of active duty. He said he just could not take it any more. He said, rather depressingly, "It's the last straw."

As sad as it was for me to hear this from him, I really understood where he was coming from, and deeply felt for him. The corrupt family court system in this country had won. It had corrupted the truth to try turning public support, although it never really achieved that before breaking the back of the protest movement. It had simply won because of its enormous power, its enormous wealth of resources and influential personnel determined to look after the goose that lays so many golden eggs for them all – keeping the mother and father at war over the kids in a loaded and bias secret world. Justice and the truth never mattered, be it in these secret family courts, giving false stories of kidnap plots contrived to mislead an entire nation, or lies to justify closing off many roads to deliberately cause inconvenience for no reason other than to influence public perception.

By and large, a lot of everyday British citizens still, over a year later, remember Fathers 4 Justice and its harmless stunts with some affection or a degree of sympathy to their cause at least. And nothing at all has changed in the UK secret family courts, it's business as usual.

CHAPTER 11

The Changes Needed

The Children Act 1989 introduced many changes to what was then considered the archaic family laws of custody and access, which usually meant if the mother objected to the father's presence in the children's lives post divorce and separation, he got excluded.

The thinking of the time was that with a soaring divorce rate, children really did need to know their fathers, and be an active part of their lives, even if the father no longer lived with their mother.

Section 11 (4) of the Act allowed, for the first time, the making of shared residence orders in favour of more than one person. Much supportive government literature commentating on the new Children Act at that time went on to state that 'Shared residence orders are likely to become the norm'. This was parliament's clear intent.

But the courts ignored this intent of the law makers from day one. Even though reading Section 11 of the Act invites the making of shared residence orders in virtually every case where a dad has his children to stay, the only changes the courts really made was substituting the old 'custody' and 'access' words with 'residence' and 'contact'.

I myself, back in 1993, asked for shared residence of my three daughters in what was my very first residence application after the judge had made clear he was not interested in moving my children to me fully, despite the physical dangers posed by the mother's new boyfriend. This judge's reaction (Recorder White of Plymouth) was simply to say, "I don't make shared residence orders." He never said my case was not one suitable for such an order, or that I had no or insufficient merits for such an order, but simply HE just did not do it.

Unfortunately, that view ran then and still runs through the entire family court judiciary today. Numerous Court of Appeal cases throughout the 90s gradually shifted the intent of parliament for shared residence orders from what the law makers expected to be 'the norm', to at first 'unusual' orders, then down to 'exceptional' orders. Nothing in the Act anywhere says they are exceptional orders, or even unusual, just an available option. But, as with the pre Children Act 1989, the placing one parent in a position of power in hostile cases causes friction and abuse. And almost always when a case has to go to court, it is usually because either of the parties cannot agree on things, or one parent is obstructive.

One very helpful amendment the Children Act really is crying out for could compel these judges to start making shared residence orders the norm, as intended a generation back.

The simple amendment could read something as follows:

"If the parents of a child lived together at the point of the child's birth and no state agency (police, local authority, etc) saw reason to have concerns regarding both parents' residency of those children, both parents will have automatic shared residency of the child should they separate."

Shared residence does not mean or suggest a 50:50 split of time, which in more recent times hostile anti-male politicians have suggested shared residence would mean (i.e. Margaret Hodge MP, "Children are not like a collection of CDs to be split up when the adults part." 2005). Shared residence can, for example, easily be six nights a week with either the mother or father, and one night a week with the other, 20 nights with one, two with the other, etc, etc.

Even if there is *no* staying contact, just day visits, while the child is in the full care of either parent, in all reality that child is in residency with the parent in charge at that time, just like when the parents were living together. Where the child actually sleeps is not of particular relevance, but who has the sole charge and care of the child at the time is.

And, of course, if both parents were to be given automatic shared residence status after separation, then if either should become obstructive of the other's residency time, then the threat of removal of the shared residence status from the obstructive parent would in all reality keep the child's relationship with both parents intact, and stop a lot of the need for court intervention in the first place.

However, it is unlikely the divorce industry, the solicitors, barristers, child psychiatrists and psychologists will ever support anything that could kill the goose that lays the golden eggs of contentious family litigation.

Another problem commonly faced by fathers with contact orders is when the resident mother moves many miles away with the children, or even emigrates. This can frustrate even a good and working contact order. It's never in the interests of any child to be separated from a parent, mother or father, unless absolutely necessary. Another simple amendment that would greatly reduce the loss of a parent in such scenarios would be to compel each parent to ensure that any child that is the subject of a residency order would remain living in the jurisdiction of any court which has become involved in contested divorce and children proceedings, unless both parents agree of course. The resistance for change and the need for stability is always raised in court if a father dares to ask for more time with his child, but stability or change is never an issue if Mum moves a variety of new partners in and out of the child's home, which can be very destabilising, or moves house to another area.

So what's wrong with ensuring a child has the stability of living in what is usually a fairly large geographical area that it has been brought up in? Why should either parent, for often their own selfish reasons, be able to move away with a child and deprive that child of the other parent, unless both parties are in agreement?

We live in a world where it's fully accepted that if a child loses a parent through death, that child will in all probability suffer some form of psychological harm for the rest of its life. There are agencies in existence that try to help children who suffer the loss of a parent through death as that loss is seen as so destructive. So why do our family courts not take a more robust – or even any –approach to preventing the loss of a parent who is still alive?

Now a lot of the anti-male brigade hoist up domestic violence as a bar to a father seeing his child. Domestic violence is an appalling thing, and must not be tolerated. Domestic violence must be prevented and punished, whether the victim is the male or the female in a relationship. Unfortunately, domestic violence is often alleged in hostile family cases to restrict a father's contact with his children, or, just as sinisterly, to get him ousted from the home on an injunction, as the proof level is virtually non-existent At present, just the allegation of being in fear of violence can prevent a father from seeing his children, have him removed from his home without warning, and have serious restrictions placed upon him as to where he can or cannot go. The retired Mr Justice Johnson, when he appeared in the *Tonight with Trevor McDonald* documentary on ITV in 2002, openly admitted that he believed "many" of the allegations of domestic violence cases he heard during his time in the family courts were based on untrue allegations.

Now, of course, if there has been violence towards a child by any parent, then that is clearly good reason to restrict or end contact. But, in nearly all domestic violence cases, it's a claim made between the adults, and in over half the cases (54%, *Mankind* study, 2003) the adult female claimed assault by the adult male (46% of domestic violence was found to be female upon male). The NSPCC had figures that somewhat concurred with the *Mankind* survey. Very rarely is domestic violence from a parent upon the child alleged by the other parent in custody and access battles.

However, the feminist lobby over recent years has managed to downgrade what constitutes domestic violence to include shouting, swearing at and other non-violent but unpleasant behaviours. Unpleasant behaviour is not violence of any kind, and the courts should not allow this manipulation to take place, but it does. Genuine domestic violence though – physical assault – is a crime, and it would be far better if the family courts, being civil courts, passed any allegations of domestic violence crime brought into family cases straight to the appropriate agency that deals with investigating crime – the police. The police are *the* investigating body who investigate criminal acts, and where there's evidence, they bring charges, and criminal courts convict on the *criminal level* of proof that's necessary to convict of crime. Currently, family courts almost always treat unproven allegations as fact in determining child, property and financial outcomes in separation and divorce proceedings every day.

All UK police forces have specialist domestic violence units. Having the police investigate what are criminal complaints would, in all probability, reduce considerably the false allegations made in family courts; like Mr Justice Johnson said he believed routinely took place. Of course, subsequent conviction in a criminal court could then be considered in family proceedings where appropriate. Needles to say, if the father has assaulted the mother (54% of the time) or the mother has assaulted the father (46% of the time), and there's no quantifiable risk to the children posed by either parent, then contact/shared residence can be planned to minimise the contact between the parents when the children move between them, rather than just ending it should an ongoing risk of harm be expected by one of the parents upon the other.

Once again, by adopting this approach, the incentive to make false allegations somewhat diminishes. Real acts of domestic violence can be properly dealt with by the appropriate authorities and real victims of domestic violence can be far better served and protected because the dishonest timewasters will be seen for what they are. Only then can the true facts be considered properly in individual children cases.

Even in cases where parents have physically attacked and assaulted each other, every avenue of effort should be explored before any court even considers ending or restricting the children's rights to have a relationship with both of their parents, providing of course, the children have not been harmed by either parent.

With school-aged children, if the parents really cannot help assaulting each other upon sight (which is in reality a very unusual situation), why not have the change of parent time taking place via school at home time when the other parent will not be there? Put simply, on a Friday, Mum takes the children to school at 9 am, Dad picks them up at home time and returns them to school on the Monday, or drops them at a point very near the Mum's home if the changeover is to be earlier (say Saturday/Sunday) at an agreed time so the parents themselves do not actually cross paths. (Even dropping off most children at the bottom of the drive or path in most circumstances is quite feasible.)

With pre-aged school children, there are already in place suitable changeover venues, they are called contact centres. Why a mother cannot take the child in one door, and the father collects from another door at the same place beggars belief. These places are staffed by people dealing with children and parents daily, so what would be wrong with using the existing network of contact centres as parent changeover points for pre-school children if no other options are available when the parents cannot be trusted not to attack each other upon sight? The parents would not have to meet. And we are only talking about some extreme cases here where the children are pre-school. The overwhelming majority of parting couples will tolerate each other for brief spells.

Also, in some cases it would be quite suitable if a trusted relative was the pick up/drop off point for changes of parent time too. There is very rarely, if ever, an excuse to cut a child off from one parent if that parent has not harmed a child.

Much of the shift in the family court's attitude regarding domestic violence has been through the 'potential danger' to the mother from the father, perceived, alleged or otherwise. In many cases, if the mother's legal team successfully convince a family court judge (and family court judges do not need much convincing) that the father poses a threat to the mother, the family court will often allow the mother to move away, with the children (and often her new man) to a secret location, thereby excluding the father from his children for ever.

Like any other civil court order, injunctions, ouster orders, etc, only really work on law abiding citizens, who are not a problem anyway. So it must follow that to a man so deranged he is determined in harming the mother of his children, then a court order forbidding him doing it is simply a waste of paper. He will not worry about a piece of paper or what it says. If he's intent on committing even the most serious of crime imaginable, let's say murder, just what is he going to care about some lousy piece of paper labelled a county court order that's handed to him?

Likewise, hiding the mother and his children is a fairly pointless exercise too. When the protest group DADS started seeking out the homes of family court judges, it proved to us that no one can really hide from anyone. DADS found judges' home addresses on the flimsiest of clues and with considerable ease. First name, last name, an approximate (i.e. city or county) area and a computer terminal with access to the Internet would often do the trick. No judge, because of the very nature of their work, willingly makes their home addresses readily available, but they were all still found with ease and some of these judges had fairly common surnames names too (Wilson, Thorpe, Johnson), which would initially make one think they would be near on impossible to find. It then goes without saying that a man looking for his ex with serious harm or even murder in his heart has a huge advantage if he really wants to find her; he knows where all her family are, he knows where all her friends and associates will be, he knows exactly where she is likely to frequent or even work, and when. He knows probably everywhere she is likely to go. You simply cannot move or hide all of a domestic violence victim's friends and family. If a madman really is hell bent on finding his ex, she will be found.

There is compelling argument that if a father, for example, is angry and a potential risk to the mother of his children, it's likely the loss of his children only adds to that anger and desire for revenge and perhaps could send him over the edge into doing something terrible to her. If that man instead lived in the knowledge that his relationship with his children is be protected by the law, so long as he behaves responsibly, even if he has split with the mother, the expected responsibility of being a [shared] resident father to his children is far more likely to have the effect of *defusing* potential danger. To heap injustices upon someone (as now routinely takes place in family courts) only fuels any anger and desire for revenge.

It has been very successfully argued by lawyers that it's better to deprive many thousands of fathers the right to see their children than get it wrong just once – where a mother gets murdered by a father hell bent on killing her because he's used access to the children as means of getting to her. Thousands of harmless and innocent men have lost all contact with much loved children because of the actions of a very small number of men over the last 30 years because of false or hyped-up fears.

But this is so very wrong – and pointless. As just stated, everyone can be traced with ease these days, so this 'hiding' of someone, especially someone you know intimately, is not realistic. Law abiding citizens, who are no real risk anyway, may go away if told to, but they are not the problem. *Everyone can be found.* More so, the fundamental principle of British law has stated for hundreds of years that it's best to let ten guilty men go that convict one innocent person. Again, the family courts are riding rough-shot over this basic principle of British law. It cannot be right to deprive thousands and thousands of parents and children the right to see each other in the misguided belief one life may be saved.

This may seem a very harsh and uncaring view on the surface, especially to the small number of victims who have been seriously harmed or killed by ex-partners collecting the children for contact over the years. It is believed to total five ex-wives and partners murdered in the UK where a father has used contact occasions with his children to do this. Many, many more husbands, wives and partners regularly murder each other while married or living in the same household. Nothing said here is intended to trivialise what happened to them. But you have to look at the world as it is, fathers *using contact* with children to murder or seriously harm their children's mother is a very rare occurrence indeed.

To take this point further, just look at the nation's approach to road safety. The motor car kills over 3,500 UK citizens each year, and the UK has a population of 58 million. That's ten people every single day that will die on UK roads because of our love of the car.

Today, tomorrow and every day, and the figures used to be much higher. Yet do the authorities ban the car? No, of course not, the benefits of the car are considered to far outweigh the ten deaths a day and the hundreds of daily serious injuries inflicted on our roads. We all have a right to apply for a licence from the age of 17 and, when we pass a 30- minute test, drive our cars anywhere and everywhere. What the authorities do though is put in place strict laws to ensure maximum safety; we test drivers for competence, we fit cars with airbags, seat belts, crumple zones, etc, etc. We MOT our vehicles every year, design roads that reduce speed and increase awareness and safety. And we still drive our cars in the knowledge that ten more people will die tomorrow...

This is the same criteria the family courts must put in place where domestic violence is alleged between parents; work towards the overall good of *all* citizens. Stick to the principles of British law, and legislate to ensure the safest possible circumstances for the children and separated parents to live in. You simply cannot continue to treat all men as guilty assassins upon allegations that are unproven. In every other area of law, you are innocent until proven guilty. The current practices are counter-productive anyway, as the feeling of being to made to suffer injustice only inflames angers and desire for revenge in any situation.

One particular case some years ago of a man finding out through the family courts where is ex-wife lived and murdering her happened in Cornwall. The father was convicted of murder. This one case was later taken up by a marginal seat Liberal Democrat MP in the ex-wife's area. His one-man campaign sparked nationwide changes in how family courts deal with allegations of domestic violence in children cases – which has ultimately led to the ending of contact for fathers and children in thousands and thousands of cases across the country since.

The final absurdity – and futility – of what currently takes place is this: assume a worse case scenario where a man *has* been terribly violent to his wife or partner. He could receive convictions for this in a criminal court and go to prison for it. While he's doing his time, ex-wife or partner moves away with the children and goes into hiding from him. Upon release, he goes to a family court for contact with his kids, fails and gets permanently excluded from his children, even being denied any knowledge as to where they live, because of his past proven violence towards the children's mother.

Assume he lacks the motivation to even try and find them, and he simply gives up. At this point it's fair to assume the mother is 'safe' from him. Maybe she is. Now on the very next Friday night out, he meets another woman, a single mum, woos her and subsequently moves into her home with this new woman and her children. That violent convict can see and live with any child other than his own, no questions asked; he starts off from the automatic position of 'presumed fine', despite his past because no one looks for it. He need make no residence or contact applications to any court to be with or live with children that are not his. If this man is to be presumed fine to be with any child, no questions asked, purely because he is now the favoured lover of this subsequent mother, then there can be no logic to deny that same man seeing his own child or children, can there? Yet that is what is happening up and down this country and facilitated by our corrupt family courts. It's the law of insanity.

To back this up, the Family Education Trust, a well established research organisation into family and youth policy, undertook a study into family types and the link between child deaths in the home. Their research looked at the period 1975-1992. Their study was published in the book *Broken Homes and Battered Children*. They took their facts and figures from NSPCC files which included nearly 50,000 children. Their study included many other high profile children cases where adults murdered or seriously abused a child (i.e. Jasmine Beckford, Maria Colwell, Christopher Pinder, to name a few). The study concluded from it's in depth study that children living in a home with a non-related male (mother's new boyfriend) were 33 times more at risk from death and abuse than in a home with the natural mother and father.

Twelve years since that report, nothing at all has been done to protect children from dangers posed by the mother's new man or men. In all practical terms, there is probably little that can be done either. There is no realistic way to police just who a mother, or any parent, brings into their child's home. It simply cannot be done. You would have to post social workers outside the home of every single parent to check who's entering and leaving. So, the authorities simply accept the hugely increased risk of death or harm to children posed by the mother's new men, like they accept the motor car will kill ten more citizens tomorrow, and every single day after. Therefore, it is completely illogical for a natural father to have to go through the absurd hoops presented in a family court just to see children he once lived with unless he has actually done something wrong to his child or children.

Enforcement. The contempt of court laws are adequate. Whatever the enforcement laws are, if these judges illegally allow mothers to break court orders with impunity and enforce nonsense orders upon fathers (i.e. my waving to my kids, off to prison), then the justice system becomes a mockery. Again the Children Act should be amended to include an 'enforceable' right for both parents to shared residence orders if the parents lived together when the child was born, unless either of them have actually done something wrong to the child or children.

The feminist lobby have, and without too much effort, successfully indoctrinated the family court's thinking with the belief that you cannot jail a mother with children, simply because it would harm those very children. Of course, the secret family courts immediately bought into this thinking so as to avoid its responsibility to enforce anything upon mothers. More often than not, if the secret court sense potential problems if they make a contact order which the mother will disobey, they routinely just do not make the order at all.

But this is completely wrong. Having a child or children is no exemption from the law in any other legal setting. If a mother on benefits takes a small part time job and fails to declare the income from her work, if that relatively minor fraud offence is committed over even just a few months, she will usually go to prison, with no thought to her children whatsoever. And many have. If any mother fails to ensure her child attends school properly, she persistently shoplifts or keeps driving a car while disqualified, the prison gates swing wide open for her and with little regard for her children. Again, many have – the law is considered to be the law.

So why do the family courts choose to become so impotent regarding enforcement of contact orders? Having children is no reason to avoid the law or punishment for breaking the law in any other court, but the unwritten rule in secret family courts is the mother is above the law. Just the real threat of being jailed for failure to comply would bring the overwhelming amount of mothers flouting contact orders straight into line. If in extreme cases where a mother declared she was still quite happy to go to prison to stop her children seeing their father, then surely the condition that the dad would have the children throughout her time in prison would almost always encourage her compliance, even at the 11th hour?

If this threat still did not encourage her compliance and realise the futility of her stance, then they should simply go ahead and move the children to the dad while she served her time, with perhaps an assessment of her mental state regarding this refusal to obey being a condition before the children could return to her residence. And just why not? This way, the court would be able to ensure the children's welfare is secure while she serves her time, as they would be with their dad.

But just the *real* threat of enforcement in these cases would work wonders in almost every case. Realistically, very few mothers would be jailed at all, if *a real threat* of punishment was in place. As things stand, mothers are routinely told by their legal advisors that they will not get punished for non-compliance of contact orders, so they drift into court feeling they are above the law. As things stand, they are above the law with how these secret courts are currently operating. This situation happened in my case, and many others too.

Obviously, prison should be the last resort in any civil proceedings. All current laws exist today are adequate to bring compliance, but the courts refuse to apply them to mothers flouting contact orders. It would be helpful if smaller and more imaginative penalties could be imposed before prison becomes the only option though. Again, the Children Act could be easily amended to facilitate this quite easily.

Contempt laws tend to suggest only fines or prison are available. The government is currently proposing the confiscation of driving licences and passports as the starting point for fathers who evade or refuse to comply with child support orders. So why not extend these powers into the Children Act as a starting point to punish broken shared residence/contact orders? Then enforcement can have an escalation of penalties to get non-compliant parents to tow the line, from inconvenience through to prison for non-compliance as the very last resort? And just what would be wrong in making refusal to comply with a contact/shared residence order grounds to move the children fully to the most co-operative parent? Again, that very small change could easily be accommodated in the Children Act.

Another invention in recent years by the family courts when seeking to evade the problem posed by a mother's refusal to allow a father to see his kids is the absurd term 'indirect contact'. The Children Act does not appear to have included this absurd term anywhere. Indirect contact appears to be a direct invention from the courtroom itself. Secret family courts often make these orders when a mother firmly opposes the dad seeing the child as a cop out from doing its duty.

This invention also enabled the establishment to manipulate the true picture about the amount of contact orders for father access that were really made. But this ability to blur what is really taking place hides the many thousand of cases where the secret courts have quite unbelievably made indirect contact orders, where a father can write to babies and children as young as two years old, telling the mother to read the father's letter to the child, then leave the case having made what corruptly passes off as a contact order. Only in secret courts could such abuse of the process be routinely passed off as justice and such utter garbage be spoken, let alone passed off as lawful. But it is, routinely. Many DADS members and Fathers 4 Justice members had indirect contact orders like this (including myself). Yet indirect contact orders, the invention of the secret family courts, are included in the figures the Lord Chancellor's spokespeople and included in press articles when misleading the public about how many contact orders for fathers were made during the Fathers 4 Justice campaigns of 2003-2006.

One of their spokespeople once had the gall to say in one interview for TV that, "The court service made over 55,000 contact orders last year…only about 50 fathers were denied all contact." That figure of "about 50 fathers were denied all contact" coincided with the approximately 50-60 fathers protesting outside the Royal Courts of Justice earlier that week.

Again, the insinuation of only 'irresponsible' fathers getting no contact was clearly there and aimed at the campaigners that day. No figures were given though to quantify just how many of the 55,000 orders were for indirect contact (the letter writing to children often not old enough to read) or indeed the amount of contact orders routinely being broken. In other words, fact was overridden with spin.

And finally, the single biggest change so desperately needed so the farcical nonsense that passes for family courts ends should be the abolishment of the closed court. The current minister responsible for family courts, Harriet Harman MP, is currently conducting a study into the feasibility of opening the family courts to public scrutiny. Even on the surface, the proposals from Ms Harman's office look full of glossy presentation but fatally doomed to instant failure. Ms Harman is already talking about judges being given the power to take courts back into closed settings at their discretion.

If these family court judges are afforded the power to revert to type, they will, and the entire change – if it happens – will fail. It cannot be permitted where a judge, sensing a case is starting to get out of hand (like my case detailed in this book) should ever be enabled to bury mistakes and wrongs by reverting the proceedings back into secrecy. If a case is going wrong, then why it has and how it is put back on the right track has to be out in the open, with hopefully the mistakes being learned from. More bizarrely, at present, any family proceedings being appealed at the Court of Appeal are held in open court. But no one can hear how the decision at the lower court was arrived at. So, although the lower court that you wish to appeal arrived at its decisions under a cloak of secrecy, a litigant can try and challenge the mistakes in an open court on appeal. There simply is no logic for closed courts in family proceedings at any level.

Furthermore, as things stand today where proceedings are in closed court, any judge can, at his whim, take selective parts of any case – as Judge Munby did in my case in 2001 – public, and the minister concerned about the current practices is in agreement the current operations are failing miserably. There would be no overall move towards progress – or even improvement – whatsoever if the same secret family court farces can possibly take place – but just from a different starting point.

Everything – not just nice, one sided cherry picked bits – should take place in fully open courts.

The identities of the parties in family cases can easily be protected by law (just as rape victims and criminals under 18 who have their identity protected in criminal courts by law) but the proceedings themselves must be fully aired in public – without exception – if the proposed changes are to have any meaningful effect. As the saying goes, justice not only has to be done, it has to be *seen to be done*.

What currently takes place in family courts needs to be seen to be believed.

The Politics of Family Destruction

An Essay by Stephen Baskerville,
(November 4th 2002)

The debate on the family is becoming increasingly politicized. President George W. Bush proposes federal programs to promote marriage and fatherhood and to enlist churches. Liberals respond that government does not belong in the family but then advocate federal programs of their own.

Yet the more polarized the issues become the less willing we are to look at the hard politics of the family crisis. Family policy is still discussed in terms set by therapists and social scientists: the rate of divorce and unwed motherhood, the level of poverty, the impact on children, the social costs. As if we don't know.

As a social scientist, I do not deny the value of data (I intend to marshal some myself). But therapeutic practitioners have established such a hold over family policy that they have paralyzed our capacity to act. Writing on single motherhood in Commentary magazine, the eminent political scientist James Q. Wilson grimly concludes, "If you believe, as I do, in the power of culture, you will realize that there is very little one can do." Like many others (including the Bush administration), Wilson is reduced to advocating counseling and "education."

What seems missing here is old-fashioned politics, the kind that did not hesitate to make moral judgments and even express outrage. The politics of the prophets, for example.

The facts are well-established among social scientists, but a kind of ideological correctness on both left and right seems to keep us from confronting the full implications of what we know. We are afraid to challenge the accepted clichés about marriage breakdown, even when it becomes clear that they don't correspond to the evidence.

We should begin, therefore, with the uncontested but seldom-mentioned facts. First, marriages do not simply "break down" by themselves. Legally, someone – and it is usually one – consciously ends it by filing official documents and calling in the government against his or her spouse. According to Frank Furstenberg and Andrew Cherlin, the authors of Divided Families, some 80 percent of divorces are unilateral. One spouse usually wishes to keep the family together.

When children are involved, the divorcing parent is overwhelmingly likely to be the mother. Scholarly studies by Sanford Braver, Margaret Brinig and Douglas Allen, and others estimate that between 67 and 75 percent of such divorces are instigated by the mother. Feminists and divorce attorneys report that the number is closer to 90 percent. Few of these divorces involve grounds like desertion, adultery, or violence. "Growing apart" or "not feeling loved or appreciated" are the usual explanations.

The divorcing parent is likely to get custody of the children and coerced financial payments from the divorced parent. Brinig and Allen even concluded that of 21 variables, "who gets the children is by far the most important component in deciding who files for divorce."

Clearly more is at work here than husbands and wives deciding to go their separate ways. Under no-fault laws, divorce has become a means not only of ending a marriage but of seizing monopoly control of the children, who become weapons conferring leverage backed by penal sanctions. The devastating effects of divorce and fatherlessness on both children and society are now so well-known that there is no need to belabor them here. What is seldom appreciated is the broader threat the divorce regime poses to ethical and constitutional government. In fact, there is today no better example of the link between personal morality and public ethics –between the fidelity of private individuals and the faithfulness of public servants – or the connection of both with the civilized order.

Significantly, as secular political sophisticates focus narrowly on the sociological, it is Pope John Paul II who has come closest to the root of the problem. In January, he issued what many saw as a surprisingly strong statement against divorce that specifically singled out lawyers and judges for criticism. For his pains he was attacked by lawyers, journalists, and politicians from both the left and right. Yet his characterization of divorce as a "festering wound" with "devastating consequences that spread in society like the plague" is as accurate politically as it is socially.

Since the advent of no-fault divorce, a multibillion-dollar industry has grown up around the divorce courts: judges, lawyers, psychotherapists, mediators, counselors, social workers, and bureaucratic police. All these people have a professional and financial stake in divorce. In fact, despite pieties to the contrary, public officials at all levels of government – including elected leaders in both parties – now have a vested interest in increasing the number of single-parent homes.

The politics of divorce begins in family court, a relatively new and little-examined institution. Family courts are usually closed to the public and their proceedings are usually unrecorded. Yet they reach further into private lives than any other arm of government. Though lowest in the hierarchy, they are "the most powerful branch of the judiciary," according to Judge Robert Page of the New Jersey family court. "The power of family court judges is almost unlimited," Page writes.

Secret courts have long been recognized as an invitation to chicanery. "Where there is no publicity, there is no justice," wrote British philosopher and jurist Jeremy Bentham. "It keeps the judge himself while trying under trial." Judges claim the secrecy protects family privacy, though in fact it seems to provide a cloak to violate family privacy and other protections with impunity.

Family court judges are appointed and promoted by commissions dominated by bar associations. That means they are answerable to those with an interest in maximizing the volume of divorce litigation. Though family courts complain of being "overburdened," it is clearly in their interest to be overburdened, since judicial powers and salaries are determined by demand. The aim of the courts, therefore, is to increase their workload by attracting customers, and the divorce industry has erected a series of financial and emotional incentives that encourage people to divorce. "With improved services, more persons will come before the court seeking their availability," Page explains. "As the court does a better job more persons will be attracted to it as a method of dispute resolution." Doing a "better job" really means attracting more divorcing parents with generous settlements.

A substantial body of federal and state case law recognizes parenthood as an "essential" constitutional right "far more precious than property rights" (May v. Anderson). In Doe v. Irwin, a federal court held that parenthood "cannot be denied without violating those fundamental principles of liberty and justice which lie at the base of all our civil and political institutions." Yet such apparently unequivocal principles are never applied in divorce cases, where judges routinely remove children from forcibly divorced parents without providing any reason.

Once a parent loses custody, he or she no longer has any say in where the children reside, attend school or day care, or worship. Worse, the parents who have been stripped of custody are in many ways treated as outlaws. A personalized criminal code is legislated around them by the judge, controlling their association with their children, their movements, and their finances. Unauthorized contact with their children can be punished with arrest. Involuntarily divorced parents have been arrested for running into their children in public places such as sporting events and church, for making unauthorized telephone calls, and for sending unauthorized birthday cards.

Parents whose spouses want a divorce are ordered to surrender personal diaries, correspondence, financial records, and other documents normally protected by the Fourth Amendment. Their personal habits, movements, conversations, writings, and purchases are all subject to inquiry by the court. Their home can be entered and their visits with their children monitored in a "supervised visitation center." Anything they say to their spouses, family, friends, counselors, and others can be used against them in court. Their children, too, can be used as informers.

Forcibly divorced parents are also ordered, on pain of incarceration, to hire cronies of the judge. In what some see as little less than a shakedown, family courts routinely order forcibly divorced and legally unimpeachable parents to pay attorneys, psychotherapists, and other professionals with the threat of jail for not complying.

Family law is now criminalizing constitutionally protected activities as basic as free speech, freedom of the press, and even private conversations. In many jurisdictions it is now a crime to criticize judges, and parents have been arrested for doing so. Following his congressional testimony critical of the family courts in 1992, Jim Wagner of the Georgia Council for Children's Rights was stripped of custody of his two children, ordered to pay $6,000 to lawyers he did not hire, and jailed when he could not pay.

The principal tool for enforcing divorce and keeping ejected parents away from their children is a restraining order. Orders separating parents from their children for months, years, and even life are routinely issued without the presentation of any evidence of wrongdoing. They are often issued at a hearing where the parent is not present; they are sometimes issued with no hearing at all. "The restraining order law is one of the most unconstitutional acts ever passed," says Massachusetts attorney Gregory Hession, who has filed a federal suit on civil rights grounds. "A court can issue an order that boots you out of your house, never lets you see your children again, and takes your money, all without you even knowing that a hearing took place."

Hession's description is confirmed by judges themselves. "Your job is not to become concerned about the constitutional rights of the man that you're violating as you grant a restraining order," New Jersey Judge Richard Russell told his colleagues at a training seminar in 1994. "Throw him out on the street, give him the clothes on his back and tell him, see ya around... We don't have to worry about the rights."

Elaine Epstein, former president of the Massachusetts Women's Bar Association, wrote in a column in the association's newsletter that divorce-connected restraining orders are doled out "like candy." "Everyone knows that restraining orders and orders to vacate are granted to virtually all who apply," and "the facts have become irrelevant," she reports. "In virtually all cases, no notice, meaningful hearing, or impartial weighing of evidence is to be had." Yet a government analysis found that fewer than half of all orders involved even an allegation of physical violence.

It doesn't take much to violate such restraining orders. "Stories of violations for minor infractions are legion," the Boston Globe reported on May 19, 1998. One father was arrested "when he put a note in his son's suitcase telling the mother the boy had been sick over a weekend visit." Another was arrested "for sending his son a birthday card." Parents are arrested for attending their children's worship services, music recitals, and sports activities – events any stranger may attend. National Public Radio broadcast a story in 1997 about a father arrested in church for attending his daughter's first communion. During the segment, an eight-year-old girl wails and begs to know when her father will be able to see her or call her. The answer, because of a "lifetime" restraining order, is never. Even accidental contact in public places is punished with arrest.

Restraining orders are in fact more likely to cause than to prevent violence, since laws separating parents from their children can provoke precisely the violence they are designed to prevent. "Few lives, if any, have been saved, but much harm, and possibly loss of lives, has come from the issuance of restraining orders," retired Dudley district court justice Milton Raphaelson wrote last year in the Western Massachusetts Law Tribune. "It is the opinion of many who remain quiet due to the political climate. Innocent men and their children are deprived of each other."

Domestic violence has now been federalized in a legislative agenda whose conscious aim is to promote easy divorce. Donna Laframboise of Canada's National Post wrote that federally funded battered women's shelters in the United States and Canada constituted "one-stop divorce shops" whose purpose was not to shelter women but to secure custody for divorcing mothers. The Violence Against Women Act, renewed by Congress in 2000, "offers abundant rewards" for making false accusations, writes Professor Susan Sarnoff of Ohio State University, "including the 'rights' to refuse custody and even visitation to accused fathers, with virtually no requirements of proof." The law's definition of domestic violence is so broad that "it does not even require that the violence be physical."

Authorities bully some women into taking out restraining orders by threatening to take away their children. The February 20, 2001, edition of the Massachusetts News described how Heidi Howard was ordered by the Massachusetts Department of Social Services to take out a restraining order against her husband and divorce him, though neither parent was charged with any wrongdoing. When she refused, the social workers seized her children. Reporter Nev Moore claims to have seen hundreds of similar cases. Government officials can now impose divorce not only on one unwilling parent but on both.

While the domestic violence industry is driven by federal funding, the main financial fuel of the divorce machinery is "child support," which subsidizes and encourages unilateral divorce. Bryce Christensen of the Howard Center for Family, Religion, and Society argues for a "linkage between aggressive child-support policies and the erosion of wedlock."

Those accused of failing to pay child support –"deadbeat dads" – are now the subject of a national demonology. Yet a federally funded study by Sanford Braver, published as Divorced Dads: Shattering the Myths, found government "estimates" of nonpayment are produced not from any official statistics but entirely from surveys of custodial parents. Braver concluded that "the single most important factor relating to nonpayment" is unemployment.

Braver is not alone. Columnist Kathleen Parker has concluded that "the 'deadbeat dad' is an egregious exaggeration, a caricature of a few desperate men who for various reasons – sometimes pretty good ones – fail to hand over their paycheck, assuming they have one." Deborah Simmons of the Washington Times likewise found "scant evidence that crackdowns...serve any purpose other than to increase the bank accounts of those special-interest groups pushing enforcement."

Child support enforcement is now a massive industry, where revolving doors, financial transfers, and other channels connect family courts with legislators, interlocking executive agencies on the federal, state, and local level, with private contractors.

To encourage divorce, child support must be set high enough to make divorce attractive for mothers, and setting it is a political process conducted by officials and groups that thrive on divorce. About half the states use guidelines devised not by the legislature but by courts and enforcement agencies. Yet even legislative enactment is no guarantee of impartiality, since legislators may divert enforcement contracts to their own firms.

The ethical conflicts extend to the private sector, where collection firms also help to decide the levels of what they are to collect. Not only does an obvious conflict of interest impel them to make the burdens as high as possible to increase their take in absolute terms (and to encourage divorce), but the firms can set the levels high enough to ensure the arrearages on which their business depends.

While working as a paid consultant with the Department of Health and Human Services (HHS) during the 1980s, Robert Williams helped to establish uniform state guidelines in the federal Child Support Guidelines Project. Predictably, Williams's guidelines sharply increased support obligations in many states. Economist Mark Rogers charges in Family Law Quarterly that they resulted in "excessive burdens" based on a "flawed economic foundation." Williams himself acknowledges that "there is no consensus among economists on the most valid theoretical model to use in deriving estimates of child-rearing expenditures." Donald Bieniewicz, author of an alternative guideline published by HHS, writes, "This is a shocking vote of 'no confidence' in the...guideline by its author" – a guideline used to incarcerate parents without trial.

Governments also profit from child support. "Most states make a profit on their child support program," according to the House Ways and Means Committee, which notes that "states are free to spend this profit in any manner the state sees fit." With substantial sums at stake, officials have no incentive to discourage divorce, regardless of their party affiliation. Notwithstanding rhetoric about strengthening the family, neither Democratic nor Republican lawmakers are likely to question any policy that fills the public coffers.

The trampling of due process in child support prosecutions parallels that in domestic violence cases, since a parent may legally be presumed guilty until proven innocent, and the parent will not necessarily have a lawyer or a jury of his or her peers. "The burden of proof may be shifted to the defendant," according to the National Conference of State Legislatures (NCSL), which approves these methods. "Not all child support contempt proceedings classified as criminal are entitled to a jury trial," adds NCSL, and "even indigent obligors are not necessarily entitled to a lawyer."

In the decades since the inception of no-fault divorce, family law has gradually become an ethical cesspool. Attorneys such as Hession charge that tapes and transcripts of hearings are routinely altered in family court. Hession's forensic evidence was published last year in the Massachusetts News. When his client, Zed McLarnon, complained about the tampering and other irregularities, he was assessed $3,500 for attorneys he had not hired and jailed without trial by the same judges whose tapes were allegedly doctored. "This is criminal misconduct," attorney Eugene Wrona says of similar practices in Pennsylvania, "and these people belong in jail." In May 1999, Insight magazine exposed a "slush fund" for Los Angeles family court judges into which attorneys and court-appointed "monitors" paid. These monitors are hired by the court to watch parents accused of spousal or child abuse while they are with their children.

The corrupting power of forced divorce now extends beyond the judiciary, validating the pope's observation that its consequences spread "like the plague." In 2000, four leading Arkansas senators were convicted on federal racketeering charges connected with divorce. One scheme involved hiring attorneys to represent children during divorce, a practice generally regarded as a pretext to appoint cronies of the judge. In the April 29, 1999, edition of the Arkansas

Democrat-Gazette, John Brummett wrote that "no child was served by that $3 million scam to set up a program ostensibly providing legal representatives to children in custody cases, but actually providing a gravy train to selected legislators and pals who were rushing around to set up corporations and send big checks to each other."

The affair illustrates one reason legislators protect judges and their associates in the courts. Divorce attorneys are prominent in state legislatures. Tony Perkins, who sponsored Louisiana's celebrated "covenant marriage" law, reports that similar measures have failed in some "seemingly sympathetic legislatures" because of "opposition from key committee chairmen who were divorce lawyers."

The potential of child support to become what one Arkansas player termed a "cash cow," providing officials with "steady income for little work," has been exploited elsewhere. The Washington Post reported in July 2000 that a top adviser to Prince George's County, Maryland, executive Wayne Curry received contracts without competitive bidding for child support enforcement within days of leaving the county payroll. In March 2002, Maryland announced a criminal investigation of Maximus, which runs Baltimore's program. The alleged misconduct included collecting money from parents even after their children had reached adulthood and then refusing to refund it. The whistle-blower expressed fear for her personal safety, according to the Baltimore Sun.

Throughout the United States and abroad, child support enforcement has been plagued with corruption. Kansas awarded a contract to Glenn and Jan Jewett, who were involved in bingo operations in Las Vegas and spent time in federal prison for drug trafficking, forgery, concealing stolen property, and writing bad checks. The DuPage County, Illinois, child support system has been under investigation for fraud. "A string of foul-ups plaguing Ohio's child support system," included "millions of dollars worth of improperly intercepted income tax refunds and child support payments," according to the Cleveland Plain-Dealer and WHIO television in Dayton. In Wisconsin, "Parents who owe nothing have been billed thousands of dollars," according to the Milwaukee

Journal Sentinel, including a man billed for children in their 40s, who "was compelled to prove his innocence."

In October 1998 the Los Angeles Times investigated fraud and due process violations in the L.A. child support enforcement system. Deputy District Attorney Jackie Myers had left office in 1996 because, he said, "I felt we were being told to do unethical, very unethical things." In December 1999, Insight reported on the case of a father left by the district attorney's office with $200 a month to care for a family of four. One month, the district attorney "took all but $1 of his $1,200 paycheck."

Following the Times series, HHS was moved to investigate criminal fraud in the city's system, but the General Accounting Office found the investigation "consisted of just two phone calls" – one to "one of the DA office employees who had engaged in misconduct." HHS apparently "did not interview any of more than a dozen people who a confidential informant claimed had firsthand knowledge of wrongdoing within the child support program."

The divorce industry depends on the widespread violation of what most people still hold to be the most solemn promise one makes in life. It is no coincidence that public officials whose livelihoods depend on encouraging citizens to betray their private trust will not hesitate to betray the trust conferred on them by the public. Likewise, a society where private citizens are encouraged not to honor their commitments is a society that will not hold public leaders to their promises. Maggie Gallagher's observation that marriage has become "the only contract where the law now sides with the party who wants to violate it" raises the question of whether we are willing to allow our government to be an active party to deceit and faithless dealing.

Our present divorce system is not only unjust but fundamentally dishonest. For all the talk of a "divorce culture," it is not clear that most people today enter the marriage contract with the intention of breaking it. "If the marital vows were changed to '...until I grow tired of you,' or '...for a period of five years unless I decide otherwise,' and the state were willing to sanction such an agreement, then divorce would not be such a significant event from a moral point of view," attorney Steven L. Varnis writes in Society. "But there is no evidence that the content of marital vows or marital expectations at the time of marriage has changed." Varnis may be only half right, but even so, the point is that the marriage contract has become unenforceable and therefore fraudulent. Until this changes, it seems pointless and even irresponsible to encourage young people to place their trust and their lives in it.

One may argue that government should not enforce the marriage contract, or any contracts for that matter (though the Constitution holds otherwise). But I am not aware of anyone who suggests the government should be forcibly abrogating contracts, let alone luring citizens into contracts that it then tears up. If we truly believe our present divorce policy is appropriate, we should at least have the honesty to tell young people up front that marriage provides them with no protection. Let us inform them at the time of their marriage that even if they remain faithful to their vows, they can lose their children, their home, their savings and future earnings, and their freedom. Not only will the government afford them no protection; it will prosecute them as criminals, though without the due process of law afforded to formally accused criminals. And let us then see how many young people are willing to start families.

It is one thing to tolerate divorce, as perhaps we must do in a free society. It is another to use the power of the state to impose it on unwilling parents and children. When courts stop dispensing justice, they must start dispensing injustice. There is no middle ground.

Stephen Baskerville teaches political science at Howard University and is author of Not Peace But a Sword: The Political Theology of the English Revolution.

ACKNOWLEDGEMENTS AND THANKS

I would like to acknowledge and personally thank the following people who have contributed in some way to the struggle of fathers for the right to see their children post divorce and seperation over the last seven years.

Although we all got shafted, there has been a significant and successful raising of public awareness to the injustices and farce that routinely takes place in the secret family court's, which, I am convinced, one day probably well into the distant future, will lead to change.

Some of the people below have also contributed directly to this book and some have also been there for me personally during the darkest times of my existance during the years I was removed from my children's lives by the corrupt UK Family Court's.

Dr Stephen Baskerville, phd, lecturer at Howard University, Washington, USA, who teaches Political Science. Stephen is also President of the American Coalition for fathers and children and a tireless campaigner for change in the States. Stephen has kindly allowed me to reproduce an artice he wrote for the USA's Crisis Magazine, which illustrates the routine injustices of the UK Family Court's also takes place in the United States too.

Matt O'Connor, founder of Fathers 4 Justice. Against all odds, Matt professionalised father protest and brought the attention of the World to what routinely takes place in the Secret Family Court's, despite the authorities efforts to discredit him as a person and the fathers rights issues generally.

Pat Lyons, of PJ L Surveys, Port Talbot, South Wales. Despite us having never met at the time, when he heard about me being jailed for waving to my children in 2001, Pat Lyons placed me upon the payroll of his company PJL Surveys while I served this completely absurd sentence.

Kate Kirk, whom I have never met. Kate made a very substantial gift of money when she heard about my jailing which combined with Pat Lyons (and others) actions, ensured I had a home to return to upon release.

Jason Hatch, AKA Batman, who successfully scaled Buckingham Palace in 2004 and single handidly brought the plight of seperated fathers and their children to international attention.

Jolly Stanesby, Devon. Probably the most determined campaigner alive. Jolly, despite a strong dislike of heights, has protested for years on behalf of seperated fathers high upon amongst many other places, London's Tower Bridge, the Tamar Bridge, the Severn Bridge, The Royal Court's of Justice London, Stonehenge, various court rooftops nationwide and even on the roof of the home of the notorious Devon Family Court Judge, David Tyzack QC.

Ron Davies, 'Flower bomber' of Tony Blair, 2004.

David Chick, 'Spiderman', who scaled a number of prominent London attractions in pursuit of contact rights.

Dave Ellison, Warrington. Father and Photographer who gave a number of photographs of protests for inclusion in this book.

Some of the very large number of supporters who came to various father protests across the UK which just a few included; Brian Robertson of Cambridge, Matthew Mudge of Cardiff, Ted Diggins of Wiltshire, Tom Aldridge, Robert Whiston, Ivor Catt and Steve Fitzgerald and the members of Mankind, Graham Goodfellow, Paul

Turner, Shaun O'Connell, Eddie Gorecki, Andrew Crook, Bridgitte Creasey, Alex Newman, Nigel Jasper, Colin White, Richard Day, Michael Cox, Paul Rushton, Len Muskiln, Gavin French, Anson Allan, Martin Connolly, Simon Blackmore, Ian Kelly, Graham Starkey, Peter Weaving, Paul Davis, Julie and 'Spike' McIntosh, Raymond Cuthill, Chris Stapleton, Garry Clarkson, many members of CASPER, members of MATCH, many members of Families Need Fathers, members of the United Kingdom Mens Movement (UKMM), The Equal Parenting Coalition, everyone who joined Fathers 4 Justice and every single person who attended any protest for the basic rights of fathers to see their children post divorce and seperation. I can only apologise to the many hundreds of people I've left out, I never met everyone and I kept no record of names of the people I did. But every single person who took part, even in the smallest way, helped the cause. Thank you everyone, on behalf of fathers and children everywhere; when the change eventually comes, you each played a very significant part.